THE BUILDERS

A STORY AND STUDY OF
FREEMASONRY

JOSEPH FORT NEWTON
1876–1950

"There will be a great spiritual revival though no one can tell what form faith will take. Let us hope it will overflow our sectarianism and sweep it away. *We can never have a religion of brotherhood on earth until we have a brotherhood of religion. . . .*"

This was Dr. Newton's sermon throughout life, and though the life is finished, the sermon lives through his books.

JOSEPH FORT NEWTON, Litt. D.

The Builders

A STORY AND STUDY OF

FREEMASONRY

MACOY PUBLISHING AND MASONIC
SUPPLY COMPANY, INC.
RICHMOND, VIRGINIA

FIRST AMERICAN EDITION, 1914
REPRINTED 1915, 1916, 1920, 1922, 1924, 1926
REVISED EDITION, 1930, REPRINTED 1945, 1946
REVISED AND ENLARGED EDITION, 1951

ISBN-0-88053-045-6

Printed in the United States of America

To all my Brethren
of
The gentle Craft of Freemasonry,
of every race and rite,
who have been the inspiration of my research,
and whose fellowship is a consecration,
I inscribe this final edition of my book,
with love, honor and gratitude.

When I was a King and a Mason—
A master proved and skilled,
I cleared me ground for a palace
Such as a King should build.
I decreed and cut down to my levels,
Presently, under the silt,
I came on the wreck of a palace
Such as a King had built.

—KIPLING

FINAL FOREWORD
"A Strange Interlude."

"We could do much with Masonry," said the Sergeant-Major in the glorious Kipling story, "in the Interests of the Brethren," one of the classics of the Craft. "Not as a substitute for a creed, but as an average plan of life," he added, after the clergyman had said that it must not take the place of religion. Thus the talk ran in the Lodge of Instruction, attached to the Faith and Works Lodge, of which the story tells. "When I think of the possibilities of the Craft, I wonder—," said Burges, staring into the fire. Such was the motive which prompted the writing of *The Builders,* the first of nine books written at various times in the effort to induce Masons to know more about Masonry, in order to do more with Masonry and for it. Written to meet a deeply felt need, my "Story and Study of Masonry" has stood the test of time, in many lands and tongues.

The Builders was first published in 1914, the black year, a Book of Brotherhood in an hour when the Brotherhood of the World was broken; yet, despite the irony of its advent, it has made its way through a long-lived storm of great events. It was revised in England in 1918, where I was living as the Minister of the City Temple in London; two Research Lodges went through it for errors. It enjoyed the benefit of all the interesting literature brought out by the bi-centenary of the Grand Lodge of England, adding many new and important facts; the celebration having been put forward until the end of the first World War in 1919. Its reception in England was most cordial, and it passed through a number of editions. As soon as the battle-smoke had lifted, in the gray interval between wars, despite economic collapse, the book was discovered and published on the Continent.

Using the English edition, in 1921 Brother H. J. van Ginkel—a dear, gracious man—translated *The Builders* into Dutch. It was published in Amsterdam, and seems to have been used as a kind of textbook in the Grand Lodge of the Netherlands. In 1926 a brilliant and gallant group of Brethren in the University of Barcelona, Spain, published two large editions in Spanish, translated by Brother Salvador Velera Aparicio. Alas, when the Franco regime came in—a harbinger of horrors to follow—the group were "liquidated," in the dialect of the Devil, which became the vocabulary of the time. Some of them faced firing squads, a few were found in concentration camps in southern France—and then vanished. A Swedish edition of *The Builders* appeared in 1929, beautifully printed, translated by Brothers Walter Hulphers and Carl A. Carleson, and was widely read. A Sanskrit version was published, first in a serial and then in a book, in the ancient city of Damascus, due to the efforts of the late Brother Dr. Adams; a man to know whom was a kind of religion. It was translated and ready to be published in Germany, when the "New Order" seized power, and all Lodges were closed, as had also happened in Italy. A Portuguese edition was projected in Brazil, and the Macoy Publishing & Masonic Supply Company have been given the right to republish it in Spanish for the use of Masons in Latin America. Thus the need which the book originally sought to meet has given it vogue all over the Masonic world.

1914! The dark date, which divided modern history into *before* and *after,* just when the race was moving toward unity and amity! It was as if some Demon of Discord—or else some deep neurotic frustration in the subconscious life of humanity—had shattered the foundations of the House of Man, releasing a vast irruption of barbarism in the heart of what was called civilization; so that we can hardly imagine life as we had known it on yonder side of the chasm. The human world cracked, and the cleavage continued to widen, one World-War, more ghastly than a devil ever dreamed, was followed, after an interval of Armistice and anarchy, by a second War more frightful than the first; "total war," with cruelties, volcanic violences, obscenities and horrors unbelievable, as if liberty, justice, and mercy had vanished from the earth—so frightful that even now it seems too terrible ever to have been true. For two decades we have lived in a dehumanized world; stark starvation has stalked the earth; the

thick stench of death has floated on every wind. Such
a human earthquake is a mystery and a terror, baffling analysis.

Here was no "wave of the future," as blind souls
decried, but the dregs of a black and tragic past
washed up by a storm; the police-state is no new invention, but as old as the inhumanity of man to
man. It was as if "the underworld" came to the top,
the criminal element grasped power, with mad fury
wrecking every fine and gracious thing slowly built
up through ages. It had the suddenness of an explosion, the swiftness of a cyclone, the force of an
avalanche, the destructiveness of a cataclysm. Even
the pace of Time seemed to be speeded up; centuries were telescoped into decades, so rapid has
been the velocity of ideas and events, leaving us
dazzled and then dazed. Truly he knows nothing
of the world in which we are trying to live who does
not realize that a thousand years of history have
swept over it between 1914 and 1948. Things in-
expressibly revolutionary have happened overnight,
upheavals and overturnings so radical that they have
altered the outward aspect and inner attitude of
men and nations. New ideas, alien ideals, challenge
all that humanity has held to be holy, not only in
our own civilization, but in all the civilizations the
race has known. So, after a phantasmagoria of terror
and an apocalypse of heroism, we find ourselves in
a strange, terrifying age, fear-haunted, hate-driven,
with a shuddering sense of insecurity and forebod-

ing. Who can describe the tearing of the world to pieces, and our fumbling efforts to put it together after another pattern!

Our concern here, however, is with what happened to the Masonic Fraternity, along with all the gentle, refining, liberating institutions and influences of mankind. In all lands where the Brutalitarians ruled—Black or Brown or Red—it is a melancholy story of ravage and ruin, of Masons killed, starved, or left to rot in concentration camps, their properties confiscated, their temples wrecked and left unfit for use, their records destroyed—having first been used to hunt down the Brethren—in an orgy of fiendish horror which made the earth a province of hell, ruled by Satan and his imps. It began in Italy, under the "sawdust Caesar," not so severe at first, since most Italian Masons are Catholics, but increased in violence; Torrigiani, Grand Master of the Grand Orient, died in prison on the Island of Lipari. Other leaders "vanished" as if they had never lived; the Craft was dissolved or driven underground. In Germany, where hatred became a mad hysteria—nay, a fratricidal mania, "All Masons Jews, all Jews Masons,"—the regime was utterly ruthless, its techniques of torture more terrible, amid such sadistic mutilations and massacres as beggar words. As the war went on and the Axis powers became more insolent and implacable, horror was added to horror in Greece, in Holland, in Austria, reaching its nadir in the agonizing ordeals of Czechoslovakia and Norway—a record of fiendish horror and heroic devotion unmatched in human annals.[1]

But enough; a new day is at hand, and Masonry will be born anew for new adventures and new and benign labors. As the symbolism of our Craft-Masonry is woven about the building, the destruction, and the re-building of a Temple—the tallest temple in the ancient world, not in its architecture, but in the lofty Faith for which it stood—so once again, by a strange, incredible irony, the Temple of Masonry itself has been blasted to rubble by new weapons in the old art of war, and lies in disarray and ruin over wide areas. But it will be rebuilt and restored, if not in its former magnificence, in stately beauty, scarred by the horror through which it has passed; let us hope and pray not to be demolished again, along with every vestige of civilization, in an ecumenical holocaust of an Atomic War. But who will heal the injury of human souls, and bring back the ancient lost reverence and passion for human dignity—for the good earth and its web of blooming life? Still, goodness is tough; it is next to impossible to destroy it; still we build on God and good men—

[1] For fuller details, by no means exhaustive, see the Report of a Committee sent abroad in 1945, by the Masonic Service Association of the United States, to study the situation with a view to aiding Masons in dire plight. Also, the restrained and noble statement of the Czechoslovak National Grand Lodge in Prague, in 1947, entitled, *A Grand Lodge Home Again After the War*, published in English by the Service Association. Also, *The Freemasons*, by Eugen Lennhoff, Part 2, chapters V to XI, and Part 3, chapters I to IV. As Lennhoff wrote in 1932, carefully documenting his account, he did not describe the second World-War, with its unspeakable atrocities.

God help us, we can do no other, whatever "black blizzards" may blow.

The first World-War—we seem to reckon time by wars—found American Masonry ill prepared for the crisis. It sought to be of service, but men of State could not deal with forty-nine different Grand Lodges, and there was no agency or method of common action. Each Grand Lodge was separate, each edgy about its sovereignty; yet all wanted to bring the gentle ministrations of Masonry to the fighting men and their families. Either the Craft must find a way to work together, or stand idle and impotent in the face of disaster. Facts do not threaten; they operate. In sheer necessity, of which there was no doubt, the Masonic Service Association of the United States was organized in 1919, amid fears, suspicions, and difficulties no end. In spite of prophecies of failure it grew and gathered power, seeking to make speculative Masonry operative by making it co-operative. Mistakes were made, but the greatest mistake is to attempt nothing. As its spirit and purpose were understood, it made its way, serving in time of disaster, and carrying on a program of education. It is in no sense a general Grand Lodge, and never can be. It is not even a federation of Grand Lodges. It is less an institution than an agency, whereby Grand Lodges can do together, in fellowship, what none can do so well alone, if at all.

To put it plainly, the Masonic Service Association, and its work of education and ministry, was the outstanding achievement in the history of Craft Masonry in America during the thirty-five years since *The Builders* was written. No argument is necessary; the facts prove it. The second World-War gave the Craft its supreme opportunity, to which it measured up magnificently, by Square, Compasses and Plumb-line. When, in an hour dark with destiny, the earth and sky suddenly became a red and blazing hell, and the gray solitudes of the sea a cemetery, Masonry was duly and truly prepared. Its slogan, *"Your son is my Brother,"* was a stroke of genius; it struck a chord that echoed in every Lodge and in every Home. Masonry, once just an Order to belong to, became an active power, a benign influence in an hour of dire tragedy and need. Superbly organized, tirelessly, tactfully, skillfully it ministered to its men on land and sea, and in the air, in social centers at home and overseas, in rest camps and hospitals, bringing the human touch, the word of cheer, the hand of fellowship, to its Brothers and Fellows. A soldier-Brother, seeing the familiar symbols, the Square and Compasses, felt happy and at home, for a brief time, in the shrieking, screaming hurricane of death. The record of *War Service Work* of the Grand Lodges of America, State by State, reads like a romance, or a chapter in a new Book of Acts. No landmark was violated, but a new "point of fellowship" was discovered, "Shoulder to Shoulder"; and if added to the munificent philanthropies of the Craft, which never paused —its homes for the aged and orphanages for crippled children,—it is an epic of Brotherly Love, Relief, and Truth.

For the rest, surely he who ever gives a thought to the life of man at large, to the waste and cruelty of existence, must reckon the spirit and service of Freemasonry among the most precious possessions of his race. What lies before us none can foresee, save dimly and in vague outline, which may melt away. Yet some things are beginning to be clear—we must learn to live spiritually and think scientifically, following "the better angels of our nature," and those great freedoms of the mind, which unveil the Truth which alone can set us free from the horrible Fear which enslaves the race and makes life a terror and a torture, and mankind a tribe of creepers. Also, we must master the art of living together, the finest of all arts, whereby men of many races and many faiths dwell in mutual respect and goodwill. While we have made great strides toward that goal, we are still far from it. Still there is racial rancor—a thing slithered with blood and black with bitterness; still there is religious bigotry which blasphemes the genius of brotherhood. For such things there is no place in this our Brotherland, where men rule themselves, and no man has any right that does not belong to all his fellows. Yet, if there is much to dismay, we must all hope much from the gradual growth of brotherly love, trusting in "the ultimate decency of things and the veiled kindness of the Father of men."

For the finer spirits of the world, a great man of France tells us, there are two dwelling places, our earthly Brotherland, and that other City above which is free, whose maker and builder is God; a City we see, afar, when the clouds are off our souls, where order no longer rests on force, but on love and truth. Of one we are builders; of the other guests. To the one let us give our lives, our labors, and "the last full measure of devotion," pledging our time and thought and service to the common life and welfare. But neither family, friend, nor aught that we value has power over the spirit. The spirit is Light! It is Truth, it is Love! It is for us to rise above tempests, to thrust aside all clouds and fogs which threaten to obscure, looking beyond the hatred of races and the injustices of nations, until we behold, in far-shining splendor, the walls of that City of the Spirit wherein the souls of the whole world shall assemble:—

> *And I saw no temple therein:*
> *For the Lord God and the Lamb*
> *are the Temple of it.*

JOSEPH FORT NEWTON.

Church of St. Luke and Epiphany,
Philadelphia, July 21st, 1948.

FOREWORD MACOY EDITION

For twenty years, or thereabouts—to be exact, since 1911, when I first became Grand Chaplain of the Grand Lodge of Iowa—outside my home I have had three great interests: the Church, the University, and the Lodge. To these widely differing fields of labor my energies have been devoted, in about equal measure, and in all three I have been trying to do one thing: to interpret the spiritual worth and meaning of life, without which our hurrying human years may easily sink to a lower octave and end in ambiguity or futility.

In Freemasonry my aim, through all variations of endeavor, has been twofold: to induce Masons to know more about Freemasonry, and to inspire them to do more with Freemasonry in behalf of the common good. In this spirit and for this purpose I wrote *The Builders,* at the request of the Grand Lodge of Iowa; and the fact that it is the most widely read Masonic book in our generation, not only in English, but in the Dutch, Swedish, Spanish and Syrian tongues, is a token that it met, however imperfectly, a deeply felt need of the Fraternity. It so happened that the appearance of the book coincided with a new impulse in American Freemasonry, the result of which is a new kind of Masonic literature, at once more accurate and more popular, and a more active and intelligent concern of Grand

Lodges for the training of Masons in Freemasonry.

As the first editor of "The Builder," the journal of the National Masonic Research Society, and, later, as editor of "The Master Mason," the journal of the Masonic Service Association of the United States, as well as in many books and on a thousand Lodge platforms, in America and in England, I have had a tiny part in the movement in behalf of Masonic education, seeking to do somewhat in the service of the gentle Craft of Freemasonry, to which my obligation is profound and my loyalty life-long. Others have done better work, but no one ever worked harder, trying to do good work, true work, square work, in the effort to expound the principle and to promote the practice of Brotherly Love, Relief, and Truth—by which I mean the Truth which makes all other truth true, which man has sought in all ages, through many systems of symbolism, in his quest for the meaning and mastery of life. All that a man can do in this world is to do his work, as best he can, or well or ill, and pass on, leaving its worth to be estimated and appraised by time, and its results with the Master of all good work to forgive or to approve.

Anyway, to my profound regret, it is no longer possible for me to devote as much time to the active service of Freemasonry as in the years gone by, having reached a time of life when one cannot do so many things, and I must conserve and concentrate my energies in order to do some things of which I have long dreamed, before the night falls and no man can work. If the Grand Master will grant me the health, strength and vision, I hope sometime to write a little book on the Symbolism of Freemasonry—which to me is the thin shadow of something very great; but that is only a dream, and may not come true, because our fleeting life is of such stuff as dreams are made on, rounded with a Sleep. Yet, if all dreams came true, life would lose its zest and lustre, and there would be nothing to look forward to out yonder in the City of the Hill.

To all the Men of the Square, at every point of the Compass, all over America, in England, in Africa, Australia and the far ends of the earth, good men and true, brothers and builders, the very thought of whom has been an inspiration in the midst of the years, whose fellowship has added a whole dimension to my life—men to know whom is a kind of religion, and whose love on earth has made the Love of God more real and radiant in the heavens—I send greetings, blessings, thanksgiving, and goodwill; and to each one I would fain whisper a tiny word—trust God, hope much, fear not at all, and love with all your heart.

JOSEPH FORT NEWTON.

St. James's Church
Philadelphia, 1930.

THE ANTEROOM

Fourteen years ago the writer of this volume entered the temple of Freemasonry, and that date stands out in memory as one of the most significant days in his life. There was a little spread on the night of his raising, and, as is the custom, the candidate was asked to give his impressions of the Order. Among other things, he made request to know if there was any little book which would tell a young man the things he would most like to know about Masonry—what it was, whence it came, what it teaches, and what it is trying to do in the world? No one knew of such a book at that time, nor has any been found to meet a need which many must have felt before and since. By an odd coincidence, it has fallen to the lot of the author to write the little book for which he made request fourteen years ago.

This bit of reminiscence explains the purpose of the present volume, and every book must be judged by its spirit and purpose, not less than by its style and contents. Written as a commission from the Grand Lodge of Iowa, and approved by that Grand body, a copy of this book is to be presented to every man upon whom the degree of Master Mason is conferred within this Grand Jurisdiction. Naturally this intention has determined the method and arrangement of the book, as well as the matter it contains; its aim being to tell a young man entering

the order the antecedents of Masonry, its development, its philosophy, its mission, and its ideal. Keeping this purpose always in mind, the effort has been
to prepare a brief, simple, and vivid account of the
origin, growth, and teaching of the Order, so written
as to provoke a deeper interest in and a more earnest
study of its story and its service to mankind.

No work of this kind has been undertaken, so far
as is known, by any Grand Lodge in this country or
abroad—at least, not since the old *Pocket Companion,* and other such works in the earlier times; and
this is the more strange from the fact that the need
of it is so obvious, and its possibilities so fruitful
and important. Every one who has looked into the
vast literature of Masonry must often have felt the
need of a concise, compact, yet comprehensive survey to clear the path and light the way. Especially
must those feel such a need who are not accustomed
to traverse long and involved periods of history, and
more especially those who have neither the time nor
the opportunity to sift ponderous volumes to find
out the facts. Much of our literature—indeed,
by far the larger part of it—was written before the
methods of scientific study had arrived, and while
it fascinates, it does not convince those who are used
to the more critical habits of research. Consequently, without knowing it, some of our most
earnest Masonic writers have made the Order a tar-
get for ridicule by their extravagant claims as to its
antiquity. They did not make it clear in what sense
it is ancient, and not a little satire has been aimed at

Masons for their gullibility in accepting as true the wildest and most absurd legends. Besides, no history of Masonry has been written in recent years, and some important material has come to light in the world of historical and archæological scholarship, making not a little that has hitherto been obscure more clear; and there is need that this new knowledge be related to what was already known. While modern research aims at accuracy, too often its results are dry pages of fact, devoid of literary beauty and spiritual appeal—a skeleton without the warm robe of flesh and blood. Striving for accuracy, the writer has sought to avoid making a dusty chronicle of facts and figures, which few would have the heart to follow, with what success the reader must decide.

Such a book is not easy to write, and for two reasons: it is the history of a private Order, much of whose lore is not to be written, and it covers a bewildering stretch of time, asking that the contents of innumerable volumes—many of them huge, disjointed, and difficult to digest—be compact within a small space. Nevertheless, if it has required a prodigious labor, it is assuredly worth while in behalf of the young men who throng our temple gates, as well as for those who are to come after us. Every line of this book has been written in the conviction that the real history of Masonry is great enough, and its simple teaching grand enough, without the embellishment of legend, much less of occultism. It proceeds from first to last upon the assurance that all that we need to do is to remove the scaffolding from the historic temple of Masonry and let it stand out in the sunlight, where all men can see its beauty and symmetry, and that it will command the respect of the most critical and searching intellects, as well as the homage of all who love mankind. By this faith the long study has been guided; in this confidence it has been completed.

To this end the sources of Masonic scholarship, stored in the library of the Grand Lodge of Iowa, have been explored, and the highest authorities have been cited wherever there is uncertainty—copious references serving not only to substantiate the statements made, but also, it is hoped, to guide the reader into further and more detailed research. Also, in respect of issues still open to debate and about which differences of opinion obtain, both sides have been given a hearing, so far as space would allow, that the student may weigh and decide the question for himself. Like all Masonic students of recent times, the writer is richly indebted to the great Research Lodges of England—especially to the Quatuor Coronati Lodge, No. 2076—without whose proceedings this study would have been much harder to write, if indeed it could have been written at all. Such men as Gould, Hughan, Speth, Crawley, Thorp, to name but a few—not forgetting Pike, Parvin, Mackey, Fort, and others in this country—deserve the perpetual gratitude of the fraternity. If, at times, in seeking to escape from mere legend, some of them seemed to go too far toward another extreme—forgetting that there is much in Masonry that cannot be traced by name and date—it was but natural in their effort in behalf of authentic history and accurate scholarship. Alas, most of those named belong now to a time that is gone and to the people who are no longer with us here, but they are recalled by an humble student who would pay them the honor belonging to great men and great Masons.

This book is divided into three parts, as everything Masonic should be: Prophecy, History, and Interpretation. The first part has to do with the hints and foregleams of Masonry in the early history, tradition, mythology, and symbolism of the race—finding its foundations in the nature and need of man, and showing how the stones wrought out by time and struggle were brought from afar to the making of Masonry as we know it. The second part is a story of the order of builders through the centuries, from the building of the Temple of Solomon to the organization of the mother Grand Lodge of England, and the spread of the Order all over the civilized world. The third part is a statement and exposition of the faith of Masonry, its philosophy, its religious meaning, its genius, and its ministry to the individual, and through the individual to society and the state. Such is a bare outline of the purpose, method, plan, and spirit of the work, and if these be kept in mind it is believed that it will tell its story and confide its message.

When a man thinks of our mortal lot—its greatness and its pathos, how much has been wrought out in the past, and how binding is our obligation to

preserve and enrich the inheritance of humanity—
there comes over him a strange warming of the heart
toward all his fellow workers; and especially toward
the young, to whom we must soon entrust all that we
hold sacred. All through these pages the wish has
been to make the young Mason feel in what a great
and benign tradition he stands, that he may the
more earnestly strive to be a Mason not merely in
form, but in faith, in spirit, and still more, in character; and so help to realize somewhat of the beauty
we all have dreamed—lifting into the light the latent
powers and unguessed possibilities of this the greatest order of men upon the earth. Everyone can do
a little, and if each does his part faithfully the sum
of our labors will be very great, and we shall leave
the world fairer than we found it, richer in faith,
gentler in justice, wiser in pity—for we pass this way
but once, pilgrims seeking a country, even a City
that hath foundations.

J. F. N.

Cedar Rapids, Iowa, September 7, 1914.

Table of Contents

Illustrations

Part 1

PROPHECY

THE FOUNDATIONS

By Symbols is man guided and commanded, made happy, made wretched. He everywhere finds himself encompassed with Symbols, recognized as such or not recognized: the Universe is but one vast Symbol of God; nay, if thou wilt have it, what is man himself but a Symbol of God; is not all that he does symbolical; a revelation to Sense of the mystic God-given force that is in him; a Gospel of Freedom, which he, the Messiah of Nature, preaches, as he can, by word and act? Not a Hut he builds but is the visible embodiment of a Thought; but bears visible record of invisible things; but is, in the transcendental sense, symbolical as well as real.

—THOMAS CARLYLE, *Sartor Resartus*

Chapter One

THE FOUNDATIONS

TWO ARTS have altered the face of the earth and given shape to the life and thought of man, Agriculture and Architecture. Of the two, it would be hard to know which has been the more intimately interwoven with the inner life of humanity; for man is not only a planter and a builder, but a mystic and a thinker. For such a being, especially in primitive times, any work was something more than itself; it was a truth found out. In becoming useful it attained some form, enshrining at once a thought and a mystery. Our present study has to do with the second of these arts, which has been called the matrix of civilization.

When we inquire into origins and seek the initial force which carried art forward, we find two fundamental factors—physical necessity and spiritual aspiration. Of course, the first great impulse of all architecture was need, honest response to the de-

mand for shelter; but this demand included a Home
for the Soul, not less than a roof over the head. Even
in this response to primary need there was something spiritual which carried it beyond provision
for the body; as the men of Egypt, for instance,
wanted an indestructible resting-place, and so built
the pyramids. As Capart says, prehistoric art shows
that this utilitarian purpose was in almost every
case blended with a religious, or at least a magical,
purpose.[1] The spiritual instinct, in seeking to re-
create types and to set up more sympathetic relations with the universe, led to imitation, to ideas of
proportion, to the passion for beauty, and to the effort after perfection.

Man has been always a builder, and nowhere has
he shown himself more significantly than in the
buildings he has erected. When we stand before
them—whether it be a mud hut, the house of a
cliff-dweller stuck like the nest of a swallow on the
side of a canyon, a Pyramid, a Parthenon, or a Pan-
theon—we seem to read into his soul. The builder
may have gone, perhaps ages before, but here he has
left something of himself, his hopes, his fears, his
ideas, his dreams. Even in the remote recesses of
the Andes, amidst the riot of nature, and where man
is now a mere savage, we come upon the remains of
vast, vanished civilizations, where art and science
and religion reached unknown heights. Wherever
humanity has lived and wrought, we find the crum-
bling ruins of towers, temples, and tombs, monu-

[1] *Primitive Art in Egypt.*

ments of its industry and its aspiration. Also, whatever else man may have been—cruel, tyrannous, vindictive—his buildings always have reference to religion. They bespeak a vivid sense of the Unseen and his awareness of his relation to it. Of a truth, the story of the Tower of Babel is more than a myth. Man has ever been trying to build to heaven, embodying his prayer and his dream in brick and stone.

For there are two sets of realities—material and spiritual—but they are so interwoven that all practical laws are exponents of moral laws. Such is the thesis which Ruskin expounds with so much insight and eloquence in his *Seven Lamps of Architecture,* in which he argues that the laws of architecture are moral laws, as applicable to the building of character as to the construction of cathedrals. He finds those laws to be Sacrifice, Truth, Power, Beauty, Life, Memory, and, as the crowning grace of all, that principle to which Polity owes its stability, Life its happiness, Faith its acceptance, and Creation its continuance—*Obedience.* He holds that there is no such thing as liberty, and never can be. The stars have it not; the earth has it not; the sea has it not. Man fancies that he has freedom, but if he would use the word Loyalty instead of Liberty, he would be nearer the truth, since it is by obedience to the laws of life and truth and beauty that he attains to what he calls liberty.

Throughout that brilliant essay, Ruskin shows how the violation of moral laws spoils the beauty of architecture, mars its usefulness, and makes it unstable. He points out, with all the variations of emphasis, illustration, and appeal, that beauty is what is imitated from natural forms, consciously or unconsciously, and that what is not so derived, but depends for its dignity upon arrangement received from the human mind, expresses, while it reveals, the quality of the mind, whether it be noble or ignoble. Thus:

> All building, therefore, shows man either as gathering or governing; and the secrets of his success are his knowing what to gather, and how to rule. These are the two great intellectual Lamps of Architecture; the one consisting in a just and humble veneration of the works of God upon earth, and the other in an understanding of the dominion over those works which has been vested in man.[1]

What our great prophet of art thus elaborated so eloquently, the early men forefelt by instinct, dimly it may be, but not less truly. If architecture was born of need it soon showed its magic quality, and all true building touched depths of feeling and opened gates of wonder. No doubt the men who first balanced one stone over two others must have looked with astonishment at the work of their hands, and have worshiped the stones they had set up. This element of mystical wonder and awe lasted long through the ages, and is still felt when work is done in the old way by keeping close to nature, necessity, and faith. From the first, ideas of sacred-

[1] Chapter iii, aphorism 2.

ness, of sacrifice, of ritual rightness, of magic stability, of likeness to the universe, of perfection of form and proportion glowed in the heart of the builder, and guided his arm. Wren, philosopher as he was, decided that the delight of man in setting up columns was acquired through worshiping in the groves of the forest; and modern research has come to much the same view, for Sir Arthur Evans shows that in the first European age columns were gods. All over Europe the early morning of architecture was spent in the worship of great stones.[1]

If we go to old Egypt, where the art of building seems first to have gathered power, and where its remains are best preserved, we may read the ideas of the earliest artists. Long before the dynastic period a strong people inhabited the land who developed many arts which they handed on to the pyramid builders. Although only semi-naked savages using flint instruments in a style much like the bushmen, they were the root, so to speak, of a wonderful artistic stock. Of the Egyptians Herodotus said, "They gather the fruits of the earth with less labor than any other people." With agriculture and settled life came trade and stored-up energy which might essay to improve on caves and pits and other rude dwellings. By the Nile, perhaps, man first aimed to overpass the routine of the barest need, and obey his soul. There he wrought out beautiful vases of fine marble, and invented square building.

[1] *Architecture*, by Lethaby, chap. i.

At any rate, the earliest known structure actually discovered, a prehistoric tomb found in the sands at Hieraconpolis, is already right-angled. As Lethaby reminds us, modern people take squareness very much for granted as being a self-evident form, but the discovery of the square was a great step in geometry.[1] It opened a new era in the story of the builders. Early inventions must have seemed like revelations, as indeed they were; and it is not strange that skilled craftsmen were looked upon as magicians. If man knows as much as he does, the discovery of the Square was a great event to the primitive mystics of the Nile. Very early it became an emblem of truth, justice, and righteousness, and so it remains to this day though uncountable ages have passed. Simple, familiar, eloquent, it brings from afar a sense of the wonder of the dawn, and it still teaches a lesson which we find it hard to learn. So also the cube, the compasses, and the keystone, each a great advance for those to whom architecture was indeed "building touched with emotion," as showing that its laws are the laws of the Eternal.

Maspero tells us that the temples of Egypt, even from earliest times, were built in the image of the earth as the builders had imagined it.[2] For them the earth was a sort of flat slab more long than wide, and the sky was a ceiling or vault supported by four great pillars. The pavement represented the earth; the four angles stood for the pillars; the ceiling,

[1] *Architecture*, by Lethaby, chap. ii.
[2] *Dawn of Civilization.*

more often flat, though sometimes curved, corresponding to the sky. From the pavement grew vege-
tation, and water plants emerged from the water;
while the ceiling, painted dark blue, was strewn with
stars of five points. Sometimes, the sun and moon
were seen floating on the heavenly ocean escorted by
the constellations, and the months and days. There
was a far withdrawn holy place, small and obscure,
approached through a succession of courts and col-
umned halls, all so arranged on a central axis as to
point to the sunrise. Before the outer gates were
obelisks and avenues of statues. Such were the
shrines of the old solar religion, so oriented that
on one day in the year the beams of the rising sun,
or of some bright star that hailed his coming, should
stream down the nave and illumine the altar.[1]

Clearly, one ideal of the early builders was that
of sacrifice, as seen in their use of the finest materials; and another was accuracy of workmanship.
Indeed, not a little of the earliest work displayed an
astonishing technical ability, and such work must
point to some underlying idea which the workers
sought to realize. Above all things they sought per-
manence. In later inscriptions relating to buildings,
phrases like these occur frequently: "it is such as
the heavens in all its quarters;" "firm as the heavens." Evidently the basic idea was that, as the
heavens were stable, not to be moved, so a building
put into proper relation with the universe would

[1] *Dawn of Astronomy*, Norman Lockyear.

acquire magical stability. It is recorded that when Ikhnaton founded his new city, four boundary stones were accurately placed, that so it might be exactly square, and thus endure forever. Eternity was the ideal aimed at, everything else being sacrificed for that aspiration:—dwellers in a world of "whispering dreams and wistful dust," they sought to make their fleeting lives eternal.

How well they realized their dream is shown us in the Pyramids, of all monuments of mankind the oldest, the most technically perfect, the largest, and the most mysterious. Ages come and go, empires rise and fall, philosophies flourish and fail, and man seeks him out many inventions, but they stand silent under the bright Egyptian night, as fascinating as they are baffling. An obelisk is simply a pyramid, albeit the base has become a shaft, holding aloft the oldest emblems of solar faith—a Triangle mounted on a Square. When and why this figure became holy no one knows, save as we may conjecture that it was one of those sacred stones which gained its sanctity in times far back of all recollection and tradition, like the *Ka'aba* at Mecca. Whether it be an imitation of the triangle of zodiacal light, seen at certain times in the eastern sky at sunrise and sunset, or a feat of masonry used as a symbol of Heaven, as the Square was an emblem of Earth, no one may affirm.[1]

[1] Churchward, in his *Signs and Symbols of Primordial Man* (chap. xv), holds that the pyramid was typical of heaven, Shu, standing on seven steps, having lifted the sky from the earth in the form of a triangle; and that at each point stood one of the gods, Sut and Shu at the base, the apex being the Pole Star where Horus of the Horizon

In the Pyramid Texts the Sun-god, when he created all the other gods, is shown sitting on the apex of the sky in the form of a Phoenix—that Supreme God to whom two architects, Suti and Hor, wrote so noble a hymn of praise.[1]

White with the worship of ages, ineffably beautiful and pathetic, is the old light-religion of humanity—a sublime nature-mysticism in which Light was love and life, and Darkness evil and death. For the early man light was the mother of beauty, the unveiler of color, the elusive and radiant mystery of the world, and his speech about it was reverent and grateful. At the gates of the morning he stood with uplifted hands, and the sun sinking in the desert at eventide made him wistful in prayer, half fear and half hope, lest the beauty return no more. His religion, when he emerged from the night of animalism, was a worship of the Light—his temple hung with stars, his altar a glowing flame, his ritual a woven hymn of night and day. No poet of our day, not even Shelley, has written lovelier lyrics in praise of the Light than those hymns of Ikhnaton in the morning of the world.[2] Memories of this religion

had his throne. This is, in so far, true; but the pyramid emblem was older than Osiris, Isis, and Horus, and runs back into an obscurity beyond knowledge.

[1] *Religion and Thought in Egypt,* by Breasted, lecture ix.

[2] Ikhnaton, indeed, was a grand, solitary, shining figure, "the first idealist in history," and a poetic thinker in whom the religion of Egypt attained its highest reach. Dr. Breasted puts his lyrics alongside the poems of Wordsworth and the great passage of Ruskin in *Modern Painters,* as celebrating the divinity of Light (*Religion and Thought in Egypt,* lecture ix). Despite the revenge of his enemies, he stands out as a lonely, heroic, prophetic soul—"the first *individual* in time."

of the dawn linger with us today in the faith that
follows the Day-Star from on high, and the Sun of
Righteousness—One who is the Light of the World
in life, and the Lamp of Poor Souls in the night of
death.

Here, then, are the real foundations of Masonry,
both material and moral: in the deep need and aspiration of man, and his creative impulse; in his
instinctive Faith, his quest of the Ideal, and his love
of the Light. Underneath all his building lay the
feeling, prophetic of his last and highest thought,
that the earthly house of his life should be in right
relation with its heavenly prototype, the world-
temple—imitating on earth the house not made with
hands, eternal in the heavens. If he erected a square
temple, it was an image of the earth; if he built a
pyramid, it was a picture of a beauty shown him in
the sky; as, later, his cathedral was modelled after
the mountain, and its dim and lofty arch a memory
of the forest vista—its altar a fireside of the soul, its
spire a prayer in stone. And as he wrought his faith
and dream into reality, it was but natural that the
tools of the builder should become emblems of the
thoughts of the thinker. Not only his tools, but, as
we shall see, the very stones with which he worked
became sacred symbols—the temple itself a vision of
that House of Doctrine, that Home of the Soul,
which, though unseen, he is building in the midst of
the years.

(See also *The Dawn of Conscience* by Breasted, one of the great books
of our generation.)

THE WORKING TOOLS

It began to shape itself to my intellectual vision into something more imposing and majestic, solemnly mysterious and grand. It seemed to me like the Pyramids in their loneliness, in whose yet undiscovered chambers may be hidden, for the enlightenment of coming generations, the sacred books of the Egyptians, so long lost to the world; like the Sphinx half buried in the desert.

In its symbolism, which and its spirit of brotherhood are its essence, Freemasonry is more ancient than any of the world's living religions. It has the symbols and doctrines which, older than himself, Zarathrustra inculcated; and it seemed to me a spectacle sublime, yet pitiful— the ancient Faith of our ancestors holding out to the world its symbols once so eloquent, and mutely and in vain asking for an interpreter.

And so I came at last to see that the true greatness and majesty of Freemasonry consist in its proprietorship of these and its other symbols; and that its symbolism is its soul.

—ALBERT PIKE, *Letter to Gould*

ALBERT PIKE

Sovereign Grand Commander of the Supreme Council, 33°, Ancient and Accepted Scottish Rite, Southern Jurisdiction, U.S.A. from 1859 to his death in 1891. He recast the old Scottish Rite rituals and brought them to their present state of beauty and perfection.

Chapter Two

THE WORKING TOOLS

NEVER WERE truer words than those of Goethe in the last lines of *Faust,* and they echo one of the oldest instincts of humanity: "All things transitory but as symbols are sent." From the beginning man has divined that the things open to his senses are more than mere facts, having other and hidden meanings. The whole world was close to him as an infinite parable, a mystical and prophetic scroll the lexicon of which he set himself to find. Both he and his world were so made as to convey a sense of doubleness, of high truth hinted in humble, nearby things. No smallest thing but had its skyey aspect which, by his winged and quick-sighted fancy, he sought to surprise and grasp.

Let us acknowledge that man was born a poet, his mind a chamber of imagery, his world a gallery of art. Despite his utmost efforts, he can in nowise strip his thought of the flowers and fruits that cling to it, withered though they often are. As a fact, he has ever been a citizen of two worlds, using the scenery of the visible to make vivid the realities of the world Unseen. What wonder, then, that trees grew in his fancy, flowers bloomed in his faith, and the victory of spring over winter gave him hope of life after death, while the march of the sun and the great stars invited him to "thoughts that wander through eternity." Symbol was his native tongue, his first form of speech—as, indeed, it is his last—whereby he was able to say what else he could not have uttered. Such is the fact, and even the language in which we state it is "a dictionary of faded metaphors," the fossil poetry of ages ago.

1

That picturesque and variegated maze of the early symbolism of the race we cannot study in detail, tempting as it is. Indeed, so luxuriant was that old picture-language that we may easily miss our way and get lost in the labyrinth, unless we keep to the right path.[1] First of all, throughout this study of

[1] There are many books in this field, but two may be named: *The Lost Language of Symbolism,* by Bayley, and the *Signs and Symbols of Primordial Man,* by Churchward, each in its own way remarkable. The first aspires to be for this field what Frazer's *Golden Bough* is for religious anthropology, and its dictum is: "Beauty is Truth; Truth Beauty." The thesis of the second is that Masonry is founded upon Egyptian eschatology, which may be true; but unfortunately the book is too polemical. Both books partake of the poetry, if not the confusion, of the subject; but not for a world of dust would one clip their wings of fancy and suggestion. Indeed, their union of scholarship and poetry is unique. When the pains of erudition fail to track a fact to its lair, they do not scruple to use the divining rod; and the result often passes

prophecy let us keep ever in mind a very simple and obvious fact, albeit not less wonderful because obvious. Socrates made the discovery—perhaps the greatest ever made—that human nature is universal. By his searching questions he found that when men think round a problem, and think deeply, they disclose a common nature and a common system of truth. So there dawned upon him, from this fact, the truth of the kinship of mankind and the unity of mind. His insight is confirmed many times over, whether we study the earliest gropings of the human mind or set the teachings of the sages side by side. Always we find, after comparison, that the final conclusions of the wisest minds as to the meaning of life and the world are harmonious, if not identical.

Here is the clue to the striking resemblances between the faiths and philosophies of widely separated peoples, and it makes them intelligible while adding to their picturesqueness and philosophic interest. By the same token, we begin to understand why the same signs, symbols, and emblems were used by all peoples to express their earliest aspiration and thought. We need not infer that one people learned them from another, or that there existed a mystic, universal order which had them in keeping. They simply betray the unity of the human mind, and show how and why, at the same stage of culture, races far removed from each other came to the same

out of the realm of pedestrian chronicle into the world of winged literature.

conclusions and used much the same symbols to body forth their thought. Illustrations are innumerable, of which a few may be named as examples of this unity both of idea and of emblem, and also as confirming the insight of the great Greek that, however shallow minds may differ, in the end all seekers after truth follow a common path, comrades in one great quest.

An example in point, as ancient as it is eloquent, is the idea of the trinity and its emblem, the triangle. What the human thought of God is depends on what power of the mind or aspect of life man uses as a lens through which to look into the mystery of things. Conceived of as the will of the world, God is one, and we have the monotheism of Moses. Seen through instinct and the kaleidoscope of the senses, God is multiple, and the result is polytheism and its gods without number. For that reason, God is a dualism made up of matter and mind, as in the faith of Zoroaster and many other cults. But when the social life of man becomes the prism of faith, God is a trinity of Father, Mother, Child. Almost as old as human thought, we find the idea of the trinity and its triangle emblem everywhere—Siva, Vishnu, and Brahma in India corresponding to Osiris, Isis, and Horus in Egypt. No doubt this idea underlay the old pyramid emblem, at each corner of which stood one of the gods. No missionary carried this profound truth over the earth. It grew out of a natural and universal human experience, and is explained by the fact of the unity of the human mind and its vision of God through the family.

Other emblems take us back into an antiquity so remote that we seem to be walking in the shadow of prehistoric time. Of these, the mysterious Swastika is perhaps the oldest, as it is certainly the most widely distributed over the earth. (Alas, in our day, by a tragic irony, it became the symbol of the foulest tryanny that ever crawled across the earth, plunging the race into an inferno of horror—by a monster whose name ought to be erased from human records.) As much a talisman as a symbol, it has been found on Chaldean bricks, among the ruins of the city of Troy, in Egypt, on vases of ancient Cyprus, on Hittite remains and the pottery of the Etruscans, in the cave temples of India, on Roman altars and Runic monuments in Britain, in Thibet, China, and Korea, in Mexico, Peru, and among the prehistoric burial grounds of North America. There have been many interpretations of it. Perhaps the meaning most usually assigned to it is that of the Sanskrit word having in its roots an intimation of the beneficence of life, *to be* and *well*. As such, it is a sign indicating "that the maze of life may bewilder, but a path of light runs through it: *It is well* is the name of the path, and the key to life eternal is in the strange labyrinth for those whom God leadeth." [1] Others hold it to have been an emblem of the Pole Star whose stability in the sky, and the procession of

[1] *The Word in the Pattern,* Mrs. G. F. Watts.

the Ursa Major around it, so impressed the ancient world. Men saw the sun journeying across the heavens every day in a slightly different track, then standing still, as it were, at the solstice, and then returning on its way back. They saw the moon changing not only its orbit, but its size and shape and time of appearing. Only the Pole Star remained fixed and stable, and it became, not unnaturally, a light of assurance and the footstool of the Most High.[1] Whatever its meaning, the Swastika shows us the efforts of the early man to read the riddle of things, and his intuition of a love at the heart of life.

Akin to the Swastika, if not an evolution from it, was the Cross, made forever holy by the highest heroism of Love. When man climbed up out of the primeval night, with his face to heaven upturned, he had a cross in his hand. Where he got it, why he held it, and what he meant by it, no one can conjecture much less affirm.[2] Itself a paradox, its arms pointing to the four quarters of the earth, it is found in almost every part of the world carved on coins, altars, and tombs, and furnishing a design for temple architecture in Mexico and Peru, in the pagodas of India, not less than in the churches of Christ. Ages before our era, even from the remote time of the cliff-dweller, the Cross seems to have been a symbol of life, though for what reason no one knows. More

[1] *The Swastika,* Thomas Carr. See essay by the same writer in which he shows that the Swastika is the symbol of the Supreme Architect of the Universe among Operative Masons today (*The Lodge of Research,* No. 2429, Transactions, 1911-12).

[2] *Signs and Symbols,* Churchward, chap. xvii.

often it was an emblem of eternal life, especially when inclosed within a Circle which ends not, nor begins—the type of Eternity. Hence the Ank Cross or Crux Ansata of Egypt, scepter of the Lord of the Dead that never die. There is less mystery about the Circle, which was an image of the disk of the Sun and a natural symbol of completeness, of eternity. With a point within the center it became, as naturally, the emblem of the Eye of the World—that All-seeing eye of the eternal Watcher of the human scene.

Square, triangle, cross, circle—oldest symbols of humanity, all of them eloquent, each of them pointing beyond itself, as symbols always do, while giving form to the invisible truth which they invoke and seek to embody. They are beautiful if we have eyes to see, serving not merely as chance figures of fancy, but as forms of reality as it revealed itself to the mind of man. Sometimes we find them united, the Square within the Circle, and within that the Triangle, and at the center the Cross. Earliest of emblems, they show us hints and foregleams of the highest faith and philosophy, betraying not only the unity of the human mind but its kinship with the Eternal—the fact which lies at the root of every religion, and is the basis of each. Upon this Faith man builded, finding a rock beneath, refusing to think of Death as the gigantic coffin-lid of a dull and mindless universe descending upon him at last.

2

From this brief outlook upon a wide field, we may pass to a more specific and detailed study of the early prophecies of Masonry in the art of the builder. Always the symbolic must follow the actual, if it is to have reference and meaning, and the real is ever the basis of the ideal. By nature an Idealist, and living in a world of radiant mystery, it was inevitable that man should attach moral and spiritual meanings to the tools, laws, and materials of building. Even so, in almost every land and in the remotest ages we find great and beautiful truth hovering about the builder and clinging to his tools.[1] Whether there were organized orders of builders in the early times no one can tell, though there may have been. No matter; man mixed thought and worship with his work, and as he cut his altar stones and fitted them together he thought out a faith by which to live.

Not unnaturally, in times when the earth was thought to be a Square the Cube had emblematical

[1] Here again the literature is voluminous, but not entirely satisfactory. A most interesting book is *Signs and Symbols of Primordial Man*, by Churchward, in that it surveys the symbolism of the race always with reference to its Masonic suggestion. Vivid and popular is *Symbols and Legends of Freemasonry*, by Finlayson but he often strains facts in order to stretch them over wide gaps of time. Dr. Mackey's *Symbolism of Freemasonry*, though written more than sixty years ago, remains a classic of the order. Unfortunately the lectures of Albert Pike on *Symbolism* are not accessible to the general reader, for they are rich mines of insight and scholarship, albeit betraying his partisanship of the Indo-Aryan race. Many minor books might be named, but we need a work brought up to date and written in the light of recent research.

meanings it could hardly have for us. From earliest ages it was a venerated symbol, and the oblong cube signified immensity of space from the base of earth to the zenith of the heavens. It was a sacred emblem of the Lydian Kubele, known to the Romans in after ages as Ceres or Cybele—hence, as some aver, the derivation of the word "cube." At first rough stones were most sacred, and an altar of hewn stones was forbidden.[1] With the advent of the cut cube, the temple became known as the House of the Hammer —its altar, always in the center, being in the form of a cube and regarded as "an index or emblem of Truth, ever true to itself." [2] Indeed, the cube, as Plutarch points out in his essay *On the Cessation of Oracles,* "is palpably the proper emblem of rest, on account of the security and firmness of the superficies." He further tells us that the pyramid is an image of the triangular flame ascending from a square altar; and since no one knows, his guess is as good as any. At any rate, Mercury, Apollo, Neptune, and Hercules were worshiped under the form of a square stone, while a large black stone was the emblem of Buddha among the Hindoos, of Manah Theus-Ceres in Arabia, and of Odin in Scandinavia. Everyone knows of the Stone of Memnon in Egypt, which was said to speak at sunrise—as, in truth, all stones spoke to man in the sunrise of time.[3]

[1] Exod. 20:25.
[2] *Antiquities of Cornwall,* Borlase.
[3] *Lost Language of Symbolism,* Bayley, chap. xviii; also in the Bible, Deut. 32:18, II Sam. 22:3, 32, Psa. 28:1, Matt. 16:18, I Cor. 10:4.

More eloquent, if possible, was the Pillar uplifted, like the pillars of the gods upholding the heavens. Whatever may have been the origin of pillars, and there is more than one theory, Evans has shown that they were everywhere worshiped as gods.[1] Indeed, the gods themselves were pillars of Light and Power, as in Egypt Horus and Sut were the twin-builders and supporters of heaven; and Bacchus among the Thebans. At the entrance of the temple of Amenta, at the door of the house of Ptah—as, later, in the porch of the temple of Solomon—stood two pillars. Still further back, in the old solar myths, at the gateway of eternity stood two pillars—Strength and Wisdom. In India, and among the Mayas and Incas, there were three pillars at the portals of the earthly and skyey temple—Wisdom, Strength, and Beauty. When man set up a pillar, he became a fellow-worker with Him whom the old sages of China used to call "the first Builder." Also, pillars were set up to mark the holy places of vision and Divine deliverance, as when Jacob erected a pillar at Bethel, Joshua at Gilgal, and Samuel at Mizpeh and Shen. Always they were symbols of stability, of what the Egyptians described as "the place of establishing forever,"—emblems of the faith "that the pillars of the earth are the Lord's, and He hath set the world upon them." [2]

Long before our era we find the working tools of the Mason used as emblems of the very truths which they teach today. In the oldest classic of China, *The*

[1] *Tree and Pillar Cult,* Sir Arthur Evans.
[2] I Sam. 2:8, Psa. 75:8, Job 26:7, Rev. 3:12.

Book of History, dating back to the twentieth century before Christ, we read the instruction: "Ye officers of the Government, apply the compasses." Even if we begin where *The Book of History* ends, we find many such allusions more than seven hundred years before the Christian era. For example, in the famous canonical work, called *The Great Learning,* which has been referred to the fifth century B. C., we read, that a man should abstain from doing unto others what he would not they should do to him; "and this," the writer adds, "is called the principle of acting on the square." So also Confucius and his great follower, Mencius. In the writings of Mencius it is taught that men should apply the square and compasses morally to their lives, and the level and the marking line besides, if they would walk in the straight and even paths of wisdom, and keep themselves within the bounds of honor and virtue.[1] In the sixth book of his philosophy we find these words:

> A Master Mason, in teaching apprentices, makes use of the compasses and the square. Ye who are engaged in the pursuit of wisdom must also make use of the compass and square.[2]

There are even evidences, in the earliest historic records of China, of the existence of a system of faith expressed in allegoric form, and illustrated by the symbols of building. The secrets of this faith seem

[1] *Freemasonry in China,* Giles. Also Gould, *His. Masonry,* vol. i, chap. i.

[2] *Chinese Classics,* by Legge, i, 219-45.

to have been orally transmitted, the leaders alone pretending to have full knowledge of them. Oddly enough, it seems to have gathered about a symbolical temple put up in the desert, and the various officers of the faith were distinguished by symbolic jewels, while at its rites they wore leather aprons.[1] From such records as we have it is not possible to say whether the builders themselves used their tools as emblems, or whether it was the thinkers who first used them to teach moral truths. In any case, they were understood; and the point here is that, thus early, the tools of the builder were teachers of wise and good and beautiful truth. Indeed, we need not go outside the Bible to find both the materials and working tools of the Mason so employed: [2]

> For every house is builded by some man; but the builder of all things is God . . . whose house we are.[3]
> Behold, I lay in Zion for a foundation a tried stone, a precious corner-stone, a sure foundation.[4]
> The stone which the builders rejected is become the head of the corner.[5]
> Ye also, as living stones, are built up into a spiritual house.[6]

[1] Essay by Chaloner Alabaster, *Ars Quatuor Coronatorum*, vol. ii, 121-24. It is not too much to say that the Transactions of this Lodge of Research are the richest storehouse of Masonic lore in the world.

[2] Matt. 16:18, Eph. 2:20-22, I Cor. 2:9-17. Woman is the house and wall of man, without whose bounding and redeeming influence he would be dissipated and lost (Song of Solomon 8:10). So also by the mystics (*The Perfect Way*).

[3] Heb. 3:4.

[4] Isa. 28:16.

[5] Psa. 118:22, Matt. 21:42

[6] I Pet. 2:5.

When he established the heavens I was there, when he set the compass upon the face of the deep, when he marked out the foundations of the earth: then was I by him as master workman.[1]

The Lord stood upon a wall made by a plumbline, with a plumbline in his hand. And the Lord said unto me, Amos, what seest thou? And I said, A plumbline. Then said the Lord, Behold, I will set a plumbline in the midst of my people Israel: I will not again pass by them any more.[2]

Ye shall offer the holy oblation foursquare, with the possession of the city.[3]

And the city lieth foursquare, and the length is as large as the breadth.[4]

Him that overcometh I will make a pillar in the temple of my God; and I will write upon him my new name.[5]

For we know that when our earthly house of this tabernacle is dissolved, we have a building of God, an house not made with hands, eternal in the heavens.[6]

If further proof were needed, it has been preserved for us in the imperishable stones of Egypt.[7] The famous obelisk, known as Cleopatra's Needle, now in Central Park, New York, the gift to our nation

[1] Prov. 8:27-30, Revised Version.
[2] Amos 7:7, 8.
[3] Ezk. 48:20.
[4] Rev. 21:16.
[5] Rev. 3:12.
[6] II Cor. 5:1.
[7] *Egyptian Obelisks*, H. H. Gorringe. The obelisk in Central Park, the expenses for removing which were paid by W. H. Vanderbilt, was examined by the Grand Lodge of New York, and its emblems pronounced to be unmistakably Masonic. This book gives full account of all obelisks brought to Europe from Egypt, their measurements, inscriptions, and transportation.

from Ismail, Khedive of Egypt in 1878, is a mute but
eloquent witness of the antiquity of the simple symbols of the Mason. Originally it stood as one of a
pair of obelisks in front of the great temple of
the Sun-god at Heliopolis, so long a seat of Egyptian
learning and religion, dating back, it is thought, to
the fifteenth century before Christ. It was removed
to Alexandria and re-erected by a Roman architect
and engineer named Pontius, B. C. 22. When it was
taken down in 1879 to be brought to America, all
the emblems of the builders were found in the
foundation. The rough Cube and the polished Cube
in pure white limestone, the Square cut in syenite,
an iron Trowel, a lead Plummet, the arc of a Circle,
the serpent-symbols of Wisdom, a stone Trestle-
board, a stone bearing the Master's Mark, and a
hieroglyphic word meaning *Temple*—all so placed
and preserved as to show, beyond doubt, that they
had high symbolic meaning. Whether they were in
the original foundation, or were placed there when
the obelisk was removed, no one can tell. Nevertheless, they were there, concrete witnesses of the fact
that the builders worked in the light of a mystical
faith, of which their tools were emblems.

Much has been written of buildings, their origin,
age, and architecture, but of the builders hardly a
word—so quickly is the worker forgotten, save as he
lives in his work. Though we have no records other
than these emblems, it is an obvious inference that
there were orders of builders even in those early
ages, to whom these symbols were sacred; and this

inference is the more plausible when we remember the importance of the builder both to religion and the State. What though the builders have fallen into dust, to which all things mortal decline, they still hold out their symbols for us to read, speaking their thoughts in a language easy to understand. Across the piled-up debris of ages they whisper the old familiar truths, and it will be a part of this study to trace those symbols through the centuries, showing that they have always had the same high meanings. They bear witness not only to the unity of the human mind, but to the existence of a common system of truth veiled in allegory and taught in symbols. As such, they are prophecies of Masonry as we know it, whose genius it is to take what is old, simple, and universal, and use it to bring men together and make them friends.

> Shore calls to shore
> That the line is unbroken!

THE DRAMA OF FAITH

And so the Quest goes on. And the Quest, as it may be, ends in attainment—we know not where and when: so long as we can conceive of our separate existence, the quest goes on—an attainment continued henceforward. And ever shall the study of the ways which have been followed by those who have passed in front be a help on our own path.

It is well, it is of all things beautiful and perfect, holy and high of all, to be conscious of the path which does in fine lead thither where we seek to go, namely, the goal which is in God. Taking nothing with us which does not belong to ourselves, leaving nothing behind us that is of our real selves, we shall find in the great attainment that the companions of our toil are with us. And the place is the Valley of Peace.

—ARTHUR EDWARD WAITE, *The Secret Tradition*

Chapter Three

THE DRAMA OF FAITH

MAN DOES not live by bread alone; he lives by Faith, Hope, and Love, and the first of these was Faith. Nothing in the human story is more striking than the persistent, passionate, profound protest of man against death. Even in the earliest time we see him daring to stand erect at the gates of the grave, disputing its verdict, refusing to let it have the last word, and making argument in behalf of his soul. For Emerson, as for Addison, that fact alone was proof enough of immortality, as revealing a universal intuition of eternal life. Others may not be so easily convinced, but no man who has the heart of a man can fail to be impressed by the ancient, heroic faith of his race.

Nowhere has this faith ever been more vivid or victorious than among the old Egyptians.[1] In the

[1] Of course, faith in immortality was in nowise peculiar to Egypt, but was universal; as vivid in *The Upanishads* of India as in the

ancient *Book of the Dead*—which is, indeed, a Book of Resurrection—occur the words: "The soul to heaven; the body to earth"; and that first faith is our faith today. Of King Unas, who lived in the third millennium, it is written: "Behold, thou hast not gone as one dead, but as one living." Nor has any one in our day set forth this faith with more simple eloquence than the Hymn to Osiris, in the Papyrus of Hunefer. So in the Pyramid Texts the dead are spoken of as Those Who Ascend, the Imperishable Ones who shine as stars, and the gods are invoked to witness the death of the king "Dawning as a Soul." There is deep prophecy, albeit touched with poignant pathos, in these broken exclamations written on the pyramid walls:

> Thou diest not! Have ye said that he would die? He diest not; this King Pepi lives forever! Live! Thou shalt not die! He has escaped his day of death! Thou livest, thou livest, raise thee up! Thou diest not, stand

Pyramid records. It rests upon the consensus of the insight, experience, and aspiration of the race; its strongest proof, perhaps, being the unquenchable conviction that the values of life are real, and that whatsoever has value for God is exempt from the touch of time, change, and death. But the records of Egypt, like its monuments, are richer than those of other nations, if not older. Moreover, the drama of faith with which we have to do here had its origin in Egypt, whence it spread to Tyre, Athens, and Rome—and, as we shall see, even to England. For brief expositions of Egyptian faith see *Egyptian Conceptions of Immortality,* by G. A. Reisner, and *Religion and Thought in Egypt,* by J. H. Breasted.

More recent opinion tends to the view that the *Book of the Dead* was really a ritual of eternal life performed, perhaps, in the dim chambers of the Pyramids. It ought to be added that when Egypt lost its faith in the immortal life—"lost its nerve" so to speak—its empire became a mummery.

up, raise thee up! Thou perishest not eternally! Thou diest not! [1]

Nevertheless, nor poetry nor chant nor solemn ritual could make death other than death; and the Pyramid Texts, while refusing to utter the fatal word, give wistful reminiscences of that blessed age "before death came forth." However high the faith of man, the masterful negation and collapse of the body was a fact, and it was to keep that daring faith alive and aglow that The Mysteries were instituted. Beginning, it may be, in incantation, they rose to heights of influence and power, giving dramatic portrayal of the unconquerable faith of man. Watching the sun rise from the tomb of night, and the spring return in glory after the death of winter, man reasoned from analogy—justifying a faith that held him as truly as he held it—that the race, sinking into the grave, would rise triumphant over death.

1

There were many variations on this theme as the drama of faith evolved, and as it passed from land to land; but the *motif* was ever the same, and they all were derived, directly or indirectly, from the old Osirian passion-play in Egypt. Against the background of the ancient Solar religion, Osiris made his advent as Lord of the Nile and fecund Spirit of vegetable life—son of Nut the sky-goddess and Geb the earth-god; and nothing in the story of the Nile-

[1] Pyramid Texts, 775, 1262, 1453, 1477.

dwellers is more appealing than his conquest of the hearts of the people against all odds.[1] Howbeit, that history need not detain us here, except to say that by the time his passion had become the drama of national faith, it had been bathed in all the tender hues of human life; though somewhat of its solar radiance still lingered in it. Enough to say that of all the gods, called into being by the hopes and fears of men who dwelt in times of yore on the banks of the Nile, Osiris was the most beloved. Osiris the benign father, Isis his sorrowful and faithful wife, and Horus whose filial piety and heroism shine like diamonds in a heap of stones—about this trinity were woven the ideals of Egyptian faith and family life. Hear now the story of the oldest drama of the race, which for more than three thousand years held captive the hearts of men.[2]

Osiris was Ruler of Eternity, but by reason of his visible shape seemed nearly akin to man—revealing a divine humanity. His success was chiefly due, however, to the gracious speech of Isis, his sister-wife,

[1] For a full account of the evolution of the Osirian theology from the time it emerged from the mists of myth until its conquest, see *Religion and Thought in Egypt*, by Breasted, the latest, if not the most brilliant, book written in the light of the completest translation of the Pyramid Texts (especially lecture v).

[2] Much has been written about the Egyptian Mysteries from the days of Plutarch's *De Iside et Osiride* and the *Metamorphoses* of Apuleius to the huge volumes of Baron Sainte Croix. For popular reading the *Kings and Gods of Egypt*, by Moret (chaps. iii-iv), and the delightfully vivid *Hermes and Plato*, by Schure, could hardly be surpassed. But Plutarch and Apuleius, both initiates, are our best authorities, even if their oath of silence prevents them from telling us what we most want to know.

whose charm men could neither reckon nor resist. Together they labored for the good of man, teaching him to discern the plants fit for food, themselves pressing the grapes and drinking the first cup of wine. They made known the veins of metal running through the earth, of which man was ignorant, and taught him to make weapons. They initiated man into the intellectual and moral life, taught him ethics and religion, how to read the starry sky, song and dance and the rhythm of music. Above all, they evoked in men a sense of immortality, of a destiny beyond the tomb. Nevertheless, they had enemies at once stupid and cunning, keen-witted but short-sighted—the dark force of evil which still weaves the fringe of crime on the borders of human life.

Side by side with Osiris, lived the impious Set-Typhon, as Evil ever haunts the Good. While Osiris was absent, Typhon—whose name means serpent—filled with envy and malice, sought to usurp his throne; but his plot was frustrated by Isis. Where-upon he resolved to kill Osiris. This he did, having invited him to a feast, by persuading him to enter a chest, offering, as if in jest, to present the richly carved chest to any one of his guests who, lying down inside it, found he was of the same size. When Osiris got in and stretched himself out, the conspirators closed the chest, and flung it into the Nile.[1] Thus

---

[1] Among the Hindoos, whose Krishna is the same as the Osiris of Egypt, the gods of summer were beneficent, making the days fruitful. But "the three wretches" who presided over winter, were cut off from the zodiac; and as they were "found missing," they were accused of the death of Krishna.

far, the gods had not known death. They had grown
old, with white hair and trembling limbs, but old
age had not led to death. As soon as Isis heard of
this infernal treachery, she cut her hair, clad herself in a garb of mourning, ran thither and yon, a
prey to the most cruel anguish, seeking the body.
Weeping and distracted, she never tarried, never
tired in her sorrowful quest.

Meanwhile, the waters carried the chest out to sea,
as far as Byblos in Syria, the town of Adonis, where
it lodged against a shrub of arica, or tamarisk—like
an acacia tree.[1] Owing to the virtue of the body, the
shrub, at its touch, shot up into a tree, growing
around it, and protecting it, until the king of that
country cut the tree which hid the chest in its bosom,
and made from it a column for his palace. At last
Isis, led by a vision, came to Byblos, made herself
known, and asked for the column. Hence the picture of her weeping over a broken column torn
from the palace, while Horus, god of Time, stands
behind her pouring ambrosia on her hair. She took
the body back to Egypt, to the city of Bouto; but
Typhon, hunting by moonlight, found the chest,

---

[1] A literary parallel in the story of *Æneas*, by Vergil, is most sug-
gestive. Priam, king of Troy, in the beginning of the Trojan war
committed his son Polydorus to the care of Polymester, king of Thrace,
and sent him a great sum of money. After Troy was taken the
Thracian, for the sake of the money, killed the young prince and
privately buried him. Æneas, coming into that country, and acci-
dentally plucking up a shrub that was near him on the side of the
hill, discovered the murdered body of Polydorus. Other legends of
such accidental discoveries of unknown graves haunted the olden
time, and may have been suggested by the story of Isis.

and having recognized the body of Osiris, mangled it and scattered it beyond recognition. Isis, embodiment of the old world-sorrow for the dead, continued her pathetic quest, gathering piece by piece the body of her dismembered husband, and giving him decent interment. Such was the life and death of Osiris, but as his career pictured the cycle of nature, it could not of course end here.

Horus fought with Typhon, losing an eye in the battle, but finally overthrew him and took him prisoner. There are several versions of his fate, but he seems to have been tried, sentenced, and executed—"cut in three pieces," as the Pyramid Texts relate. Thereupon the faithful son went in solemn procession to the grave of his father, opened it, and called upon Osiris to rise: "Stand up! Thou shalt not end, thou shalt not perish!" But death was deaf. Here the Pyramid Texts recite the mortuary ritual, with its hymns and chants; but in vain. At length Osiris awakes, weary and feeble, and by the aid of the strong grip of the lion-god he gains control of his body, and is lifted from death to life.[1] Thereafter, by virtue of his victory over death, Osiris becomes Lord of the Land of Death, his scepter an Ank Cross, his throne a Square.

2

Such, in brief, was the ancient allegory of eternal life, upon which there were many elaborations as

---

[1] *The Gods of the Egyptians*, by E. A. W. Budge; *La Place des Victores*, by Austin Fryar, especially the colored plates.

the drama unfolded; but always, under whatever variation of local color, of national accent or emphasis, its central theme remained the same. Often perverted and abused, it was everywhere a dramatic expression of the great human aspiration for triumph over death and union with God, and the belief in the ultimate victory of Good over Evil. Not otherwise would this drama have held the hearts of men through long ages, and won the eulogiums of the most enlightened men of antiquity—of Pythagoras, Socrates, Plato, Euripides, Plutarch, Pindar, Isocrates, Epictetus, and Marcus Aurelius. Writing to his wife after the loss of their little girl, Plutarch commends to her the hope set forth in the mystic rites and symbols of this drama, as, elsewhere, he testifies that it kept him "as far from superstition as from atheism," and helped him to approach the truth. For deeper minds this drama had a double meaning, teaching not only immortality after death, but the awakening of man upon earth from animalism to a life of purity, justice, and honor. How nobly this practical aspect was taught, and with what fineness of spiritual insight, may be seen in *Secret Sermon on the Mountain* in the Hermetic lore of Greece: [1]

> What may I say, my son? I can but tell thee this. Whenever I see within myself the Simple Vision brought to birth out of God's mercy, I have passed through myself into a Body that can never die. Then I am not what I was before. . . . They who are thus

[1] *Quests New and Old,* by G. R. S. Mead.

born are children of a Divine race. This race, my son, is never taught; but when He willeth it, its memory is restored by God. It is the "Way of Birth in God." . . . Withdraw into thyself and it will come. *Will,* and it comes to pass.

Isis herself is said to have established the first temple of the Mysteries, the oldest being those practiced at Memphis. Of these there were two orders, the Lesser to which the many were eligible, and which consisted of dialogue and ritual, with certain signs, tokens, grips, passwords; and the Greater, reserved for the few who approved themselves worthy of being entrusted with the highest secrets of science, philosophy, and religion. For these the candidate had to undergo trial, purification, danger, austere asceticism, and, at last, regeneration through dramatic death amid rejoicing. Such as endured the ordeal with valor were then taught, orally and by symbol, the highest wisdom to which man had attained, including geometry, astronomy, the fine arts, the laws of nature, as well as the truths of faith. Awful oaths of secrecy were exacted, and Plutarch describes a man kneeling, his hands bound, a cord round his body, and a knife at his throat—death being the penalty of violating the obligation. Even then, Pythagoras had to wait almost twenty years to learn the hidden wisdom of Egypt, so cautious were they of candidates, especially of foreigners. But he made noble use of it when, later, he founded a secret order of his own at Crotona, in Greece, in which, among other things, he taught geometry, using numbers as symbols of spiritual truth.[1]

From Egypt the Mysteries passed with little change to Asia Minor, Greece, and Rome, the names of local gods being substituted for those of Osiris and Isis. The Grecian or Eleusinian Mysteries, established 1800 B. C., represented Demeter and Persephone, and depicted the death of Dionysius with stately ritual which led the neophyte from death into life and immortality. They taught the unity of God, the immutable necessity of mortality, and a life after death, investing initiates with signs and passwords by which they could know each other in the dark as well as in the light. The Mithraic or Persian Mysteries celebrated the eclipse of the Sun-god, using the signs of the zodiac, the procession of the seasons, the death of nature, and the birth of spring. The Adoniac or Syrian cults were similar, Adonis being killed, but revived to point to life through death. In the Cabiric Mysteries on the island of Samothrace, Atys the Sun was killed by his brothers the Seasons, and at the vernal equinox was restored to life. So, also, the Druids, as far north as England, taught of one God the tragedy of winter and summer, and conducted the initiate through the valley of death to life everlasting.[2]

[1] *Pythagoras,* by Edouard Schure—a fascinating story of that great thinker and teacher. The use of numbers by Pythagoras must not, however, be confounded with the mystical, or rather fantastic, mathematics of the Kabbalists of a later time.

[2] For a vivid account of the spread of the Mysteries of Isis and Mithra over the Roman Empire, see *Roman Life from Nero to*

Shortly before the Christian era, when faith was failing and the world seemed reeling to its ruin, there was a great revival of the Mystery-religions. Imperial edict was powerless to stay it, much less to stop it. From Egypt, from the far East, they came rushing in like a tide, Isis "of the myriad names" vying with Mithra, the patron saint of the soldier, for the homage of the multitude. If we ask the secret reason for this influx of mysticism, no single answer can be given to the question. What influence the reigning mystery-cults had upon the new, uprising Christianity is also hard to know, and the issue is still in debate. That they did influence the early Church is evident from the writings of the Fathers, and some go so far as to say that the Mysteries died at last only to live again in the ritual of the Church. St. Paul in his missionary journeys came in contact with the Mysteries, and even makes use of some of their technical terms in his epistles; [1] but he condemned them on the ground that what they sought

Aurelius, by Dill (bk. iv, chaps. v-vi). Franz Cumont is the great authority on Mithra, and his *Mysteries of Mithra* and *Oriental Religions* trace the origin and influence of that cult with accuracy, insight, and charm. W. W. Reade, brother of Charles Reade the novelist, left a study of *The Veil of Isis, or Mysteries of the Druids,* finding in the vestiges of Druidism "the Emblems of Masonry."

[1] Col. 2:8-19. See *Mysteries Pagan and Christian,* by C. Cheethan; also *Monumental Christianity,* by Lundy, especially chapter on "The Discipline of the Secret." For a full discussion of the attitude of St. Paul, see *St. Paul and the Mystery-Religions,* by Kennedy, a work of fine scholarship. That Christianity had its esoteric is plain—as it was natural—from the writings of the Fathers, including Origen, Cyril, Basil, Gregory, Ambrose, Augustine, and others. Chrysostom often uses the word *initiation* in respect of Christian teaching, while Tertullian denounces the pagan mysteries as counterfeit imitations by Satan

to teach in drama can be known only by spiritual experience—a sound insight, though surely drama may assist to that experience, else public worship might also come under ban.

3

Toward the end of their power, the Mysteries fell into the mire and became corrupt, as all things human are apt to do: even the Church itself being no exception. But that at their highest and best they were not only lofty and noble, but elevating and refining, there can be no doubt, and that they served a high purpose is equally clear. No one who has read in the *Metamorphoses* of Apuleius the initiation of Lucius into the Mysteries of Isis can doubt that the effect on the votary was profound and purifying. He tells us that the ceremony of initiation "is, as it were, to suffer death," and that he stood in the presence of the gods, "ay, stood near and worshiped." *Far hence ye profane, and all who are polluted by sin,* was the motto of the Mysteries, and Cicero testifies that what a man learned in the house of the hidden place made him want to live nobly, and gave him happy hopes for the hour of death.

Indeed, the Mysteries, as Plato said,[1] were established by men of great genius who, in the early ages,

of the Christian secret rites and teachings: "He also baptizes those who believe in him, and promises that they shall come forth, cleansed of their sins." Other Christian writers were more tolerant, finding in Christ the answer to the aspiration uttered in the Mysteries; and therein, it may be, they were right.

[1] *Phaedo.*

strove to teach purity, to ameliorate the cruelty of the race, to refine its manners and morals, and to restrain society by stronger bonds than those which human laws impose. No mystery any longer attaches to what they taught, but only as to the particular rites, dramas, and symbols used in their teaching. They taught faith in the unity and spirituality of God, the sovereign authority of the moral law, heroic purity of soul, austere discipline of character, and the hope of a life beyond the tomb. Thus in ages of darkness, of complexity, of conflicting peoples, tongues, and faiths, these great orders toiled in behalf of friendship, bringing men together under a banner of faith, and training them for a nobler moral life. Tender and tolerant of all faiths, they formed an all-embracing moral and spiritual fellowship which rose above barriers of nation, race, and creed, satisfying the craving of men for unity, while evoking in them a sense of that eternal mysticism out of which all religions were born. Their ceremonies, so far as we know them, were stately dramas of the moral life and the fate of the soul. Mystery and secrecy added impressiveness, and fable and enigma disguised in imposing spectacle the laws of justice, piety, and the hope of immortality.

Masonry stands in this tradition; and if we may not say that it is historically related to the great ancient orders, it is their spiritual descendant, and renders much the same ministry to our age which the Mysteries rendered to the olden world. It is, indeed, the same stream of sweetness and light flowing in our day—like the fabled river Alpheus which, gathering the waters of a hundred rills along the hillsides of Arcadia, sank, lost to sight, in a chasm in the earth, only to reappear in the fountain of Arethusa. This at least is true: the Greater Ancient Mysteries were prophetic of Masonry whose drama is an epitome of universal initiation, and whose simple symbols are the depositaries of the noblest wisdom and hope of mankind. As such, it brings men together at the altar of prayer, keeps alive the truths that make us men, seeking, by every resource of art, to make tangible the power of love, the worth of beauty, and the reality of the ideal.

THE SECRET DOCTRINE

The value of man does not consist in the truth which he possesses, or means to possess, but in the sincere pain which he hath taken to find it out. For his powers do not augment by possessing truth, but by investigating it, wherein consists his only perfectibility. Possession lulls the energy of man, and makes him idle and proud. If God held inclosed in his right hand absolute truth, and in his left only the inward lively impulse toward truth, and if He said to me: Choose! even at the risk of exposing mankind to continual erring, I most humbly would seize His left hand, and say: Father, give! absolute truth belongs to Thee alone.

G. E. LESSING, Fragments

Chapter Four

THE SECRET DOCTRINE

1

OD EVER shields us from premature ideas, said the gracious and wise Emerson; and so does nature. She holds back her secrets until man is fit to be entrusted with them, lest by rashness he destroy himself. Those who seek find, not because the truth is far off, but because the discipline of the quest makes them ready for the truth, and worthy to receive it. By a certain sure instinct the great teachers of our race have regarded the highest truth less as a gift bestowed than as a trophy to be won. Everything must not be told to everybody. Truth is power, and when held by untrue hands it may become a plague. Even Jesus had His "little flock" to whom He confided much which He kept from the world, or else taught it in parables cryptic and veiled.[1] One of His sayings in explana-

[1] Matt. 13:10, 11.

tion of His method is quoted by Clement of Alexandria in his *Homilies*:

> It was not from grudgingness that our Lord gave the
> charge in a certain Gospel: *"My mystery is for Me and
> the sons of My house."* [1]

This more withdrawn teaching, hinted in the
saying of the Master, with the arts of spiritual culture employed, has come to be known as the Secret
Doctrine, or the Hidden Wisdom. A persistent tradition affirms that throughout the ages, and in every
land, behind the system of faith accepted by the
masses an inner and deeper doctrine has been held
and taught by those able to grasp it. This hidden
faith has undergone many changes of outward expression, using now one set of symbols and now another, but its central tenets have remained the same;
and necessarily so, since the ultimates of thought are
ever immutable. By the same token, those who have
eyes to see have no difficulty in penetrating the varying veils of expression and identifying the underlying truths; thus confirming in the arcana of faith
what we found to be true in its earliest forms—the
oneness of the human mind and the unity of truth.

There are those who resent the suggestion that
there is, or can be, secrecy in regard to spiritual
truths which, if momentous at all, are of common
moment to all. For this reason Demonax, in the
Lucian play, would not be initiated, because, if the
Mysteries were bad, he would not keep silent as a

---

[1] *Unwritten Sayings of Our Lord*, David Smith, vii.

warning; and if they were good, he would proclaim them as a duty. The objection is, however, unsound, as a little thought will reveal. Secrecy in such matters inheres in the nature of the truths themselves, not in any affected superiority of a few elect minds —for, to say no more, the presence of vanity is proof that the highest truth is far away. Qualification for the knowledge of higher things is, and must always be, a matter of personal fitness. Other qualification there is none. For those who have that fitness the Secret Doctrine is as clear as sunlight, and for those who have it not the truth would still be secret though shouted from the housetop. The Grecian Mysteries were certainly secret, yet the fact of their existence was a matter of common knowledge, and there was no more secrecy about their sanctuaries than there is about a cathedral. Their presence testified to the public that a deeper than the popular faith did exist, but the right to admission into them depended upon the whole-hearted wish of the aspirant, and his willingness to fit himself to know the truth. The old maxim applies here, that when the pupil is ready the teacher is found waiting, and he passes on to know a truth hitherto hidden because he lacked either the aptitude or the desire.

All is mystery as of course, but mystification is another thing, and the tendency to befog a theme which needs to be clarified, is to be regretted. Here lies, perhaps, the real reason for the feeling of resentment against the idea of a Secret Doctrine, and one must admit that it is not without justification. For example, we are told that behind the age-long struggle of man to know the truth there exists a hidden fraternity of initiates, adepts in esoteric lore, known to themselves but not to the world, who have had in their keeping, through the centuries, the high truths which they permit to be dimly adumbrated in the popular faiths, but which the rest of the race are too obtuse, even yet, to grasp save in an imperfect and limited degree. These hidden sages, it would seem, look upon our eager aspiring humanity much like the patient masters of an idiot school, watching it go on forever seeking without finding, while they sit in seclusion keeping the keys of the occult.[1] All of which would be very wonderful, if true. It is, however, only one more of those fascinating fictions with which mystery-mongers entertain themselves, and deceive others. Small wonder that thinking men turn from such fanciful folly with mingled feelings of pity and disgust. Sages there have been in every land and time, and their lofty wisdom has the unity which inheres in all high human thought, but that there is now, or has ever been, a conscious, much less a continuous, fellow-

---

[1] By occultism is meant the belief in, and the claim to be able to use, a certain range of forces neither natural nor technically supernatural, but more properly to be called preternatural—often, though by no means always, for evil or selfish ends. Some extend the term occultism to cover mysticism and the spiritual life generally, but that is not a legitimate use of either word. Occultism seeks to get; mysticism to give. The one is audacious and seclusive, the other humble and open; and if we are not to end in blunderland we must not confound the two (*Mysticism*, by E. Underhill, part i, chap. vii). Mysticism seeks to explore God; occultism to exploit God. One is religion, the other magic—or akin to it.

ship of superior souls holding as secrets truths denied to their fellow-men, verges upon the absurd.

Indeed, what is called the Secret Doctrine differs not one whit from what has been taught openly and earnestly, so far as such truth can be taught in words or pictured in symbols, by the highest minds of almost every land and language. The difference lies less in what is taught than in the way in which it is taught; not so much in matter as in method. Also, we must not forget that, with few exceptions, the men who have led our race farthest along the way toward the Mount of Vision, have not been men who learned their lore from any coterie of esoteric experts, but, rather, men who told in song what they had been taught in sorrow—initiates into eternal truth, to be sure, but by the grace of God and the divine right of genius! [1] Seers, sages, mystics, saints—these are they who, having sought in sincerity, found in reality, and the memory of them is a

---

[1] Much time would have been saved, and not a little confusion avoided, had this obvious fact been kept in mind. Even so charming a book as *Jesus, the Last Great Initiate,* by Schure—not to speak of *The Great Work,* by J. E. Richardson and *Mystic Masonry,* by the late Dr. Buck—is clearly, though not intentionally, misleading. Of a piece with this is the effort, apparently deliberate and concerted, to rob the Hebrew race of all spiritual originality, as witness so able a work as *Our Own Religion in Persia,* by Mills, to name no other. Our own religion? Assuredly, if by that is meant the one great, universal religion of humanity. But the sundering difference between the Bible and any other book that speaks to mankind about God and Life and Death, sets the Hebrew race apart as supreme in its religious genius, as the Greeks were in philosophical acumen and artistic power, and the Romans in executive skill. Leaving all theories of inspiration out of account, facts are facts, and the Bible has no peer in the literature of mankind.

kind of religion. Some of them, like Pythagoras, were trained for their quest in the schools of the Secret Doctrine, but others went their way alone, though never unattended, and, led by "the vision splendid," they came at last to the gate and passed into the City.

Why, then, it may be asked, speak of such a thing as the Secret Doctrine at all, since it were better named the Open Secret of the world? For two rea-sons, both of which have been intimated: first, in the olden times unwonted knowledge of any kind was deemed a very dangerous possession, and the truths of science and philosophy, equally with reli-gious ideas other than those in vogue among the multitude, had to seek the protection of obscurity. If this necessity gave designing priestcraft its oppor-tunity, it nevertheless offered the security and silence needed by the thinker and seeker after truth in dark times. Hence there arose in the ancient world, wherever the human mind was alive and spiritual, systems of exoteric and esoteric instruc-tion; that is, of truth taught openly and truth con-cealed. Disciples were advanced from the outside to the inside of this divine philosophy, as we have seen, by degrees of initiation. Whereas, by symbols, dark sayings, and dramatic ritual the novice received only hints of what was later made plain to those who per-severed in their quest and proved themselves trust-worthy.

Second, this hidden teaching may indeed be de-scribed as the open secret of the world, because it is open, yet understood only by those fit to receive it, those who do not seek the secret merely to satisfy curiosity—who are not content to see the truth and not to be changed by it. Hence, the familiar refrain in the teaching of Jesus: "He that hath ears to hear, let him hear." What kept it hidden was no arbitrary restriction, but only a lack of insight and fineness of mind to appreciate and assimilate it. Nor could it be otherwise; and this is as true today as ever it was in the days of the Mysteries, and so it will be until whatever is to be the end of mortal things. Fitness for the finer truths cannot be conferred; it must be developed. Without it the teachings of the sages are enigmas that seem unintelligible, if not contradictory. In so far, then, as the discipline of initiation, and its use of art in drama and symbol, help toward purity of soul and spiritual awakening, by so much do they prepare men for the truth; by so much and no further. So that, the Secret Doctrine, whether as taught by the ancient Mysteries or by modern Masonry, is less a doctrine than a discipline —a method of organized spiritual culture, and as such has a place and a ministry among men.

2

Perhaps the greatest student in this field of esoteric teaching and method, certainly the greatest now living,[1] is Arthur Edward Waite, to whom it is a pleasure to pay tribute. By nature a symbolist, if not a sacramentalist, he found in such studies a task for

[1] Arthur Edward Waite died May 19, 1942.

which he was almost ideally fitted by temperament, training, and genius. Engaged in business, but not absorbed by it, years of quiet, leisurely toil have made him master of the vast literature and lore of his subject, to the study of which he brought a religious nature, the accuracy and skill of a scholar, a sureness and delicacy of insight at onc~ sympathetic and critical, the soul of a poet, and a patience as untiring as it is rewarding; qualities rare indeed, and still more rarely blended. Prolific but seldom prolix, he writes with grace, ease, and lucidity, albeit in a style often opulent, and touched at times with lights and jewels from old alchemists, antique liturgies, remote and haunting romance, secret orders of initiation, and other recondite sources not easily traced. Much learning and many kinds of wisdom are in his pages, and withal an air of serenity, of tolerance; and if he is of those who turn down another street when miracles are performed in the neighborhood, it is because, having found the inner truth, he asks for no sign.

Always he writes in the conviction that all great subjects bring us back to the one subject which is alone great, and that scholarly criticisms, folk-lore, and deep philosophy are little less than useless if they fall short of directing us to our true end—the attainment of that living Truth which is about us everywhere. He conceives of our mortal life as one eternal Quest of that living Truth, taking many phases and forms, yet ever at heart the same aspiration, to trace which he has made it his labor and joy

to essay. Through all his pages he is following out
the tradition of this Quest, in its myriad aspects,
especially since the Christian era, disfigured though
it has been at times by superstition, and distorted
at others by bigotry, but still, in what guise soever,
containing as its secret the meaning of the life of
man from his birth to his reunion with God who
is his Goal. And the result is a series of volumes
noble in form, united in aim, unique in wealth of
revealing beauty, and of unequalled worth.[1]

Beginning as far back as 1886, Waite issued his
study of the *Mysteries of Magic,* a digest of the writings of Eliphas Levi, to whom Albert Pike was more
indebted than he let us know. Then followed the
Real History of the Rosicrucians, which traces, as
far as any mortal may trace, the thread of fact
whereon is strung the romance of a fraternity the
very existence of which has been doubted and denied by turns. Like all his work, it bears the impress
of knowledge from the actual sources, betraying his
extraordinary learning and his exceptional experi-

---

[1] Some there are who think that much of the best work of Mr.
Waite is in his poetry, of which there are two volumes, *A Book of
Mystery and Vision,* and *Strange Houses of Sleep.* There one meets
a fine spirit, alive to the glory of the world and all that charms the
soul and sense of man, yet seeing past these; rich and significant
thought so closely wedded to emotion that each seems either. Other
books not to be omitted are his slender volume of aphorisms, *Steps
to the Crown,* his *Life of Saint-Martin,* and his *Studies in Mysticism;*
for what he touches he adorns. His later volume, *The Way of Divine
Union,* is perhaps the masterpiece of modern expositions of Mysticism, the more so because he writes from the inside, as one who has
in his experience that which gives him a key to much that is hidden
to others.

ence in this kind of inquiry. Of the Quest in its distinctively Christian aspect, he has written in *The Hidden Church of the Holy Graal;* a work of rare beauty, of bewildering richness, written in a style which, partaking of the quality of the story told, is not at all after the manner of these days. But the Graal Legend is only one aspect of the old-world sacred Quest, uniting the symbols of chivalry with Christian faith. Masonry is another; and no one may ever hope to write of *The Secret Tradition in Masonry* with more insight and charm, or a touch more sure and revealing, than this gracious student for whom Masonry perpetuates the instituted Mysteries of antiquity, with much else derived from innumerable store-houses of treasure. His last work is a survey of *The Secret Doctrine in Israel,* being a study of the *Zohar,*[1] or Hebrew "Book of Splendor," a feat for which no Hebrew scholar has had the heart. This Bible of Kabbalism is indeed so confused and confusing that only a "golden dustman" would have had the patience to sift out its gems from the mountain of dross and attempt to reduce its wide-weltering chaos to order. Even Waite, with all his gift of research and narration, finds little more than gleams of dawn in a dim forest, brilliant vapors,

---

[1] Even the *Jewish Encyclopedia,* and such scholars as Zunz, Graetz, Luzzatto, Jost, and Munk avoid this jungle, as well they might, remembering the legend of the four sages in "the enclosed garden": one of whom looked around and died; another lost his reason; a third tried to destroy the garden; and only one came out with his wits. See *The Cabala,* by Pick, and *The Kabbalah Unveiled,* by Mac-Gregor Mathers.

and glints that tell by their very perversity and strangeness.

Whether this age-old legend of the Quest be woven about the Cup of Christ, a Lost Word, or a design left unfinished by the death of a Master Builder, it has always these things in common: first, the memorials of a great *loss* which has befallen humanity by sin, making our race a pilgrim host ever in search; second, the intimation that what was lost still exists somewhere in time and the world, although deeply buried; third, the faith that it will ultimately be found and the vanished glory restored; fourth, the substitution of something temporary and less than the best, albeit never in a way to adjourn the quest; fifth, and more rarely, the felt presence of that which was lost under veils close to the hands of all. What though it take many forms, from the pathetic pilgrimage of the *Wandering Jew* to the journey to fairyland in quest of *The Blue Bird,* it is ever and always the same. These are but so many symbols of the fact that men are made of one blood and born to one need; that they should seek the Lord, if haply they might feel after Him, and find Him, though He is not far from every one of us; for in Him we live and move and have our being.[1]

What, then, is the Secret Doctrine, of which this seer-like scholar has written with so many improvisations of eloquence and emphasis, and of which each of us is in quest? What, indeed, but that which all the world is seeking—knowledge of Him whom to

[1] Acts 17:26-28.

know aright is the fulfillment of every human need: the kinship of the soul with God; the life of purity, honor, and piety demanded by that high heredity; the unity and fellowship of the race in duty and destiny; and the faith that the soul is deathless as God its Father is deathless! Now to accept this faith as a mere philosophy is one thing, but to realize it as an experience of the innermost heart is another and a deeper thing. *No man knows the Secret Doctrine until it has become the secret of his soul, the reigning reality of his thought, the inspiration of his acts, the form and color and glory of his life.* Happily, owing to the growth of the race in spiritual intelligence and power, the highest truth is no longer held as a sacred secret. Still, if art has efficacy to surprise and reveal the elusive Spirit of Truth, when truth is dramatically presented it is made vivid and impressive, strengthening the faith of the strongest and bringing a ray of heavenly light to many a baffled seeker.

Ever the Quest goes on, though it is permitted some of us to believe that the Lost Word has been found, in the only way in which it can ever be found —even in the life of Him who was "the Word made flesh," who dwelt among us and whose grace and beauty we know. Of this Quest Masonry is an aspect, continuing the high tradition of humanity, asking men to unite in the search for the thing most worth finding, that each may share the faith of all—fellowship being its very genius, since no one can find the highest truth for another and no one can find it alone. Apart from its rites, there is no mystery in Masonry, save the mystery of all great and simple things. So far from being hidden or occult, its glory lies in its openness, and its emphasis upon the realities which are to the human world what light and air are to nature. Its mystery is of so great a kind that it is easily overlooked; its secret almost too simple to be found out. "We know as much as we do," said Francis of Assisi. It is not enough to enact a truth in a ritual; it must become *both an incarnation and an act.*

THE COLLEGIA

This society was called the Dionysian Artificers, as Bacchus was supposed to be the inventor of building theaters; and they performed the Dionysian festivities. From this period, the Science of Astronomy which had given rise to the Dionysian rites, became connected with types taken from the art of building. The Ionian societies . . . extended their moral views, in conjunction with the art of building, to many useful purposes, and to the practice of acts of benevolence. They had significant words to distinguish their members; and for the same purpose they used emblems taken from the art of building.

—JOSEPH DA COSTA, *Dionysian Artificers*

We need not then consider it improbable, if in the dark centuries when the Roman empire was dying out, and its glorious temples falling into ruin; when the arts and sciences were falling into disuse or being enslaved; and when no place was safe from persecution and warfare, the guild of the Architects should fly for safety to almost the only free spot in Italy; and here, though they could no longer practice their craft, they preserved the legendary knowledge and precepts which, as history implies, came down to them through Vitruvius from older sources, some say from Solomon's builders themselves.

—LEADER SCOTT, *The Cathedral Builders*

Chapter Five

THE COLLEGIA

1

O FAR in our study we have found that from
earliest time architecture was related to
religion; that the working tools of the
builder were emblems of moral truth; that there
were great secret orders using the Drama of Faith
as a rite of initiation; and that a hidden doctrine
was kept for those accounted worthy, after trial, to
be entrusted with it. Secret societies, born of the
nature and need of man, there have been almost
since recorded history began;[1] but as yet we have

[1] All secret orders, it may be added, are a reminiscence, if not a
survival, of the Men's House of primitive society, a tribal Lodge in
which every young man, when he came to maturity, was initiated into
the secret law, legend, tradition, and religion of his people. Recent
research has brought this long hidden institution to light, showing
that it was really the center of early tribal life, the council-chamber,
the guest-house, the place where laws were made and courts held,
and where the trophies of war were treasured. Indeed, primitive
society was really a secret society so far as the men were concerned,
and unless we keep this fact in mind we can hardly understand it

come upon no separate and distinct order of builders. For aught we know there may have been such
in plenty, but we have no intimation, much less a
record, of the fact. That is to say, history has a vague
story to tell us of the earliest orders of the builders.

However, it is more than a mere plausible inference that from the beginning architects were members of secret orders; for, as we have seen, not only
the truths of religion and philosophy, but also the
facts of science and the laws of art, were held as
secrets to be known only to the few—the idea of education in the ancient world being exactly opposite
to ours, which tells everything to everybody. This
was so, apparently without exception, among all ancient peoples; so much so, indeed, that we may take it
as certain that the builders of old time were initiates.
Of necessity, then, the arts of the craft were secrets

at all. Every man was an initiate. Methods of initiation differed
in different times and places, but they had, nevertheless, a certain
likeness, as they had always the same purpose. Ordeals, often severe
and frightful, were required—exposing the candidate not only to
physical torture, but to the peril of unseen spirits—as tests to prove
youth worthy, by reason of virtue and valor, to be entrusted with
the secret lore of his tribe. The ceremonies included vows of
chastity, of loyalty and secrecy, and, almost universally, a mimic
representation of the death and resurrection of the novice. After
his "initiation into manhood," for such it really was, he was given a
new name, and a new language of signs, grips, and tokens. No
doubt it was this antiquity of the idea and necessity of initiation that
our Masonic fathers had in mind when they said that Masonry began
with the beginning of history—and, so interpreted, they were right.
At any rate the Men's House, with its initiatory rites and secret
teaching, was one of the great institutions of humanity which
Masonry perpetuates today. (For a scientific account of the Men's
House, see *Primitive Secret Societies*, by Prof. Hutton Webster and
Secret Societies of all Ages and Countries, by W. C. Heckethorn.)

jealously guarded, and the architects themselves, while they may have employed and trained ordinary workmen, were men of learning and influence. Such glimpses of early architects as we have confirm this inference, as, for example, the noble hymn to the Sun-god written by Suti and Hor, two architects employed by Amenhotep III, of Egypt.[1] Just when the builders began to form orders of their own no one knows, but it was perhaps when the Mystery-cults began to journey abroad into other lands. What we have to keep in mind is that all the arts had their home in the temple, from which, as time passed, they spread out fan-wise along all the paths of culture.

Keeping in mind the secrecy of the laws of building, and the sanctity with which all science and art were regarded, we have a key whereby to interpret the legends woven about the building of the temple of Solomon. Few realize how high that temple on Mount Moriah towered in the history of the olden world, and how the story of its building haunted the legends and traditions of the times following. Of these legends there were many, some of them wildly improbable, but the persistence of the tradition, and its consistency withal, despite many varia-

[1] We may add the case of Weshptah, one of the viziers of the Fifth Dynasty in Egypt, about 2700 B. C., and also the royal architect, for whom the great tomb was built, endowed, and furnished by the king (*Religion in Egypt*, by Breasted, lecture ii); also the statue of Semut, chief of Masons under Queen Hatasu, now in Berlin. (Publisher's note: Since the bombing of Berlin, this may no longer be true, 1951.)

tions, is a *fact of no small moment*. Nor is this tradition to be wondered at, since time has shown that the building of the temple at Jerusalem was an event of world-importance, not only to the Hebrews, but to other nations, more especially the Phoenicians. The histories of both peoples make much of the building of the Hebrew temple, of the friendship of Solomon and Hiram I, of Tyre, and of the harmony between the two peoples; and Phoenician tradition has it that Solomon presented Hiram with a duplicate of the temple, which was erected in Tyre.[1]

Clearly, the two nations were drawn closely together, and this fact carried with it a mingling of religious influences and ideas, as was true between the Hebrews and other nations, especially Egypt and Phoenicia, during the reign of Solomon. Now the religion of the Phoenicians at this time, as all agree, was the Egyptian religion in a modified form, Dionysius having taken the role of Osiris in the drama of faith in Greece, Syria, and Asia Minor. Thus we have the Mysteries of Egypt, in which Moses was learned, brought to the very door of the temple of Solomon, and that, too, at a time favorable to their impress. The Hebrews were not architects, and it is plain from the records that the temple—and, indeed, the palaces of Solomon—were designed and erected by Phoenician builders, and for the most

---

[1] *Historians His. World,* vol. ii, chap. iii. Josephus gives an elaborate account of the temple, including the correspondence between Solomon and Hiram of Tyre (*Jewish Antiquities,* bk. viii, chaps. 2-6).

part by Phoenician workmen and materials. Josephus adds that the architecture of the temple was of the style called Grecian. So much would seem to be fact, whatever may be said of the legends flowing from it.

If, then, the laws of building were secrets known only to initiates, there must have been a secret order of architects who built the temple of Solomon. Who were they? They were almost certainly the *Dionysian Artificers*—not to be confused with the play-actors called by the same name later—an order of builders who erected temples, stadia, and theaters in Asia Minor, and who were at the same time an order of the Mysteries under the tutelage of Bacchus before that worship declined, as it did later in Athens and Rome, into mere revelry.[1] As such, they united the art of architecture with the old

[1] *Symbolism of Masonry*, Mackey, chap. vi; also in Mackey's *Encyclopedia of Masonry*, both of which were drawn from *History of Masonry*, by Laurie, chap. i; and Laurie in turn derived his facts from a *Sketch for the History of the Dionysian Artificers, A Fragment*, by H. J. Da Costa (1820). Why Waite and others brush the Dionysian architects aside as a dream is past finding out in view of the evidence and authorities put forth by Da Costa, nor do they give any reason for so doing. "Lebedos was the seat and assembly of the *Dionysian Artificers*, who inhabit Ionia to the Hellespont; there they had annually their solemn meetings and festivities in honor of Bacchus," wrote Strabo (lib. xiv, 921). They were a secret society having signs and words to distinguish their members (Robertson's *Greece*), and used emblems taken from the art of building (Eusebius, *de Prep. Evang.* iii, c. 12). They entered Asia Minor and Phoenicia fifty years before the temple of Solomon was built, and Strabo traces them on into Syria, Persia, and India. Surely here are facts not to be swept aside as romance because, forsooth, they do not fit certain theories. Moreover, they explain many things, as we shall see.

Egyptian drama of faith, representing in their ceremonies the murder of Dionysius by the Titans and
his return to life. So that, blending the symbols of
Astronomy with those of Architecture, by a slight
change made by a natural process, how easy for the
master-artist of the temple-builders to become the
hero of the ancient drama of immortality.[1] Whether
or not this fact can be verified from history, such is
the form in which the tradition has come down to
us, surviving through long ages and triumphing over
all vicissitude.[2] Secret orders have few records and
their story is hard to tell, but this account is per-

[1] Rabbinic legend has it that all the workmen on the temple were
killed, so that they should not build another temple devoted to
idolatry (*Jewish Encyclopedia*, article "Freemasonry"). Other legends
equally absurd cluster about the temple and its building, none of
which is to be taken literally. As a fact, Hiram, the architect, or
rather artificer in metals, did not lose his life, but, as Josephus tells
us, lived to good age and died at Tyre. What the legend is trying
to tell us, however, is that at the building of the temple the Mysteries
mingled with Hebrew faith, each mutually influencing the other.

[2] Strangely enough, there is a sect or tribe called the Druses,
now inhabiting the Lebanon district, who claim to be not only the
descendants of the Phoenicians, but *the builders of King Solomon's
temple*. So persistent and important among them is this tradition
that their religion is built about it—if indeed it be not something
more than a legend. They have Khalwehs, or temples, built after
the fashion of lodges, with three degrees of initiation, and, though
an agricultural folk, they use signs and tools of building as emblems
of moral truth. They have signs, grips, and passwords for recognition. In the words of their lawgiver, Hamze, their creed reads:
"The belief in the Truth of One God shall take the place of Prayer;
the exercise of brotherly love shall take the place of Fasting; and
the daily practice of acts of Charity shall take the place of Alms-
giving." Why such a people, having such a tradition? Where did
they get it? What may this fact set in the fixed and changeless
East mean? (See the essay of Hackett Smith on "The Druses and
Their Relation to Freemasonry," and the discussion following, *Ars
Quatuor Coronatorum*, iv. 7-19.)

fectly in accord with the spirit and setting of the situation, and there is neither fact nor reason against it. While this does not establish it as true historically, it surely gives it validity as a prophecy, if nothing more.[1]

After all, then, the tradition that Masonry, not unlike the Masonry we now know, had its origin while the temple of King Solomon was building, and was given shape by the two royal friends, may not be so fantastic as certain superior folk seem to think it. One need not affirm that Freemasonry, as we know it, can be traced historically to the building of the temple of Solomon, but it is none the less a significant tradition. How else can we explain the fact that when the Knights of the Crusades went to the Holy Land they came back a secret, oath-bound fraternity? Also, why is it that, through the ages, we see bands of builders coming from the East calling themselves "sons of Solomon," and using his interlaced-triangle seal as their emblem? Strabo, as we have seen, traced the Dionysiac builders eastward into Syria, Persia, and even India. They may also be traced westward. Traversing Asia Minor, they entered Europe by way of Constantinople, and we follow them through Greece to Rome, where already several centuries before Christ we find them bound together in corporations called *Collegia*. These

[1] Rawlinson, in his *History of Phoenicia*, says the people "had for ages possessed the mason's art, it having been brought in very early days from Egypt." Sir C. Warren found on the foundation stones at Jerusalem mason's marks in Phoenician letters (*A. Q. C.*, ii, 125; iii, 68).

lodges flourished in all parts of the Roman Empire, traces of their existence having been discovered in England as early as the middle of the first century of our era.

2

Krause [1] was the first to point out a prophecy of Masonry in the old orders of builders, following their footsteps—not connectedly, of course, for there are many gaps—through the Dionysiac fraternity of Tyre, through the Roman Collegia, to the architects and Masons of the Middle Ages. Since he wrote, however, much new material has come to light, but the date of the advent of the builders in Rome is still uncertain. Some trace it to the very founding of the city, while others go no further back than King Numa, the friend of Pythagoras.[2] By any account, they were of great antiquity, and their influence in Roman history was far-reaching. They followed the Roman legions to remote places, building cities, bridges, and temples, and it was but natural that Mithra, the patron god of soldiers, should have influenced their orders. Of this an example

[1] See the noble lecture on Krause by Prof. Roscoe Pound in *Philosophy of Masonry*.

[2] See essay on "A Masonic Built City," by S. R. Forbes, a study of the plan and building of Rome, *Ars Quatuor Coronatorum*, iv, 86. As there will be many references to the proceedings of the Coronatorum Lodge of Research, it will be convenient hereafter to use only its initials, *A. Q. C.*, in behalf of brevity. For an account of the Collegia in early Christian times, see *Roman Life from Nero to Aurelius*, by Dill (bk. ii, chap. iii); also *De Collegia*, by Mommsen. There is an excellent article in Mackey's *Encyclopedia of Freemasonry*, and Gould, *His. Masonry*, vol. i, chap. i.

may be seen in the remains of the ancient Roman villa at Morton, on the Isle of Wight.[1]

As Rome grew in power and became a vast, all-embracing empire, the individual man felt, more and more, his littleness and loneliness. This feeling, together with the increasing specialization of industry, begat a passion for association, and Collegia of many sorts were organized. Even a casual glance at the inscriptions, under the heading *Artes et Opificia*, will show the enormous development of skilled handicrafts, and how minute was their specialization. Every trade soon had its secret order, or union, and so powerful did they become that the emperors found it necessary to abolish the right of free association. Yet even such edicts, though effective for a little time, were helpless as against the universal craving for combination. Ways were easily found whereby to evade the law, which had exempted from its restrictions orders consecrated by their antiquity or their religious character. Most of the Collegia became funerary and charitable in their labors, humble folk seeking to escape the dim, hopeless obscurity of plebeian life, and the still more hopeless obscurity of death. Pathetic beyond words are some of the inscriptions telling of the horror and loneliness of the grave, of the day when no kindly eye would read the forgotten name, and no hand bring offerings of flowers. Each collegium held memorial services and marked the tomb of its dead with the

[1] See *Masonic Character of Roman Villa at Morton,* by J. F. Crease (*A. Q. C.,* iii, 38-59).

emblems of its trade: if a baker, with a loaf of bread; if a builder, with a square, compasses, and level.

From the first the Colleges of Architects seem to have enjoyed special privileges and exemptions, owing to the value of their service to the State, and while we do not find them called Free-masons they were such in law and fact long before they wore the name. They were permitted to have their own constitutions and regulations, both secular and religious. In form, in officers, in emblems a Roman Collegium resembled very much a modern Masonic Lodge. For one thing, no College could consist of less than three persons, and so rigid was this rule that the saying, "three make a college," became a maxim of law. Each College was presided over by a Magister, or Master, with two *decuriones,* or Wardens, each of whom extended the commands of the Master to "the brethren of his column." There were a secretary, a treasurer, and a keeper of archives, and, as the colleges were in part religious and usually met near some temple, there was a *sacerdos,* or, as we would say, a priest, or chaplain. The members were of three orders, not unlike apprentices, fellows, and masters, or colleagues. What ceremonies of initiation were used we do not know, but that they were of a religious nature seems certain, as each College adopted a patron deity from among the many then worshiped. Also, as the Mysteries of Isis and Mithra ruled the Roman world by turns, the ancient drama of eternal life was never far away.

Of the emblems of the Collegia, it is enough to say that here again we find the simple tools of the builder used as teachers of truth for life and hope in death. Upon a number of sarcophagi, still extant, we find carved the square, the compasses, the cube, the plummet, the circle, and always the level. There is, besides, the famous Collegium uncovered at the excavation of Pompeii in 1878, having been buried under the ashes and lava of Mount Vesuvius since the year 79 A. D. It stood near the Tragic Theater, not far from the Temple of Isis, and by its arrangement, with two columns in front and interlaced triangles on the walls, was identified as an ancient lodge room. Upon a pedestal in the room was found a rare bit of art, unique in design and exquisite in execution, now in the National Museum at Naples. It is described by S. R. Forbes, in his *Rambles in Naples,* as follows:

It is a mosaic table of square shape, fixed in a strong wooden frame. The ground is of grey green stone, in the middle of which is a human skull, made of white, grey, and black colors. In appearance the skull is quite natural. The eyes, nostrils, teeth, ears, and coronal are all well executed. Above the skull is a level of colored wood, the points being of brass; and from the top to the point, by a white thread, is suspended a plumb-line. Below the skull is a wheel of six spokes, and on the upper rim of the wheel there is a butterfly with wings of red, edged with yellow, its eyes blue. . . . On the left is an upright spear, resting on the ground; from this there hangs, attached to a golden cord, a garment of scarlet, also a purple robe; whilst the upper part of the spear is surrounded by a white braid of diamond pattern. To the right is a gnarled thorn stick, from which hangs a coarse, shaggy piece of cloth in yellow, grey, and brown colors, tied with a ribbon; and above it is a leather knapsack. . . . Evidently this work of art, by its composition, is mystical and symbolical.

No doubt; and for those who know the meaning of these emblems there is a feeling of kinship with those men, long since fallen into dust, who gathered about such an altar. They wrought out in this work of art their vision of the old-worn pilgrim way of life, with its vicissitude and care, the level of mortality to which all are brought at last by death, and the winged, fluttering hope of man. Always a journey with its horny staff and wallet, life is sometimes a battle needing a spear, but for him who walks uprightly by the plumb-line of rectitude, there is a true and victorious hope at the end.

> Of wounds and sore defeat
> I made my battle stay,
> Winged sandals for my feet
> I wove of my delay.
>
> Of weariness and fear
> I made a shouting spear,
> Of loss and doubt and dread
> And swift on-coming doom
> I made a helmet for my head,
> And a waving plume.

3

Christianity, whose Founder was a Carpenter, made a mighty appeal to the working classes of Rome. As Deissmann and Harnack have shown, the secret of its expansion in the early years was that it came down to the man in the street with its message of hope and joy. Its appeal was hardly heard in high places, but it was welcomed by the men who were weary and heavy ladened. Among the Collegia it made rapid progress, its Saints taking the place of pagan deities as patrons, and its spirit of love welding men into closer, truer union. When Diocletian determined to destroy Christianity, he was strangely lenient and patient with the Collegia, so many of whose members were of that faith. Not until they refused to make a statue of Æsculapius did he vow vengeance and turn on them, venting his fury. In the persecution that followed four Master Masons and one humble apprentice suffered cruel torture and death, but they became the Four Crowned Martyrs, the story of whose heroic fidelity unto death haunted the legends of later times.[1] They were the

[1] Their names were Claudius, Nicostratus, Simphorianus, Castorius, and Simplicius. Later their bodies were brought from Rome to Toulouse where they were placed in a chapel erected in their honor in the church of St. Sernin (*Martyrology*, by Du Saussay). They became patron saints of Masons in Germany, France, and England (*A. Q. C.*, xii, 196). In a fresco on the walls of the church of St. Lawrence at Rotterdam, partially preserved, they are painted with compasses and trowel in hand. With them, however, is another figure, clad in oriental robe, also holding compasses, but with a royal, not a martyr's, crown. Is he Solomon? Who else can he be? The fresco dates from 1641, and was painted by F. Wounters (*A. Q. C.*,

patron saints alike of Lombard and Tuscan builders, and, later, of the working Masons of the Middle
Ages, as witness the poem in their praise in the oldest record of the Craft, the *Regius MS.*

With the breaking up of the College of Architects and their expulsion from Rome, we come upon
a period in which it is hard to follow their path.
Happily the task has been made less baffling by recent research, and if we are unable to trace them
all the way, much light has been let into the darkness. Hitherto there has been a hiatus also in the
history of architecture between the classic art of
Rome, which is said to have died when the Empire
fell to pieces, and the rise of Gothic art. Just so, in
the story of the builders one finds a gap of like
length, between the Collegia of Rome and the cathedral artists. While the gap cannot, as yet, be per-
fectly bridged, much has been done to that end by
Leader Scott in *The Cathedral Builders: The Story
of a Great Masonic Guild.* Her thesis is that the
missing link is to be found in the Magistri Comacini,
a guild of architects who, on the break-up of the
Roman Empire, fled to Comacina, a fortified island
in Lake Como, and there kept alive the traditions
of classic art during the Dark Ages; that from them
were developed in direct descent the various styles
of Italian architecture; and that, finally, they carried

xii, 202). Even so, those humble workmen, faithful to their faith,
became saints of the church, and reign with Solomon! Once the
fresco was whitewashed, but the coating fell off and they stood forth
with compasses and trowel as before.

the knowledge and practice of architecture and sculpture into France, Spain, Germany, and England. Such a thesis is difficult, and, from its nature, not susceptible of absolute proof.

While she does not positively affirm that the Comacine Masters were the veritable stock from which the Freemasonry of the present day sprang, "we may admit," she says, "that they were the link between the classic Collegia and all other art and trade Guilds of the Middle Ages. *They were Freemasons because they were builders of a privileged class, absolved from taxes and servitude, and free to travel about in times of feudal bondage.*" The name Freemason—*Libera muratori*—may not actually have been used thus early, but the Comacines were *in fact free builders long before the name was employed*—free to travel from place to place, as we see from their migrations; free to fix their own prices, while other workmen were bound to feudal lords, or by the Statutes of Wages. The author quotes in the original Latin an Edict of the Lombard King Rotharis, dated November 22, 643, in which certain privileges are confirmed to the *Magistri Comacini* and their *colligantes*. From this Edict it is clear that it is no new order that is alluded to, but an old and powerful body of Masters capable of acting as architects, with men who executed work under them. For the Comacines were not ordinary workmen, but artists, including architects, sculptors, painters, and decorators, and if affinities of style left in stone be adequate evidence, to them were due

the changing forms of architecture in Europe during the cathedral-building period. Everywhere they
left their distinctive impress in a way so unmistake-
able as to leave no doubt.

Under Charlemagne the Comacines began their
many migrations, and we find them following the
missionaries of the Church into remote places, from
Sicily to Britain, building churches. When Augustine went to convert the British, the Comacines
followed to provide shrines, and Bede, as early as
674, in mentioning that builders were sent for from
Gaul to build the church at Wearmouth, uses
phrases and words found in the Edict of King Rotharis. For a long time the changes in style of architecture, appearing simultaneously everywhere over
Europe, from Italy to England, puzzled students.[1]
Further knowledge of this powerful and widespread
order explains it. It also accounts for the fact that
no individual architect can be named as the designer
of any of the great cathedrals. Those cathedrals were
the work, not of individual artists, but of an order
who planned, built, and adorned them. In 1355
the painters of Siena seceded, as the German Masons
did later, and the names of individual artists who
worked for fame and glory begin to appear; but up
to that time the Order was supreme. Artists from
Greece and Asia Minor, driven from their homes,
took refuge with the Comacines, and Leader Scott
finds in this order a possible link, by tradition at

[1] *History of Middle Ages*, Hallam, vol. ii, 547.

least, with the temple of Solomon. At any rate, all through the Dark Ages the name and fame of the Hebrew king lived in the minds of the builders.

An inscribed stone, dating from 712, shows that the Comacine Guild was organized as *Magistri* and *Discipuli,* under a *Gastaldo,* or Grand Master, the very same terms as were kept in the lodges later. Moreover, they called their meeting places *loggia,* a long list of which the author recites from the records of various cities, giving names of officers, and, often, of members. They, too, had their masters and wardens, their oaths, tokens, grips, and passwords which formed a bond of union stronger than legal ties. They wore white aprons and gloves, and revered the Four Crowned Martyrs of the Order. Square, compasses, level, plumb-line, and arch appear among their emblems. "King Solomon's Knot" was one of their symbols, and the endless, interwoven cord, symbol of Eternity, which has neither beginning nor end, was another. Later, however, the Lion's Paw seems to have become their chief emblem. From illustrations given by the author they are shown in their regalia, with apron and emblems, clad as the keepers of a great art and teaching of which they were masters.

Here, of a truth, is something more than prophecy, and those who have any regard for facts will not again speak lightly of an order having such ancestors as the great Comacine Masters. Had Fergusson known their story, he would not have paused in his *History of Architecture* to belittle the Free-masons as incapable of designing a cathedral, while puzzling the while as to who did draw the plans for those dreams of beauty and prayer. Hereafter, if any one asks to know who uplifted those massive piles in which was portrayed the great drama of mediaeval worship, he need not remain uncertain. With the decline of Gothic architecture the order of Free-masons also suffered decline, as we shall see, but did not cease to exist—continuing its symbolic tradition amidst varying, and often sad, vicissitude until 1717, when it became a fraternity teaching spiritual faith by allegory and moral science by symbols.

NOTE—Whatever the origin of Freemasonry, its practical value remains the same. The Nile blesses Egypt whether the source of it is the Mountains of the Moon, or a Lake in Central Africa; so of the fertilizing stream of Masonry. None the less we should go as far back as we can in search of the source, and so far we have been picking our way amidst many cults and rites in quest of hints and prophecies of the Craft. Naturally, the record is less definite than in the pages following, but it has its value and much remains to be explored in the Museum of Antiquity. Meanwhile we may observe:

I—The Dionysiac Artificers are the first order of architects, of which we have record, who were a secret order practicing the rites of the Mysteries. Prof. Robinson writes: "We know that the Dionysiacs of Ionia were a great corporation of architects and engineers, who undertook, and even monopolized, the building of temples and stadia, precisely as the fraternity of Freemasons monopolized the building of cathedrals and conventual churches in the Middle Ages. Indeed, the Dionysiacs resembled in many respects the mystic fraternity now called Freemasons. They allowed no strangers to interfere in their employment; they recognized each other by signs and tokens; they professed certain mysterious doctrines under the tutelage of Bacchus (who represented the Sun, and was the outward symbol of One God, so that the worship of the Dionysiacs resolved itself into a worship of the One God), to whom they built a magnificent temple at Teos, where they celebrated his mysteries at solemn festivals, and they called all other men profane because not admitted to their mysteries." (Article on the *Arch* in *Brewster's Edinburgh Encyclopedia*.)

II—While the contention of Leader Scott that the Comacine Masters were the real ancestors of Freemasonry has not yet been entirely established and may never be put beyond question, it is believed that it puts us on the track of the truth. Further researches by W. Ravenscroft, in his essay on *The Comacines, Their Predecessors and Successors*, tend to confirm it, albeit we may not be able to accept his theory about their predecessors. Still, the investigation is not yet adjourned, and we may wisely wait its further results. It does offer an explanation, first, of the building of the cathedrals, which could not have been erected by Guild-masons; and the Comacines did have the forms and symbols of Masonry very like what they are today. They were an order of Artists, an aristocracy, to be sure, but an aristocracy of service, of talent, such as Carlyle and Ruskin would have admired. They were also democratic, because industry and merit enabled a worthy workman to attain the highest honors. In spirit, therefore, as well as in form and symbol, they were Masonic. (See a noble passage in Michelet's *History of France* on the spirit of cathedral Masonry.)

III—If in the following pages emphasis is laid upon the *historical* development of Masonry, it is because this is a book of history. Many mystical influences entered into the making of Masonry, but they are of a kind which cannot be traced historically or estimated accurately. Traces of Gnosticism, of Mithraism, are found, remnants of rites long forgotten; and the impress of the Kabalah is unmistakable, as Bro. Waite has shown in his lecture on *Some Deeper Aspects of Masonic Symbolism* (see also "Freemasonry Illustrated by the Kabalah," by W. W. Westcott. *A. Q. C.* i, 55). It has been deemed better, in a book of Introduction, to fix attention on the historical aspects of Craft, leaving the student free to follow further as his inclination and studies may direct.

Part 2

HISTORY

FREE-MASONS

The curious history of Freemasonry has unfortunately been treated only by its panegyrists or calumniators, both equally mendacious. I do not wish to pry into the mysteries of the craft; but it would be interesting to know more of their history during the period when they were literally architects. They are charged by an Act of Parliament with fixing the price of their labor in their annual chapters, contrary to the Statute of Laborers, and such chapters were consequently prohibited. This is their first persecution; they have since undergone others, and are perhaps reserved for still more. It is remarkable, that Masons were never legally incorporated, like other traders; their bond of union being stronger than any charter.

—HENRY HALLAM, *The Middle Ages*

Chapter One

FREE-MASONS

1

ROM THE foregoing pages it must be evident that Masonry, as we find it in the Middle Ages, was not a novelty. Already, if we accept its own records, it was hoary with age, having come down from a far past, bringing with it a remarkable deposit of legendary lore. Also, it had in its keeping the same simple, eloquent emblems which, as we have seen, are older than the oldest living religion, which it received as an inheritance and has transmitted as a treasure. Whatever we may think of the legends of Masonry, as recited in its oldest documents, its symbols, older than the order itself, link it with the earliest thought and faith of the race. No doubt those emblems lost some of their luster in the troublous time of transition we are about to traverse, but their beauty never wholly faded, and they had only to be touched to shine.

If not the actual successors of the Roman College

of Architects, the great order of Comacine Masters was founded upon its ruins, and continued its tradition both of symbolism and of art. Returning to Rome after the death of Diocletian, we find them busy there under Constantine and Theodosius; and from remains recently brought to knowledge it is plain that their style of building at that time was very like that of the churches built at Hexham and York in England, and those of the Ravenna, also nearly contemporary. They may not have been actually called Free-masons as early as Leader Scott insists they were,[1] but *they were free in fact,* traveling far and near where there was work to do, following the missionaries of the Church as far as England. When there was need for the name *Free-masons,* it was easily suggested by the fact that the cathedral-builders were quite distinct from the Guild-masons, the one being a universal order whereas the other was local and restricted. Older than Guild-masonry, the order of the cathedral-builders was more powerful, more artistic, and, it may be added, more religious; and it is from this order that the Masonry of today is descended.

Since the story of the Comacine Masters has come to light, no doubt any longer remains that during the building period the order of Masons was at the height of its influence and power. At that time the building art stood above all other arts, and made the other arts bow to it, commanding the services of the most brilliant intellects and of the greatest artists

[1] *The Cathedral Builders,* chap. i.

of the age. Moreover, its symbols were wrought into stone long before they were written on parchment, if indeed they were ever recorded at all. Efforts have been made to rob those old masters of their honor as the designers of the cathedrals, but it is in vain.[1] Their monuments are enduring and still tell the story of their genius and art. High upon the cathedrals they left cartoons in stone, of which Findel gives a list,[2] portraying with searching satire abuses current in the Church. Such figures and devices would not have been tolerated but for the strength of the order, and not even then had the Church known what they meant to the adepts.

History, like a mirage, lifts only a part of the past into view, leaving much that we should like to know

[1] "The honor due to the original founders of these edifices is almost invariably transferred to the ecclesiastics under whose patronage they rose, rather than to the skill and design of the Master Mason, or professional architect, because the only historians were monks. . . . They were probably not so well versed in geometrical science as the Master Masons, for mathematics formed a part of monastic learning in a very limited degree."—James Dallaway, *Architecture in England;* and his words are the more weighty for that he is not a Mason.

[2] *History of Masonry.* In the St. Sebaldus Church, Nuremburg, is a carving in stone showing a nun in the embrace of a monk. In Strassburg a hog and a goat may be seen carrying a sleeping fox as a sacred relic, in advance a bear with a cross and a wolf with a taper. An ass is reading mass at an altar. In Wurzburg Cathedral are the pillars of Boaz and Jachin, and in the altar of the Church of Doberan, in Mecklenburg, placed as Masons use them, and a most significant scene in which priests are turning a mill grinding out dogmatic doctrines; and at the bottom the Lord's Supper in which the Apostles are shown in well-known Masonic attitudes. In the Cathedral of Brandenburg a fox in priestly robes is preaching to a flock of geese; and in the Minster at Berne the Pope is placed among those who are lost in perdition. These were bold strokes which even heretics hardly dared to indulge in.

in oblivion. At this distance the Middle Ages wear an aspect of smooth uniformity of faith and opinion, but that is only one of the many illusions of time by which we are deceived. What looks like uniformity was only conformity, and underneath its surface there was almost as much variety of thought as there is today, albeit not so freely expressed. Science itself, as well as religious ideas deemed heretical, sought seclusion; but the human mind was alive and active none the less, and a great secret order like Masonry, enjoying the protection of the Church, yet independent of it, invited freedom of thought and faith.[1] The Masons, by the very nature of their art, came into contact with all classes of men, and they had opportunities to know the defects of the Church. Far ahead of the masses and most of the clergy in education, in their travels to and fro, not only in Europe, but often extending to the far East, they became familiar with widely differing religious views. They had learned to practice toleration, and their Lodges became a sure refuge for those who were persecuted for the sake of opinion by bigoted fanaticism.

While, as an order, the Comacine Masters served the Church as builders, the creed required for ad-

---

[1] *History of Masonry*, by Steinbrenner, chap. iv. There were, indeed, many secret societies in the Middle Ages, such as the Catharists, Albigenses, Waldenses, and others, whose initiates and adherents traveled through all Europe, forming new communities and making proselytes not only among the masses, but also among nobles, and even among the monks, abbots, and bishops. Occultists, Alchemists, Kabbalists, all wrought in secrecy, keeping their flame aglow under the crust of conformity.

mission to their fraternity was never narrow, and, as we shall see, it became every year broader. Unless this fact be kept in mind, the influence of the Church upon Masonry, which no one seeks to minify, may easily be exaggerated. Not until cathedral building began to decline by reason of the impoverishment of the nations by long wars, the dissolution of the monasteries, and the advent of Puritanism, did the Church greatly influence the order; and not even then to the extent of diverting it from its original and unique mission. Other influences were at work betimes, such as the persecution of the Knights Templar and the tragic martyrdom of De Molai, making themselves felt,[1] and Masonry began to be suspected of harboring heresy. So tangled were the tendencies of that period that they are not easily followed, but the fact emerges that Masonry rapidly broadened until its final break with the Church. Hardly more than a veneer, by the time of the German Reformation almost every vestige of the impress of the Church had vanished never to return. Critics of the order have been at pains to

[1] *Realities of Masonry,* by Blake (chap. ii). While the theory of the descent of Masonry from the Order of the Temple is untenable, a connection between the two societies, in the sense in which an artist may be said to be connected with his employer, is more than probable; and a similarity may be traced between the ritual of reception in the Order of the Temple and that used by Masons, but that of the Temple was probably derived from, or suggested by, that of the Masons; or both may have come from an original source further back. That the Order of the Temple, as such, did not actually coalesce with the Masons seems clear, but many of its members sought refuge under the Masonic apron (*History of Freemasonry and Concordant Orders,* by Hughan and Stillson).

trace this tendency, not knowing, apparently, that by so doing they only make more emphatic the chief glory of Masonry.

2

Unfortunately, as so often happens, no records of old Craft-masonry, save those wrought into stone, were made until the movement had begun to decline; and for that reason such documents as have come down to us do not show it at its best. Nevertheless, they range over a period of more than four centuries, and are justly held to be the title-deeds of the Order. Turning to these *Old Charges* and *Constitutions*,[1] as they are called, we find a body of quaint and curious writing, both in poetry and prose, describing the Masonry of the late cathedral-building period, with glimpses at least of greater days of old. Of these, there are more than half a hundred—seventy-eight, to be exact[2]—most of which have come to light since 1860, and all of them, it would seem, copies of documents still older. Naturally they have suffered at the hands of unskilled or unlearned copyists, as is evident from errors, embellishments, and interpola-

[1] Every elaborate History of Masonry—as, for example, that of Gould —reproduces these old documents in full or in digest, with exhaustive analyses of and commentaries upon them. Such a task obviously does not come within the scope of the present study. One of the best brief comparative studies of the *Old Charges* is an essay by W. H. Upton, "The True Text of the Book of Constitutions," in that it applies approved methods of historical criticism to all of them (*A. Q. C.*, vii, 119). See also *Masonic Sketches and Reprints*, by Hughan. No doubt these *Old Charges* are familiar, or should be familiar, to every intelligent member of the order, as a man knows the deeds of his estate.

[2] Now over one hundred (1951).

tions. They were called *Old Charges* because they contained certain rules as to conduct and duties which, in a bygone time, were read or recited to a newly admitted member of the craft. While they differ somewhat in details, they relate substantially the same legend as to the origin of the order, its early history, its laws and regulations, usually beginning with an invocation and ending with an Amen.

Only a brief account need here be given of the dates and characteristics of these documents, of the two oldest especially, with a digest of what they have to tell us, first, of the Legend of the order; second, its early History; and third, its Moral teachings, its workings, and the duties of its members. The first and oldest of the records is known as the *Regius MS.* which, owing to an error of David Casley, who in his catalogue of the MSS. in the King's Library marked it *A Poem of Moral Duties,* was overlooked until James Halliwell discovered its real nature in 1839. Although not a Mason, Halliwell was attracted by the MS. and read an essay on its contents before the Society of Antiquaries, after which he issued two editions bearing date of 1840 and 1844. Experts give it date back to 1390, that is to say, fifteen years after the first recorded use of the name *Free*-mason in the history of the Company of Masons of the City of London, in 1375.[1]

[1] *The Hole Craft and Fellowship of Masonry,* by Conder. Also exhaustive essays by Conder and Speth, *A. Q. C.,* ix, 29; x, 10. Too much, it seems to me, has been made of both the name and the date, since the *fact* was older than either. Findel finds the name *Free*-mason as early as 1350 (*History of Freemasonry,* p. 79), and Leader Scott goes

More poetical in spirit than in form, the old manuscript begins by telling of the number of unemployed in early days and the necessity of finding work, "that they myght gete there lyvyngs therby." Euclid was consulted, and recommended the "onest craft of good masonry," and the origin of the order is found "yn Egypte lande." Then, by a quick shift, we are landed in England "yn tyme of good Kinge Adelstonus day," who is said to have called an assembly of Masons, when fifteen articles and as many points were agreed upon as rules of the craft, each point being duly described. The rules resemble the Ten Commandments in an extended form, closing with the legend of the Four Crowned Martyrs, as an incentive to fidelity. Then the writer takes up again the question of origins, going back this time to the days of Noah and the Flood, mentioning the tower of Babylon and the great skill of Euclid, who is said to have commenced "the syens seven." The seven sciences are then named, to wit, Grammar, Logic, Rhetoric, Music, Astronomy, Arithmetic, Geometry, and each explained. Rich reward is held out to those who use the seven sciences aright, and the MS. proper closes with the benediction:

> Amen! Amen! so mote it be!
> So say we all for Charity.

There follows a kind of appendix, evidently added by a priest, consisting of one hundred lines in which

still farther back; but the fact may be traced back to the Roman Collegia.

pious exhortation is mixed with instruction in etiquette, such as lads and even men unaccustomed to polite society and correct deportment would need. These lines were in great part extracted from *Instructions for Parish Priests,* by Mirk, a manual in use at the time. The whole poem, if so it may be called, is imbued with the spirit of freedom, of gladness, of social good will; so much so, that both Gould and Albert Pike think it points to the existence of symbolic Masonry at the date from which it speaks, and may have been recited or sung by some club commemorating the science, but not practicing the art, of Masonry. They would find intimation of the independent existence of speculative Masonry thus early, in a society from whom all but the memory or tradition of its ancient craft had departed. One hesitates to differ with writers so able and distinguished, yet this inference seems far-fetched, if not forced. Of the existence of symbolic Masonry at that time there is no doubt, but of its independent existence it is not easy to find even a hint in this old poem. Nor would the poem be suitable for a mere social, or even a symbolic guild, whereas the spirit of genial, joyous comradeship which breathes through it is of the very essence of Masonry, and has ever been present when Masons meet.

Next in order of age is the *Cooke MS.,* dating from the early part of the fifteenth century, and first published in 1861. If we apply the laws of higher criticism to this old document a number of things appear, as obvious as they are interesting. Not only is it a copy of an older record, like all the MSS. we have, but it is either an effort to join two documents together, or else the first part must be regarded as a long preamble to the manuscript which forms the second part. For the two are quite unlike in method and style, the first being diffuse, with copious quotations and references to authorities,[1] while the second is simple, direct, unadorned, and does not even allude to the Bible. Also, it is evident that the compiler, himself a Mason, is trying to harmonize two traditions as to the origin of the order, one tracing it through Egypt and the other through the Hebrews; and it is hard to tell which tradition he favors most. Hence, a duplication of the traditional history, and an odd mixture of names and dates, often, indeed, absurd, as when he makes Euclid a pupil of Abraham. What is clear is that, having found an old Constitution of the Craft, he thought to write a kind of commentary upon it, adding proofs and illustrations of his own, though he did not manage his materials very successfully.

After his invocation,[2] the writer begins with a list

[1] He refers to Herodotus as the Master of History; quotes from the *Polychronicon*, written by a Benedictine monk who died in 1360; from *De Imagine Mundi*, Isodorus, and frequently from the Bible. Of more than ordinary learning for his day and station, he did not escape a certain air of pedantry in his use of authorities.

[2] These invocations vary in their phraseology, some bearing more visibly than others the mark of the Church. Toulmin Smith, in his *English Guilds*, notes the fact that the form of the invocations of the Masons "differs strikingly from that of most other Guilds. In almost every other case, God the Father Almighty would seem to have been forgotten." But Masons never forgot the corner-stone upon which their order and its teachings rest; not for a day.

of the Seven Sciences, giving quaint definitions of each, but in a different order from that recited in the *Regius Poem;* and he exalts Geometry above all the rest as "the first cause and foundation of all crafts and sciences." Then follows a brief sketch of the sons of Lamech, much as we find it in the book of Genesis which, like the old MS. we are here studying, was compiled from two older records: the one tracing the descent from Cain, and the other from Seth. Jabal and Jubal, we are told, inscribed their knowledge of science and handicraft on two pillars, one of marble, the other of lateres; and after the Flood one of the pillars was found by Hermes, and the other by Pythagoras, who taught the sciences they found written thereon. Other MSS. give Euclid the part here assigned to Hermes. Surely this is all fantastic enough, but the blending of the names of Hermes, the "father of Wisdom," who is so supreme a figure in the Egyptian Mysteries, and Pythagoras who used numbers as spiritual emblems, with old Hebrew history, is significant. At any rate, by this route the record reaches Egypt where, like the *Regius Poem,* it locates the origin of Masonry. In thus ascribing the origin of Geometry to the Egyptians the writer was but following a tradition that the Egyptians were compelled to invent it in order to restore the landmarks effaced by the inundations of the Nile; a tradition confirmed by modern research.

Proceeding, the compiler tells us that during their sojourn in Egypt the Hebrews learned the art and secrets of Masonry, which they took with them to the promised land. Long years are rapidly sketched, and we come to the days of David, who is said to have loved Masons well, and to have given them "wages nearly as they are now." There is but a meager reference to the building of the Temple of Solomon, to which is added: "In other chronicles and old books of Masonry, it is said that Solomon confirmed the charges that David had given to Masons; and that Solomon taught them their usages, differing but slightly from the customs now in use." While allusion is made to the master-artist of the temple, his name is not mentioned, *except in disguise.* Not one of the *Old Charges* of the order ever makes use of his name, but always employs some device whereby to conceal it.[1] Why so, when the name was well known, written in the Bible which lay upon the altar for all to read? Why such reluctance, if it be not that the name and the legend linked with it had an esoteric meaning, as it most certainly did have long before it was wrought into a drama? At this point the writer drops the old legend and traces the Masons into France and England, after the manner of the *Regius MS.,* but with more detail. Having noted these items, he returns to Euclid and brings that phase of the tradition up to the advent

[1] Such names as Aynone, Aymon, Ajuon, Dynon, Amon, Anon, Annon, and Benaim are used, deliberately, it would seem, and of set design. The *Inigo Jones MS.* uses the Bible name, but, though dated 1607, it has been shown to be apocryphal. See Gould's *History*, appendix. Also *Bulletin* of Supreme Council S. J., U. S. (vii, 200), that the Strassburg builders pictured the legend in stone.

of the order into England, adding, in conclusion, the articles of Masonic law agreed upon at an early assembly, of which he names nine, instead of the fifteen recited in the *Regius Poem.*

What shall we say of this Legend, with its recurring and insistent emphasis upon the antiquity of the order, and its linking of Egypt with Israel? For one thing, it explodes the fancy that the idea of the symbolical significance of the building of the Temple of Solomon originated with, or was suggested by, Bacon's *New Atlantis.* Here is a body of tradition uniting the Egyptian Mysteries with the Hebrew history of the Temple in a manner unmistakable. Wherefore such names as Hermes, Pythagoras, and Euclid, and how did they come into the old craft records if not through the Comacine artists and scholars? With the story of that great order before us, much that has hitherto been obscure becomes plain, and we recognize in these *Old Charges* the inaccurate and perhaps faded tradition of a lofty symbolism, an authentic scholarship, and an actual history. As Leader Scott observes, after reciting the old legend in its crudest form:

> The significant point is that all these names and Masonic emblems point to something real which existed in some long-past time, and, as regards the organization and nomenclature, we find the whole thing in its vital and actual working form in the Comacine Guild.[1]

Of interest here, as a kind of bridge between old

[1] *The Cathedral Builders,* bk. i, chap. i.

legend and the early history of the order in England, and also as a different version of the legend itself, is another document dating far back. There was a MS. discovered in the Bodleian Library at Oxford about 1696,—called the Laylande-Lock MS.—supposed to have been written in the year 1436, which purports to be an examination of a Mason by King Henry VI, albeit not allowed by all to be genuine. Its title runs as follows: *"Certain questions with answers to the same concerning the mystery of masonry written by King Henry the Sixth and faithfully copied by me, John Laylande, antiquarian, by command of his highness."* Written in quaint old English, it would doubtless be unintelligible to all but antiquaries, but it reads after this fashion:

What mote it be?—It is the knowledge of nature, and the power of its various operations; particularly the skill of reckoning, of weights and measures, of constructing buildings and dwellings of all kinds, and the true manner of forming all things for the use of man.

Where did it begin?—It began with the first men of the East, who were before the first men of the West, and coming with it, it hath brought all comforts to the wild and comfortless.

Who brought it to the West?—The Phoenicians, who, being great merchants, came first from the East into Phoenicia, for the convenience of commerce, both East and West, by the Red and Mediterranean Seas.

How came it into England?—Pythagoras, a Grecian, traveled to acquire knowledge in Egypt and Syria, and in every other land where the Phoenicians had planted Masonry; and gaining admittance into all lodges of

Masons, he learned much, and returned and dwelt in Grecia Magna, growing and becoming mighty wise and greatly renowned. Here he formed a great lodge at Crotona, and made many Masons, some of whom traveled into France, and there made many more, from whence, in process of time, the art passed into England.

3

With the conquest of Britain by the Romans, the *Collegia,* without which no Roman society was complete, made their advent into the island, traces of their work remaining even to this day. Under the direction of the mother College at Rome, the Britons are said to have attained to high degree of excellence as builders, so that when the cities of Gaul and the fortresses along the Rhine were destroyed, Chlorus, A. D. 298, sent to Britain for architects to repair or rebuild them. Whether the *Collegia* existed in Britain after the Romans left, as some affirm, or were suppressed, as we know they were on the Continent when the barbarians overran it, is not clear. Probably they were destroyed, or nearly so, for with the revival of Christianity in 598 A. D., we find Bishop Wilfred of York joining with the Abbott of Wearmouth in sending to France and Italy to induce Masons to return and build in stone, as he put it, "after the Roman manner." This confirms the Italian chroniclists who relate that Pope Gregory sent several of the fraternity of *Liberi muratori* with St. Augustine, as, later, they followed St. Boniface into Germany.

Again, in 604, Augustine sent the monk Pietro back to Rome with a letter to the same Pontiff, begging him to send more architects and workmen, which he did. As the *Liberi muratori* were none other than the Comacine Masters, it seems certain that they were at work in England *long before the period with which the* OLD CHARGES *begin their story of English Masonry.*[1] Among those sent by Gregory was Paulinus, and it is a curious fact that he is spoken of under the title of *Magister,* by which is meant, no doubt, that he was a member of the Comacine order, for they so described their members; and we know that many monks were enrolled in their lodges, having studied the art of building under their instruction. St. Hugh of Lincoln was not the only Bishop who could plan a church, instruct the workman, or handle a hod. Only, it must be kept in mind that these ecclesiastics who became skilled in architecture *were taught by the Masons,* and that it was not the monks, as some seem to imagine, who taught the Masons their art. Speaking of this early and troublous time, Giuseppe Merzaria says that only one lamp remained alight, making a

[1] See the account of "The Origin of Saxon Architecture," in the *Cathedral Builders* (bk. ii, chap. iii), written by Dr. W. M. Barnes in England independently of the author, who was living in Italy; and it is significant that the facts led both of them to the same conclusions. They show quite unmistakably that the Comacine builders were in England as early as 600 A. D., both by documents and by a comparative study of styles of architecture. More recent researches of a sort similar by Bro. W. Ravenscroft tend to confirm this view. "The Builder," vol. iv, published by the National Masonic Research Society of America.

bright spark in the darkness that extended over
Europe:

> It was from the *Magistri Comacini.* Their respec-
> tive names are unknown, their individual works un-
> specialized, but the breadth of their spirit might be
> felt all through those centuries, and their name col-
> lectively is legion. We may safely say that of all the
> works of art between A. D. 800 and 1000, the greater
> and better part are due to that brotherhood—always
> faithful and often secret—of the *Magistri Comacini.*
> The authority and judgment of learned men justify
> the assertion.[1]

Among the learned men who agree with this judgment are Kugler of Germany, Ramée of France, and
Selvatico of Italy, as well as Quatremal de Quincy,
in his *Dictionary of Architecture,* who, in the article
on the Comacine, remarks that "to these men, who
were both designers and executors, architects, sculptors, and mosaicists, may be attributed the renaissance of art, and its propagation in the southern
countries, where it marched with Christianity. Certain it is that we owe it to them, that the heritage of
antique ages was not entirely lost, and it is only by
their tradition and imitation that the art of building
was kept alive, producing works which we still ad-
mire, and which become surprising when we think
of the utter ignorance of all science in those dark
ages." The English writer, Hope, goes further and
credits the Comacine order with being the cradle of
the associations of Free-masons, who were, he adds,

---

[1] *Maestri Comacini,* vol. i, chap. ii.

"the first after Roman times to enrich architecture with a complete and well-ordinated system, which dominated wherever the Latin Church extended its influence."[1] So then, even if the early records of old Craft-masonry in England are confused, and often confusing, we are not left to grope our way from one dim tradition to another, having the history and monuments of this great·order which *spans the whole period,* and links the fraternity of Free-masons with one of the noblest chapters in the annals of art.

Almost without exception the *Old Charges* begin their account of Masonry in England at the time of Athelstan, the grandson of Alfred the Great; that is, between 925 and 940. Of this prince, or knight, they record that he was a wise and pacific ruler; that "he brought the land to rest and peace, and built many great buildings of castles and abbeys, for he loved Masons well." He is also said to have called an assembly of Masons at which laws, rules, and charges were adopted for the regulation of the craft. Despite these specific details, the story of Athelstan and St. Alban is hardly more than a legend, albeit dating at no very remote epoch, and well within the reasonable limits of tradition. Still, so many difficulties beset it that it has baffled the acutest critics, most of whom throw it aside.[2] That is, how-

---

[1] *Story of Architecture,* chap. xxii.

[2] Gould, in his *History of Masonry* (i, 31, 65), rejects the legend as having not the least foundation in fact, as indeed, he rejects almost everything that cannot prove itself in a court of law. For the other side see a "Critical Examination of the Alban and Athelstan Legends," by C. C. Howard (*A. Q. C.,* vii, 73). Meanwhile, Upton points out that

ever, too summary a way of disposing of it, since the record, though badly blurred, is obviously trying to preserve a fact of importance to the order.

Usually the assembly in question is located at York, in the year 926, of which, however, no slightest record remains. Whether at York or elsewhere, some such assembly must have been convoked, either as a civil function, or as a regular meeting of Masons authorized by legal power for upholding the honor of the craft; and its articles became the laws of the order. It was probably a civil assembly, a part of whose legislation was a revised and approved code for the regulation of Masons, and not unnaturally, by reason of its importance to the order, it became known as a Masonic assembly. Moreover, the Charge agreed upon was evidently no ordinary charge, for it is spoken of as *"the* Charge," called by one MS. "a deep charge for the observation of such articles as belong to Masonry," and by another MS. "a rule to be kept forever." Other assemblies were held afterwards, either annually or semi-annually, until the time of Inigo Jones who, in 1607, became superintendent-general of royal buildings and at the same time head of the Masonic order in England; and he is held by some to have instituted

St. Albans was the name of a town, not of a man, and shows how the error may have crept into the record (*A. Q. C.*, vii, 119-131). The nature of the tradition, its details, its motive, and the absence of any reason for fiction, should deter us from rejecting it. See two able articles, pro and con, by Begemann and Speth, entitled "The Assembly" (*A. Q. C.*, vii). Older Masonic writers, like Oliver and Mackey, accepted the York assembly as a fact established (*American Quarterly Review of Freemasonry*, vol. i, 546; ii, 245).

quarterly gatherings instead of the old annual assemblies.

Writers not familiar with the facts often speak of
Freemasonry as an evolution from Guild-masonry,
but that is to err. They were never at any time
united or the same, though working almost side by
side through several centuries. Free-masons existed
in large numbers long before any city guild of Masons was formed, and even after the Guilds became
powerful the two were entirely distinct. The
Guilds, as Hallam says,[1] "were Fraternities by voluntary compact, to relieve each other in poverty, and
to protect each other from injury. Two essential
characteristics belonged to them: the common banquet, and the common purse. They had also, in
many instances, a religious and sometimes a secret
ceremonial to knit more firmly the bond of fidelity.
They readily became connected with the exercises of
trades, with training of apprentices, and the traditional rules of art." Guild-masons, it may be added,

---

[1] *History of the English Constitution.* Of course the Guild was
indigenous to almost every age and land, from China to ancient Rome
(*The Guilds of China,* by H. B. Morse), and they survive in the trade
and labor unions of our day. The story of *English Guilds* has been
told by Toulmin Smith, and in the histories of particular com-
panies by Herbert and Hazlitt, leaving little for any one to add. No
doubt the Guilds were influenced by the Free-masons in respect of
officers and emblems, and we know that some of them, like the German Steinmetzen, attached moral meanings to their working tools, and
that others, like the French Companionage, even held the legend of
Hiram; but these did not make them Free-masons. English writers
like Speth go too far when they deny to the Steinmetzen any esoteric
lore, and German scholars like Krause and Findel are equally at fault
in insisting that they were Free-masons. (See essay by Speth, *A. Q. C.,*
i, 17, and *History of Masonry,* by Steinbrenner, chap. iv.)

had many privileges, one of which was that they were allowed to frame their own laws, and to enforce obedience thereto. Each Guild had a monopoly of the building in its city or town, except of ecclesiastical buildings, but with this went serious restrictions and limitations. No member of a local Guild could undertake work outside his town, but had to hold himself in readiness to repair the castle or town walls, whereas Free-masons journeyed the length and breadth of the land wherever their labor called them. Often the Free-masons, when at work in a town, employed Guild-masons, but only for rough work, and as such called them "rough-masons." No Guild-mason was admitted to the order of Free-masons unless he displayed unusual aptitude both as a workman and as a man of intellect. Such as adhered only to the manual craft and cared nothing for intellectual aims, were permitted to go back to the Guilds. For the Free-masons, be it once more noted, were not only artists doing a more difficult and finished kind of work, but an intellectual order, having a great tradition of science and symbolism which they guarded.

Following the Norman Conquest, which began in 1066, England was invaded by an army of ecclesiastics, and churches, monasteries, cathedrals, and abbeys were commenced in every part of the country. Naturally the Free-masons were much in demand, and some of them received rich reward for their skill as architects—Robertus Cementarius, a Master Mason employed at St. Albans in 1077, receiving a grant of land and a house in the town.[1] In the reign of Henry II no less than one hundred and fifty-seven religious buildings were founded in England, and it is at this period that we begin to see evidence of a new style of architecture—the Gothic. Most of the great cathedrals of Europe date from the eleventh century—the piety of the world having been wrought to a pitch of intense excitement by the expected end of all things, unaccountably fixed by popular belief to take place in the year one thousand. When the fatal year—and the following one, which some held to be the real date for the sounding of the last trumpet—passed without the arrival of the dreaded catastrophe, the sense of general relief found expression in raising magnificent temples to the glory of God who had mercifully abstained from delivering all things to destruction. And it was the order of Free-masons who made it possible for men to "sing their souls in stone," leaving for the admiration of after times what Goethe called the "frozen music" of the Middle Ages—monuments of the faith and gratitude of the race which adorn and consecrate the earth.

Little need be added to the story of Freemasonry during the cathedral-building period; its monuments are its best history, alike of its genius, its faith, and its symbols—as witness the triangle and the cir-

[1] *Notes on the Superintendents of English Buildings in the Middle Ages,* by Wyatt Papworth. Cementerius is also mentioned in connection with the Salisbury Cathedral, again in his capacity as a Master Mason.

cle which form the keystone of the ornamental
tracery of every Gothic temple. Masonry was then
at the zenith of its power, in its full splendor, the
Lion of the tribe of Judah its symbol, strength, wisdom, and beauty its ideals; its motto to be faithful
to God and the Government; its mission to lend itself to the public good and fraternal charity. Keeper
of an ancient and high tradition, it was a refuge for
the oppressed and a teacher of art and morality to
mankind. In 1270, we find Pope Nicholas III confirming all the rights previously granted to the Free-
masons, and bestowing on them further privileges.
Indeed, all the Popes up to Benedict XII appear to
have conceded marked favors to the order, even to
the length of exempting its members from the necessity of observance of the statutes, from municipal
regulations, and from obedience to royal edicts.

What wonder, then, that the Free-masons, ere
long, took *Liberty* for their motto, and by so doing
aroused the animosity of those in authority, as well
as the Church which they had so nobly served. Already forces were astir which ultimately issued in
the Reformation, and it is not surprising that a great
secret order was suspected of harboring men and fos-
tering influences sympathetic with the impending
change felt to be near at hand. As men of the most
diverse views, political and religious, were in the
lodges, the order began first to be accused of refusing to obey the law, and then to be persecuted. In
England a statute was enacted against the Free-masons in 1356, prohibiting their assemblies under

severe penalties, but the law seems never to have
been rigidly enforced, though the order suffered
greatly in the civil commotions of the period. However, with the return of peace after the long War
of the Roses, Freemasonry revived for a time, and
regained much of its prestige; and, at last, added
lustre to its fame in the rebuilding of London after
the Great Fire in 1666, its crowning monument being St. Paul's Cathedral.[1]

When cathedral-building ceased, and the demand
for highly skilled architects decreased, the order fell
into decline, but never at any time lost its identity,
its organization, and its ancient emblems. The Masons' Company of London, though its extant records
date only from 1620, is considered by its historian,
Conder, to have been established in 1220, if not
earlier, at which time there was great activity in
building, owing to the building of London Bridge,
begun in 1176, and of Westminster Abbey in 1221;
thus reaching back into the cathedral period. At one
time the Free-masons seem to have been stronger in
Scotland than in England, or at all events to have
left behind more records—for the minutes of the

[1] Hearing that the Masons had certain secrets that could not be revealed to her (for that she could not be Grand Master) Queen Elizabeth
sent an armed force to break up their annual Grand Lodge at York,
on St. John's Day, December 27, 1561. But Sir Thomas Sackville took
care to see that some of the men sent were Free-masons, who, joining
in the communication, made "a very honorable report to the Queen,
who never more attempted to dislodge or disturb them; but esteemed
them a peculiar sort of men, that cultivated peace and friendship,
arts and sciences, without meddling in the affairs of Church or State"
(Book of Constitutions, by Anderson).

Lodge of Edinburgh go back to 1599, and the *Schaw Statutes* to an earlier date; yet, it is a fact that the minutes of Aitchison Haven Lodge, from 1598, and of Mary's Chapel, from 1599, point almost entirely to operative guild practices. Nevertheless, as the art of architecture declined, Masonry declined with it, not a few of its members identifying themselves with the Guilds of ordinary "rough-masons," whom they formerly held in contempt; while others, losing sight of high aims, turned its lodges into social clubs. Always, however, despite defection and decline, there were those, as we shall see, who were faithful to the ideals of the order, devoting themselves more and more to its moral and spiritual teaching until what has come to be known as "the revival of 1717."

FELLOWCRAFTS

Noe person (of what degree soever) shalbee accepted a Free Mason, unless hee shall have a lodge of five Free Masons at least; whereof one to be a master, or warden, of that limitt, or division, wherein such Lodge shalbee kept, and another of the trade of Free Masonry.

That noe person shalbee accepted a Free Mason, but such as are of able body, honest parentage, good reputation, and observers of the laws of the land.

That noe person shalbee accepted a Free Mason, or know the secrets of said Society, until hee hath first taken the oath of secrecy hereafter following: "I, A. B., doe in the presence of Almighty God, and my fellows, and brethren here present, promise and declare, that I will not at any time hereafter, by any act or circumstance whatsoever, directly or indirectly, publish, discover, reveal, or make known any of the secrets, privileges, or counsels, of the fraternity or fellowship of Free Masonry, which at this time, or any time hereafter, shalbee made known unto mee soe helpe mee God, and the holy contents of this booke."

—HARLEIAN MS, 1600-1650

Chapter Two

FELLOWCRAFTS

1

HAVING FOLLOWED the Free-masons over a long period of history, it is now in order to give some account of the ethics, organization, laws, emblems, and workings of their lodges. Such a study is at once easy and difficult by turns, owing to the mass of material, and to the further fact that in the nature of things much of the work of a secret order is not, and has never been, matter for record. By this necessity, not a little must remain obscure, but it is hoped that even those not of the order may derive a definite notion of the principles and practices of the old Craft-masonry, from which the Masonry of today is descended. At least, such a sketch will show that, from times of old, the order of Masons has been a teacher of morality, charity, and truth, unique in its genius, noble in its spirit, and benign in its influence.

Taking its ethical teaching first, we have only to

turn to the *Old Charges* or *Constitutions* of the order, with their quaint blending of high truth and homely craft-law, to find the moral basis of universal Masonry. These old documents were a part of the earliest ritual of the order, and were recited or read to every young man at the time of his initiation as an Entered Apprentice. As such, they rehearsed the legends, laws, and ethics of the craft for his information, and, as we have seen, they insisted upon the antiquity of the order, as well as its service to mankind—a fact peculiar to Masonry, for *no other order has ever claimed such a legendary or traditional history*. Having studied that legendary record and its value as history, it remains to examine the moral code laid before the candidate who, having taken a solemn oath of loyalty and secrecy, was instructed in his duties as an Apprentice and his conduct as a man. What that old code lacked in subtlety is more than made up in simplicity, and it might all be stated in the words of the Prophet: "To do justly, to love mercy, and to walk humbly before God,"—the old eternal moral law, founded in faith, tried by time, and approved as valid for men of every clime, creed, and condition.

Turning to the *Regius MS.*, we find fifteen "points" or rules set forth for the guidance of Fellowcrafts, and as many for the rule of Master Masons.[1] Later the number was reduced to nine,

[1] Our present craft nomenclature is all wrong; the old order was first Apprentice, then Master, then Fellowcraft—mastership being, not a degree conferred, but a reward of skill as a workman and of

but so far from being an abridgement, it was in fact
an elaboration of the original code; and by the time
we reach the *Roberts* and *Watson* MSS. a similar set
of requirements for Apprentices had been adopted
—or rather recorded, for they had been in use long
before. It will make for clearness if we reverse the
order and take the Apprentice charge first, as it
shows what manner of men were admitted to the
order. No man was made a Mason save by his own
free choice, and he had to prove himself a freeman
of lawful age, of legitimate birth, of sound body, of
clean habits, and of good repute, else he was not
eligible. Also, he had to bind himself by solemn
oath to serve under rigid rules for a period of seven
years, vowing absolute obedience—for the old-time
Lodge was a school in which young men studied, not
only the art of building and its symbolism, but the
seven sciences as well. At first the Apprentice was
little more than a servant, doing the most menial

merit as a man. The confusion today is due, no doubt, to the custom of the German Guilds, where a Fellowcraft had to serve an
additional two years as a journeyman before becoming a Master.
No such restriction was known in England. Indeed, the reverse
was true, and it was not the Fellowcraft but the Apprentice who
prepared his masterpiece, and if it was accepted, he became a Master.
Having won his mastership, he was entitled to become a Fellowcraft—
that is, a peer and fellow of the fraternity which hitherto he had
only served. Also, we must distinguish between a Master and the
Master of the Work, now represented by the Master of the Lodge.
Between a Master and the Master of the Work there was no difference, of course, except an accidental one; they were both Masters
and Fellows. Any Master (or Fellow) could become a Master of the
Work at any time, provided he was of sufficient skill and had the
luck to be chosen as such either by the employer, or the Lodge, or
both.

work, his period of endenture being at once a test of his character and a training for his work. If he proved himself trustworthy and proficient, his wages were increased, albeit his rules of conduct were never relaxed. How austere the discipline was may be seen from a summary of its rules:

Confessing faith in God, an Apprentice vowed to honor the Church, the State, and the Master under whom he served, agreeing not to absent himself from the service of the order, by day or night, save with the license of the Master. He must be honest, truthful, upright, faithful in keeping the secrets of the craft, or the confidence of the Master, or of any Freemason, when communicated to him as such. Above all he must be chaste, never committing adultery or fornication, and he must not marry, or contract himself to any woman, during his appenticeship. He must be obedient to the Master without argument or murmuring, respectful to all Free-masons, courteous, avoiding obscene or uncivil speech, free from slander, dissension, or dispute. He must not haunt or frequent any tavern or ale-house, or so much as go into them except it be upon an errand of the Master or with his consent, using neither cards, dice, nor any unlawful game, "Christmas-time excepted." He must not steal anything even to the value of a penny, or suffer it to be done, or shield anyone guilty of theft, but report the fact to the Master with all speed.

After seven long years the Apprentice brought his masterpiece to the Lodge—or, in earlier times, to the annual Assembly [1]—and on strict trial and due examination was declared a Master. Thereupon he ceased to be a pupil and servant, passed into the ranks of Fellowcrafts, and became a free man capable, for the first time in his life, of earning his living and choosing his own employer. Having selected a Mark [2] by which his work could be identified, he could then take his kit of tools and travel as a Master of his art, receiving the wages of a Master—not, however, without first reaffirming his vows of honesty, truthfulness, fidelity, temperance, and chastity, and assuming added obligations to uphold the honor of the order. Again he was sworn not to lay bare, nor to tell to any man what he heard or saw done in the Lodge, and to keep the secrets of a fellow Mason as inviolably as his own—unless such a secret imperiled the good name of the craft. He furthermore promised to act as mediator between his Master and his

---

[1] The older MSS. indicate that initiations took place, for the most part, at the annual Assemblies, which were bodies not unlike the Grand Lodges of today, presided over by a President—a Grand Master in fact, though not in name. Democratic in government, as Masonry has always been, they received Apprentices, examined candidates for mastership, tried cases, adjusted disputes, and regulated the craft; but they were also occasions of festival and social good will. At a later time they declined, and the functions of initiation more and more reverted to the Lodges.

[2] The subject of Mason's Marks is most interesting, particularly with reference to the origin and growth of Gothic architecture, but too intricate to be entered upon here. As for example, an essay entitled "Scottish Mason's Marks Compared with Those of Other Countries," by Prof. T. H. Lewis, *British Archaeological Association*, 1888, and the theory there advanced that some great unknown architect introduced Gothic architecture from the East, as shown by the difference in Mason's Marks as compared with those of the Norman period. (Also proceedings of *A. Q. C.*, iii, 65-81.)

Fellows, and to deal justly with both parties. If he saw a Fellow hewing a stone which he was in a fair way to spoil, he must help him without loss of time, if able to do so, that the whole work be not ruined. Or if he met a fellow Mason in distress, or sorrow, he must aid him so far as lay within his power. In short, he must live in justice and honor with all men, especially with the members of the order, "that the bond of mutual charity and love may augment and continue."

Still more binding, if possible, were the vows of a Fellowcraft when he was elevated to the dignity of Master of the Lodge or of the Work. Once more he took solemn oath to keep the secrets of the order unprofaned, and more than one old MS. quotes the Golden Rule as the law of the Master's office. He must be steadfast, trusty, and true; pay his Fellows truly; take no bribe; and as a judge stand upright. He must attend the annual Assembly, unless disabled by illness, if within fifty miles—the distance varying, however, in different MSS. He must be careful in admitting Apprentices, taking only such as are fit both physically and morally, and keeping none without assurance that he would stay seven years in order to learn his craft. He must be patient with his pupils, instruct them diligently, encourage them with increased pay, and not permit them to work at night, "unless in the pursuit of knowledge, which shall be a sufficient excuse." He must be wise and discreet, and undertake no work he cannot both perform and complete equally to the profit of his

employer and the craft. Should a Fellow be overtaken by error, he must be gentle, skilful, and for-
giving, seeking rather to help than to hurt, abjuring
scandal and bitter words. He must not attempt to
supplant a Master of the Lodge or of the Work, or
belittle his work, but recommend it and assist him
in improving it. He must be liberal in charity to
those in need, helping a Fellow who has fallen upon
evil lot, giving him work and wages for at least a
fortnight, or if he has no work, "relieve him with
money to defray his reasonable charges to the next
Lodge." For the rest, he must in all ways act in a
manner befitting the nobility of his office and his
order.

Such were some of the laws of the moral life by
which the old Craft-masonry sought to train its
members, not only to be good workmen, but to be
good and true men, serving their Fellows; to which,
as the Rawlinson MS. tells us, "divers new articles
have been added by the free choice and good consent
and best advice of the Perfect and True Masons,
Masters, and Brethren." If, as an ethic of life, these
laws seem simple and rudimentary, they are none
the less fundamental, and they remain to this day
the only gate and way by which those must enter
who would go up to the House of the Lord. As such
they are great and saving things to lay to heart and
act upon, and if Masonry taught nothing else its
title to the respect of mankind would be clear. They
have a double aspect: first, the building of a spiritual
man upon immutable moral foundations; and sec-

ond, the great and simple religious faith in the Fatherhood of God, the Brotherhood of man, and the Life Eternal, taught by Masonry from its earliest history to this good day. Morality and theistic religion—upon these two rocks Masonry has always stood, and they are the only basis upon which man may ever hope to rear the spiritual edifice of his life, even to the capstone thereof.

2

Imagine, now, a band of these builders, bound together by solemn vows and mutual interests, journeying over the most abominable roads toward the site selected for an abbey or cathedral. Traveling was attended with many dangers, and the company was therefore always well armed, the disturbed state of the country rendering such a precaution necessary. Tools and provisions belonging to the party were carried on pack-horses or mules, placed in the center of the convoy, in charge of keepers. The company consisted of a Master Mason directing the work, Fellows of the craft, and Apprentices serving their time. Besides these we find subordinate laborers, not of the Lodge though in it, termed layers, setters, tilers, and so forth. Masters and Fellows wore a distinctive costume, which remained almost unchanged in its fashion for no less than three centuries.[1] Withal, it was a serious company, but in

[1] *History of Masonry*, Steinbrenner. It consisted of a short black tunic—in summer made of linen, in winter of wool—open at the sides, with a gorget to which a hood was attached; round the waist was a

nowise solemn, and the tedium of the journey was no doubt beguiled by song, story, and the humor incident to travel.

"Wherever they came," writes Mr. Hope in his *Essay on Architecture,* "in the suite of missionaries, or were called by the natives, or arrived of their own accord, to seek employment, they appeared headed by a chief surveyor, who governed the whole troop, and named one man out of every ten, under the name of warden, to overlook the other nine, set themselves to building temporary huts for their habitation around the spot where the work was to be carried on, regularly organized their different departments, fell to work, sent for fresh supplies of their brethren as the object demanded, and, when all was finished, again they raised their encampment, and went elsewhere to undertake other work."

Here we have a glimpse of the methods of the Free-masons, of their organization, almost military in its order and dispatch, and of their migratory life; although they had a more settled life than this ungainly sentence allows, for long time was required for the building of a great cathedral. Sometimes, it would seem, they made special contracts with the

leathern girdle, from which depended a sword and a satchel. Over the tunic was a black scapulary, similar to the habit of a priest, tucked under the girdle when they were working, but on holydays allowed to hang down. No doubt this garment also served as a coverlet at night, as was the custom of the Middle Ages, sheets and blankets being luxuries enjoyed only by the rich and titled (*History of Agriculture and Prices in England,* T. Rogers). On their heads they wore large felt or straw hats, and tight leather breeches and long boots completed the garb.

inhabitants of a town where they were to erect a church, containing such stipulations as, that a Lodge covered with tiles should be built for their accommodation, and that every laborer should be provided with a white apron of a peculiar kind of leather and gloves to shield the hands from stone and lime.[1] At all events, the picture we have is that of a little community or village of workmen, living in rude dwellings, with a Lodge room at the center adjoining a slowly rising cathedral—the Master busy with his plans and the care of his craft; Fellows shaping stones for walls, arches, or spires; Apprentices fetching tools or mortar, and, when necessary, tending the sick, and performing all offices of a similar nature. Always the Lodge was the center of interest and activity, a place of labor, of study, of devotion, as well as the common room for the social life of the order. Every morning, as we learn from the Fabric Rolls of York Minster, began with devotion, followed by the directions of the Master for the work

[1] Gloves were more widely used in the olden times than now, and the practice of giving them as presents was common in mediaeval times. Often, when the harvest was over, gloves were distributed to the laborers who gathered it (*History of Prices in England,* Rogers), and richly embroidered gloves formed an offering gladly accepted by princes. Indeed, the bare hand was regarded as a symbol of hostility, and the gloved hand a token of peace and goodwill. For Masons, however, the white gloves and apron had meanings hardly guessed by others, and their symbolism remains to this day with its simple and eloquent appeal. (See chapter on "Masonic Clothing and Regalia," in *Things a Freemason Should Know,* by J. W. Crowe, an interesting article by Rylands, *A. Q. C.,* vol. v, and the delightful essay on "Gloves," by Dr. Mackey, in his *Symbolism of Freemasonry.*) Not only the tools of the builder, but his clothing, had moral meaning.

of the day, which no doubt included study of the laws of the art, plans of construction, and the mystical meaning of ornaments and emblems. Only Masons were in attendance at such times, the Lodge being closed to all others, and guarded by a Tiler [1] against "the approach of cowans [2] and eavesdroppers." Thus the work of each day was begun, moving forward amidst the din and litter of the hours, until the craft was called from labor to rest and refreshment; and thus a cathedral was uplifted as a monument to the Order, albeit the names of the builders are faded and lost. Employed for years on

[1] *Tiler*—like the word *cable-tow*—is a word peculiar to the language of Masonry, and means one who guards the Lodge to see that only Masons are within ear-shot. It probably derives from the Middle Ages when the makers of tiles for roofing were also of migratory habits (*History of Prices in England,* Rogers), and accompanied the Free-masons to perform their share of the work of covering buildings. Some tiler was appointed to act as sentinel to keep off intruders, and hence, in course of time, the name of Tiler came to be applied to any Mason who guarded the Lodge.

[2] Much has been written of the derivation and meaning of the word *cowan,* some finding its origin in a Greek term meaning "dog." (See "An Inquiry Concerning Cowans," by D. Ramsay, *Review of Freemasonry,* vol. i.) But its origin is still to seek, unless we accept it as an old Scotch word of contempt (*Dictionary of Scottish Language,* Jamieson). Sir Walter Scott uses it as such in *Rob Roy,* "she doesna' value a Cawmil mair as a cowan" (chap. xxix). Masons used the word to describe a "dry-diker, one who built without cement," or a Mason without the word. Unfortunately, we still have cowans in this sense—men who try to be Masons without using the cement of brotherly love. If only they *could* be kept out! Blackstone describes an eavesdropper as a "common nuisance punishable by fine." Legend says that the old-time Masons punished such prying persons, who sought to learn their signs and secrets, by holding them under the eaves until the water ran in at the neck and out at the heels. What penalty was inflicted in dry weather, we are not informed. At any rate, they had contempt for a man who tried to make use of the signs of the craft without knowing its art and ethics.

the same building, and living together in the Lodge, it is not strange that Free-masons came to know and love one another, and to have a feeling of loyalty to their craft, unique, peculiar, and enduring. Traditions of fun and frolic, of song and feast and gala-day, have floated down to us, telling of a comradeship as joyous as it was genuine. If their life had hardship and vicissitude, it had also its grace and charm of friendship, of sympathy, service, and community of interest, and the joy that comes of devotion to a high and noble art.

When a Mason wished to leave one Lodge and go elsewhere to work, as he was free to do when he desired, he had no difficulty in making himself known to the men of his craft by certain signs, grips, and words.[1] Such tokens of recognition were necessary

---

[1] This subject is most fascinating. Even in primitive ages there seems to have been a kind of universal sign-language employed, at times, by all peoples. Among widely separated tribes the signs were very similar, owing, perhaps, to the fact that they were natural gestures of greeting, of warning, or of distress. There is intimation of this in the Bible, when the life of Ben-Hadad was saved by a sign given (I Kings, 20:30-35). Even among the North American Indians a sign-code of like sort was known (*Indian Masonry*, R. C. Wright, chap iii). "Mr. Ellis, by means of his knowledge as a Master Mason, actually passed himself into the sacred part or adytum of one of the temples of India" (*Anacalypsis*, G. Higgins, vol. i, 767). See also the experience of Hackett Smith among the Druses, already referred to (*A. Q. C.*, iv, 11). Kipling has a rollicking story with the Masonic sign-code for a theme, entitled *The Man Who Would be King*, and his imagination is positively uncanny. If not a little of the old sign-language of the race lives to this day in Masonic Lodges, it is due not only to the exigencies of the craft, but also to the instinct of the order for the old, the universal, the *human*; its genius for making use of all the ways and means whereby men may be brought to know and love and help one another.

to men who traveled afar in those uncertain days, especially when references or other means of identification were oft-times impossible. All that many people knew about the order was that its members had a code of secret signs, and that no Mason need be friendless or alone when other Masons were within sight or hearing; so that the very name of the craft came to stand for any mode of hidden recognition. Steele, in the *Tatler,* speaks of a class of people who have "their signs and tokens like Freemasons." There were more than one of these signs and tokens, as we are more than once told—in the *Harleian MS.,* for example, which speaks of "words and signs." What they were may not be here discussed, but it is safe to say that a Master Mason of the Middle Ages, were he to return from the land of shadows, could perhaps make himself known as such in a Fellowcraft Lodge of today. No doubt some things would puzzle him at first, but he would recognize the officers of the Lodge, its form, its emblems, its great altar Light, and its moral truth taught in symbols. Besides, he could tell us, if so minded, much that we should like to learn about the craft in the olden times, its hidden mysteries, the details of its rites, and the meaning of its symbols when the poetry of building was yet alive.

3

This brings us to one of the most hotly debated questions in Masonic history—the question as to the number and nature of the degrees made use of in the old craft lodges. Hardly any other subject has so deeply engaged the veteran archaeologists of the order, and while it ill becomes any one glibly to decide such an issue, it is at least permitted us, after studying all of value that has been written on both sides, to sum up what seems to be the truth arrived at.[1] While such a thing as a written record of an ancient degree—aside from the *Old Charges,* which formed a part of the earliest rituals—is unthinkable, we are not left altogether to the mercy of conjecture in a matter so important. Cesare Cantu tells us that the Comacine Masters "were called together in the Loggie by a grand-master to treat of affairs common to the order, to receive novices, and *confer superior degrees on others."* [2] Evidence of a sort similar is abundant, but not a little confusion will be avoided if the following considerations be kept in mind:

First, that during its purely operative period the ritual of Masonry was naturally less formal and ornate than it afterwards became, from the fact that its very life was a kind of ritual and its symbols were always visibly present in its labor. By the same

[1] Once more it is a pleasure to refer to the *Transactions* of the Quatuor Coronati Lodge of Research, whose essays and discussions of this issue, as of so many others, are the best survey of the whole question from all sides. The paper by W. J. Hughan arguing in behalf of only one degree in the old time lodges, and a like paper by G. W. Speth in behalf of two degrees, with the materials for the third, cover the field quite thoroughly and in full light of all the facts (*A. Q. C.,* vol. x, 127; vol. xi, 47). As for the Third Degree, that will be considered further along.

[2] *Storia di Como,* vol. i, 440.

token, as it ceased to be purely operative, and others not actually architects were admitted to its fellowship, of necessity its rites became more formal—*"very formall,"* as Aubrey said in 1686,[1]—portraying in ceremony what had long been present in its symbolism and practice.

Second, that with the decline of the old religious art of building—for such it was in very truth—some of its symbolism lost its luster, its form surviving but its meaning obscured, if not entirely faded. Who knows, for example—even with the Klein essay on *The Great Symbol* [2] in hand—what Pythagoras meant by his lesser and greater Tetractys? That they were more than mathematical theorems is plain, yet even Plutarch missed their meaning. In the same way, some of the emblems in our Lodges are veiled, or else wear meanings invented after the fact, in lieu of deeper meanings hidden, or but dimly discerned. Albeit, the great emblems still speak in truths simple and eloquent, and remain to refine, instruct, and exalt.

Third, that when Masonry finally became a purely speculative or symbolical fraternity, no longer an order of practical builders, its ceremonial inevitably became more elaborate and imposing—its old habit and custom, as well as its symbols and teachings, being enshrined in its ritual. More than this, knowing how "Time the white god makes all things holy,

[1] *Natural History of Wiltshire,* by John Aubrey, written, but not published, in 1686.
[2] *A. Q. C.,* vol. x, 82.

and what is old becomes religion," it is no wonder
that its tradition became every year more authoritative; so that the tendency was not, as many have
imagined, to add to its teaching, but to preserve and
develop its rich deposit of symbolism, and to avoid
any break with what had come down from the past.

Keeping in mind this order of evolution in the history of Masonry, we may now state the facts, so far
as they are known, as to its early degrees; dividing
it into two periods, the Operative and the Speculative.[1] An Apprentice in the olden days was "entered" as a novice of the craft, first, as a purely business proceeding, not unlike our modern indentures,
or articles. Then, or shortly afterwards—probably at
the annual Assembly—there was a ceremony of initiation making him a Mason—including an oath, the
recital of the craft legend as recorded in the *Old
Charges,* instruction in moral conduct and deportment as a Mason, and the imparting of certain
secrets. At first this degree, although comprising

[1] Roughly speaking, the year 1600 may be taken as a date dividing the two periods. Addison, writing in the *Spectator,* March 1,
1711, draws the following distinction between a speculative and an
operative member of a trade or profession: "I live in the world
rather as a spectator of mankind, than as one of the species, by
which means I have made myself a speculative statesman, soldier,
merchant, and *artisan,* without ever meddling with any practical
part of life." By a Speculative Mason, then, is meant a man who,
though not an actual architect, sought and obtained membership
among Free-masons. Such men, scholars and students, began to enter the order as early as 1600, if not earlier. If by Operative Mason
is meant one who attached no moral meaning to his tools, there
were none such in the olden time—all Masons, even those in the
Guilds, using their tools as moral emblems in a way quite unknown
to builders of our day. 'Tis a pity that this light of poetry has
faded from our toil, and with it the joy of work.

secrets, does not seem to have been mystic at all, but a simple ceremony intended to impress upon the mind of the youth the high moral life required of him. Even Guild-masonry had such a rite of initiation, as Hallam remarks, and if we may trust the Findel version of the ceremony used among the German Stone-masons, it was very like the first degree as we now have it—though one has always the feeling that it was embellished in the light of later time.[1]

So far there is no dispute, but the question is whether any other degree was known in the early lodges. All the probabilities of the case, together with such facts as we have, indicate that there was another and higher degree. For, if all the secrets of the order were divulged to an Apprentice, he could, after working four years, and just when he was becoming valuable, run away, give himself out as a Fellow, and receive work and wages as such. If there was only one set of secrets, this deception might be practiced to his own profit and the injury of the craft —unless, indeed, we revise all our ideas held hitherto, and say that his initiation did not take place until he was out of his articles. This, however, would land us in worse difficulties later on. Knowing the fondness of the men of the Middle Ages for ceremony, it is hardly conceivable that the day of all days when an Apprentice, having worked for seven long years, acquired the status of a Fellow, was allowed to go unmarked, least of all in an order of men to whom building was at once an art and an allegory. So that,

[1] *History of Masonry,* p. 66.

not only the exigencies of his occupation, but the importance of the day to a young man, and the spirit of the order, justify such a conclusion.

Have we any evidence tending to confirm this inference? Most certainly; so much so that it is not easy to interpret the hints given in the *Old Charges* upon any other theory. For one thing, in nearly all the MSS., from the *Regius Poem* down, we are told of two rooms or resorts, the Chamber and the Lodge —sometimes called the Bower and the Hall—and the Mason was charged to keep the "counsells" proper to each place. This would seem to imply that an Apprentice had access to the Chamber or Bower, but not to the Lodge itself—at least not at all times. It may be argued that the "other counsells" referred to were merely technical secrets, but that is to give the case away, since they were secrets held and communicated as such. By natural process, as the order declined and actual building ceased, *its technical secrets became ritual secrets,* though they must always have had symbolical meanings. Further, while we have record of only one oath—which does not mean that there *was* only one—signs, tokens, and words are nearly always spoken of in the plural; and if the secrets of a Fellowcraft were purely technical —which some of us do not believe—they were at least accompanied and protected by certain signs, tokens, and passwords. From this it is clear that the advent of an Apprentice into the ranks of a Fellow was in fact a degree, or contained the essentials of a degree, including a separate set of signs and secrets.

When we pass to the second period, and men of wealth and learning who were not actual architects began to enter the order—whether as patrons of the art or as students and mystics attracted by its symbolism—other evidences of change appear. They, of course, were not required to serve a seven year apprenticeship, and they would naturally be Fellows, not Masters, because they were in no sense masters of the craft. Were these Fellows made acquainted with the secrets of an Apprentice? If so, then the two degrees were either conferred in one evening, or else—what seems to have been the fact—they were welded into one; since we hear of men being made Masons in a single evening.[1] Customs differed, no doubt, in different Lodges, some of which were chiefly operative, or made up of men who had been working Masons, with only a sprinkling of men not workmen who had been admitted; while others were purely symbolical Lodges as far back as 1645. Naturally, in Lodges of the first kind the two degrees were kept separate, and in the second they were merged —the one degree becoming all the while more elaborate. Gradually the men who had been Operative Masons became fewer in the Lodges—chiefly those of higher position, such as master builders, architects, and so on—until the order became a purely speculative fraternity, having no longer any trade object in view.

Not only so, but throughout this period of transi-

[1] For a single example, the *Diary* of Elias Ashmole, under date of 1646.

tion, and even earlier, we hear intimations of "the
Master's Part," and those hints increase in number
as the office of Master of the Work lost its practical
aspect after the cathedral-building period. What
was the Master's Part? Unfortunately, while the
number of degrees may be indicated, their nature
and details cannot be discussed without grave indis-
cretion; but nothing is plainer than that *we need not
go outside Masonry itself to find the materials out of
which all three degrees, as they now exist, were developed.*[1] Even the French Companionage, or Sons
of Solomon, had the legend of the Third Degree
long before 1717, when some imagine it to have
been invented. If little or no mention of it is found
among English Masons before that date, that is no
reason for thinking that it was unknown. *Not until 1841 was it known to have been a secret of the
Companionage in France, so deeply and carefully
was it hidden.*[2] Where so much is dim one may not

---

[1] Time out of mind it has been the habit of writers, both within
the order and without, to treat Masonry as though it were a kind
of agglomeration of archaic remains and platitudinous moralizings,
made up of the heel-taps of Operative legend and the fag-ends of
Occult lore. Far from it! If this were the fact the present writer
would be the first to admit it, but it is not the fact. Instead, the
idea that an order so noble, so heroic in its history, so rich in symbolism, so skilfully adjusted, and with so many traces of remote
antiquity, was the creation of pious fraud, or else of an ingenious
conviviality, passes the bounds of credulity and enters the domain
of the absurd. This fact will be further emphasized in the chapter
following, to which those are respectfully referred who go everywhere
else, *except to Masonry itself,* to learn what Masonry is and how it
came to be.

[2] *Livre du Compagnonnage,* by Agricol Perdiguier, 1841. **George
Sand's** novel, *Le Compagnon du Tour de France,* was published the

be dogmatic, but what seems to have taken place in 1717 was, not the *addition* of a third degree made out of whole cloth, but the *conversion* of two degrees into three.

That is to say, Masonry is too great an institution to have been made in a day, much less by a few men, but was a slow evolution through long time, unfolding its beauty as it grew. Indeed, it was like one of its own cathedrals upon which one generation of builders wrought and vanished, and another followed, until, amidst vicissitudes of time and change, of decline and revival, the order itself became a temple of Freedom and Fraternity—its history a disclosure of its innermost soul in the natural process of its transition from actual architecture to its "more noble and glorious purpose." For, since what was evolved from Masonry must always have been involved in it—not something alien added to it from extraneous sources, as some never tire of trying to show—we need not go outside the order itself to learn what Masonry is, certainly not to discover its motif and its genius; its later and more elaborate form being only an expansion and exposition of its inherent nature and teaching. Upon this fact the present study insists with all emphasis, as over against those who go hunting in every odd nook and corner to find whence Masonry came, and where it got its symbols and degrees.

same year. See full account of this order in Gould. *History of Masonry,* vol. i, chap. v.

ACCEPTED MASONS

The SYSTEM, *as taught in the regular* LODGES, *may have some Redundancies or Defects, occasion'd by the Ignorance or Indolence of the old members. And indeed, considering through what Obscurity and Darkness the* MYSTERY *has been deliver'd down; the many Centuries it has survived; the many Countries and Languages, and* SECTS *and* PARTIES *it has run through; we are rather to wonder that it ever arrived to the present Age, without more Imperfection. It has run long in muddy Streams, and as it were, under Ground. But notwithstanding the great Rust it may have contracted, there is much of the* OLD FABRICK *remaining: the essential Pillars of the Building may be discov'd through the Rubbish, tho' the Superstructure be overrun with Moss and Ivy, and the Stones, by Length of Time, be disjointed. And therefore, as the Bust of an* OLD *Hero is of great Value among the Curious, tho' it has lost an Eye, the Nose or the Right Hand; so Masonry with all its Blemishes and Misfortunes, instead of appearing ridiculous, ought to be receiv'd with some Candor and Esteem, from a Veneration of its* ANTIQUITY.
—Defence of Masonry, 1730*

Chapter Three

ACCEPTED MASONS

1

WHATEVER MAY be dim in the history of Freemasonry, and in the nature of things much must remain hidden, its symbolism may be traced in unbroken succession through the centuries; and its symbolism is its soul. So much is this true, that it may almost be said that had the order ceased to exist in the period when it was at its height, its symbolism would have survived and developed, so deeply was it wrought into the mind of mankind. When, at last, the craft finished its labors and laid down its tools, its symbols, having served the faith of the worker, became a language for the thoughts of the thinker.

Few realize the service of the science of numbers to the faith of man in the morning of the world, when he sought to find some kind of key to the mighty maze of things. Living amidst change and seeming chance, he found in the laws of numbers a path by which to escape the awful sense of life as a series of accidents in the hands of a capricious Power; and, when we think of it, his insight was not invalid. "All things are in numbers," said the wise Pythagoras; "the world is a living arithmetic in its development—a realized geometry in its repose." Nature is a realm of numbers; crystals are solid geometry. Music, of all arts the most divine and exalting, moves with measured step, using geometrical figures, and cannot free itself from numbers without dying away into discord. Surely it is not strange that a science whereby men obtained such glimpses of the unity and order of the world should be hallowed among them, imparting its form to their faith.[1] Having revealed so much, mathematics came to wear mystical meanings in a way quite alien to our prosaic habit of thinking—faith in our day having betaken itself to other symbols.

Equally so was it with the art of building—a living allegory in which man imitated in miniature the world-temple, and sought by every device to discover

[1] There is a beautiful lecture on the moral meaning of Geometry by Dr. Hutchinson, in *The Spirit of Masonry*—one of the oldest, as it is one of the noblest, books in our Masonic literature. Plutarch reports Plato as saying, "God is always geometrizing" (*Diog. Laert.*, iv, 2). Elsewhere Plato remarks that "Geometry rightly treated is the knowledge of the Eternal" (*Republic,* 527b), and over the porch of his Academy at Athens he wrote the words, "Let no one who is ignorant of Geometry enter my doors." So Aristotle and all the ancient thinkers, whether in Egypt or India. Pythagoras, Proclus tells us, was concerned only with number and magnitude: number absolute, in arithmetic; number applied, in music; and so forth—whereof we read in the *Old Charges* (see "The Great Symbol," by Klein, *A. Q. C.*, x, 82).

the secret of its stability. Already we have shown how, from earliest times, the simple symbols of the builder became a part of the very life of humanity, giving shape to its thought, its faith, its dream. Hardly a language but bears their impress, as when we speak of a Rude or Polished mind, of an Upright man who is a Pillar of society, of the Level of equality, or the Golden Rule by which we would Square our actions. They are so natural, so inevitable, and so eloquent withal, that we use them without knowing it. Sages have always been called Builders, and it was no idle fancy when Plato and Pythagoras used imagery drawn from the art of building to utter their highest thought. Everywhere in literature, philosophy, and life it is so, and naturally so. Shakespeare speaks of "square-men," and when Spenser would build in stately lines the Castle of Temperance, he makes use of the Square, Circle, and Triangle: [1]

> The frame thereof seem'd partly circulaire
> And part triangular: O work divine!
> Those two the first and last proportions are;
> The one imperfect, mortal, feminine.
>
> The other immortal, perfect, masculine,
> And twixt them both a quadrate was the base,
> Proportion'd equally by seven and nine;
> Nine was the circle set in heaven's place
> All which compacted made a goodly diapase.

During the Middle Ages, as we know, men revelled in symbolism, often of the most recondite kind, and

[1] *Faerie Queene*, bk. ii, canto ix, 22.

the emblems of Masonry are to be found all through the literature, art, and thought of that time. Not only on cathedrals, tombs, and monuments, where we should expect to come upon them, but in the designs and decorations of dwellings, on vases, pottery, and trinkets, in the water-marks used by papermakers and printers, and even as initial letters in books—everywhere one finds the old, familiar emblems.[1] Square, Rule, Plumb-line, the perfect Ashlar, the two Pillars, the Circle within the parallel lines, the Point within the Circle, the Compasses, the Winding Staircase, the numbers Three, Five, Seven, Nine, the double Triangle—these and other such symbols were used alike by Hebrew Kabbalists and Rosicrucian Mystics. Indeed, so abundant is the evidence—if the matter were in dispute and needed proof—especially after the revival of symbolism under Albertus Magnus in 1249, that a whole book might be filled with it. Typical are the lines left by a poet who, writing in 1623, sings of God as the great Logician whom the conclusion never fails, and whose counsel rules without command: [2]

> Therefore can none foresee his end
> Unless on God is built his hope.
> And if we here below would learn

[1] *Lost Language of Symbolism*, by Bayley, also *A New Light on the Renaissance*, by the same author; *Architecture of the Renaissance in England*, by J. A. Gotch; and "Notes on Some Masonic Symbols," by W. H. Rylands, *A. Q. C.*, viii, 84. Indeed, the literature is as prolific as the facts.

[2] J. V. Andreae, *Ehreneich Hohenfelder von Aister Haimb*. A verbatim translation of the second line quoted would read, "Unless in God he has his building."

By Compass, Needle, Square, and Plumb,
We never must o'erlook the mete
Wherewith our God hath measur'd us.

For all that, there are those who never weary of trying to find where, in the misty mid-region of conjecture, the Masons got their immemorial emblems.
One would think, after reading their endless essays,
that the symbols of Masonry were loved and preserved by all the world—*except by the Masons themselves.* Often these writers imply, if they do not
actually assert, that our order begged, borrowed, or
cribbed its emblems from Kabbalists or Rosicrucians, whereas the truth is exactly the other way
round—those impalpable fraternities, whose vague,
fantastic thought was always seeking a local habitation and a body, making use of the symbols of Masonry the better to reach the minds of men. Why
all this unnecessary mystery—not to say mystification
—when the facts are so plain, written in records and
carved in stone? While Kabbalists were contriving
their curious cosmogonies, the Masons went about
their work, leaving record of their symbols in deeds,
not in creeds, albeit holding always to their simple
faith, and hope, and duty—as in the lines left on an
old brass Square, found in an ancient bridge near
Limerick, bearing date of 1517:

Strive to live with love and care
Upon the Level, by the Square.

Some of our Masonic writers [1]—more than one likes

[1] When, for example, Albert Pike, in his letter, "Touching Ma-

to admit—have erred by confusing Freemasonry with
Guild-masonry, to the discredit of the former. Even
Oliver once concluded that the secrets of the working Masons of the Middle Ages were none other than
the laws of Geometry—hence the letter G; forgetting,
it would seem, that Geometry had mystical meanings
for them long since lost to us. As well say that the
philosophy of Pythagoras was repeating the Multi-
plication Table! Albert Pike held that we are "not
warranted in assuming that, among Masons generally—in the *body* of Masonry—the symbolism of
Freemasonry is of earlier date than 1717." [1] Surely

sonic Symbolism," speaks of the "poor, rude, unlettered, uncultivated
working Stone-masons," who attended the Assemblies, he is obviously confounding Free-masons with the rough Stone-masons of
the Guilds. Over against these words, read a brilliant article in
the *Contemporary Review*, October, 1913, by L. M. Phillips, entitled, "The Two Ways of Building," showing how the Free-masons,
instead of working under architects outside the order, chose the finer
minds among them as leaders and created the different styles of
architecture in Europe. "Such," he adds, "was the high limit of
talent and intelligence which the creative spirit fostered among
workmen. . . . The entire body being trained and educated in the
same principles and ideas, the most backward and inefficient, as
they worked at the vaults which their own skillful brethren had
planned, might feel the glow of satisfaction arising from the conscious realization of their own aspirations. Thus the whole body
of constructive knowledge maintained its unity. . . . Thus it was
by free associations of workmen training their own leaders that
the great Gothic edifices of the medieval ages were constructed. . . .
A style so imaginative and so spiritual might almost be the dream
of a poet or the vision of a saint. Really it is the creation of the
sweat and labor of workingmen, and every iota of the boldness,
dexterity, and knowledge which it embodies was drawn out of the
practical experience and experiments of manual labor." This describes the Comacine Masters, but not the poor, rude, unlettered Stone-
masons whom Pike had in mind.
[1] Letter "Touching Masonic Symbolism."

that is to err. If we had only the Masons' Marks that
have come down to us, nothing else would be needed
to prove it an error. Of course, for deeper minds all
emblems have deeper meanings, and there may have
been many Masons who did not fathom the symbolism of the order. No more do we; but the symbolism itself, of hoar antiquity, was certainly the
common inheritance and treasure of the working
Masons of the Lodges in England and Scotland before, indeed centuries before, the year 1717.

2

Therefore it is not strange that men of note and
learning, attracted by the wealth of symbolism in
Masonry, as well as by its spirit of fraternity—perhaps, also, by its secrecy—began at an early date to
ask to be accepted as members of the order: hence
Accepted Masons.[1] How far back the custom of admitting such men to the Lodges goes is not clear, but
hints of it are discernible in the oldest documents of
the order; and this whether or no we accept as historical the membership of Prince Edwin in the tenth
century, of whom the *Regius Poem* says,

Of speculatyfe he was a master.

This may only mean that he was amply skilled in
the knowledge, as well as the practice, of the art,

[1] Some Lodges, however, would never admit such members. As
late as April 24, 1786, two brothers were proposed as members of
Domatic Lodge, No. 177, London, and were rejected because they
were not Operative Masons (*History Lion and Lamb Lodge, 192,
London,* by Abbott).

although, as Gould points out, the *Regius MS.* contains intimations of thoughts above the heads of many to whom it was read.[1] Similar traces of Accepted Masons are found in the *Cooke MS.*, compiled in 1400 or earlier. Hope suggests [2] that the earliest members of this class were ecclesiastics who wished to study to be architects and designers, so as to direct the erection of their own churches; the more so, since the order had "so high and sacred a destination, was so entirely exempt from all local, civil jurisdiction," and enjoyed the sanction and protection of the Church. Later, when the order was in disfavor with the Church, men of another sort—scholars, mystics, and lovers of liberty—sought its degrees.

At any rate, the custom began early and continued through the years, until Accepted Masons were in the majority. Noblemen, gentlemen, and scholars entered the order as Speculative Masons, and held office as such in the old Lodges, the first name recorded in actual minutes being John Boswell, who was present as a member of the Lodge of Edinburgh in 1600. Of the forty-nine names on the roll of the Lodge of Aberdeen in 1670, thirty-nine were Accepted Masons not in any way connected with the building trade. In England the earliest reference to the initiation of a Speculative Mason, in Lodge minutes, is of the year 1641. On the 20th of May that year, Robert Moray, "General Quarter-

---

[1] "On the Antiquity of Masonic Symbolism," *A. Q. C.,* iii, 7.
[2] *Historical Essay on Architecture,* chap. xxi.

master of the Armie off Scottland," as the record runs, was initiated at Newcastle by members of the "Lodge of Edinburgh" who were with the Scottish Army. A still more famous example was that of Ashmole, whereof we read in the *Memoirs of the Life of that Learned Antiquary, Elias Ashmole, Drawn up by Himself by Way of Diary,* published in 1717, which contains two entries as follows, the first dated in 1646:

> Oct: 16. 4.H. 30′ P.M. I was made a Free Mason at Warrington in Lancashire, with Coll: Henry Mainwaring of Karincham in Cheshire. The names of those that were then of the Lodge; Mr. Rich Penket Warden, Mr. James Collier, Mr. Rich: Sankey, Henry Littler, John Ellam, Rich: Ellam & Hugh Brewer.

Such is the record, complete; and it has been shown, by hunting up the wills of the men present, that the members of the Warrington Lodge in 1646 were, nearly all of them—every one in fact, so far as is known—Accepted Masons. Thirty-five years pass before we discover the only other Masonic entries in the *Diary,* dated March, 1682, which read as follows:

> About 5H: P.M. I recd a Sumons to appe at a Lodge to be held the next day, at Masons Hall London.
> Accordingly I went, & about Noone were admitted into the Fellowship of Free Masons. Sr. William Wilson Knight, Capt. Rich: Borthwick, Mr. Will: Woodman, Mr. Wm Grey, Mr. Samuell Taylour & Mr William Wise.
> I was the Senior Fellow among them (it being 35

years since I was admitted) There were pesent beside
my selfe the Fellowes after named.

Mr Tho: Wise Mr of the Masons Company this
pesent yeare. Mr. Thomas Shorthose, Mr Thomas
Shadbolt, Waindsford Esqr Mr. Nich: Young. Mr
John Shorthose, Mr. William Hamon, Mr. John
Thompson, & Mr Will: Stanton.

Wee all dyned at the halfe Moone Taverne in
Cheapeside, at a Noble Dinner prepaired at the
charge of the New-accepted Masons.

Space is given to those entries, not because they are
very important, but because Ragon and others have
actually held that Ashmole made Masonry—as if any
one man made Masonry! 'Tis surely strange, if this
be true, that only two entries in his *Diary* refer to
the order; but that does not disconcert the theorists
who are so wedded to their idols as to have scant
regard for facts. No, the circumstance that Ashmole
was a Rosicrucian, an Alchemist, a delver into occult
lore, is enough, the absence of any allusion to him
thereafter only serving to confirm the fancy—the
theory being that a few adepts, seeing Masonry
about to crumble and decay, seized it, introduced
their symbols into it, making it the mouthpiece of
their high, albeit hidden, teaching. How fascinating! and yet how baseless in fact! There is no evidence that a Rosicrucian fraternity existed—save on
paper, having been woven of a series of romances
written as early as 1616, and ascribed to Andrea—
until a later time; and even when it did take form,
it was quite distinct from Masonry. Occultism, to be

sure, is elusive, coming we know not whence, and hovering like a mist trailing over the hills. Still, we ought to be able to find in Masonry *some* trace of Rosicrucian influence, some hint of the lofty wisdom it is said to have added to the order; but no one has yet done so. Did all that high, Hermetic mysticism evaporate entirely, leaving not a wraith behind, going as mysteriously as it came to that far place which no mortal may explore? [1]

Howbeit, the *fact* to be noted is that, thus early —and earlier, for the Lodge had been in existence some time when Ashmole was initiated—the Warrington Lodge was made up of Accepted Masons. Of the ten men present in the London Lodge, mentioned in the second entry in the *Diary,* Ashmole was the senior, but he was not a member of the Masons' Company, though the other nine were, and also two of the neophytes. No doubt this is the

[1] Those who wish to pursue this Quixotic quest will find the literature abundant and very interesting. For example, such essays as that by F. W. Brockbank in *Manchester Association for Research,* vol. i, 1909-10; and another by A. F. A. Woodford, *A. Q. C.,* i, 28. Better still is the *Real History of the Rosicrucians,* by Waite (chap. xv), and for a complete and final explosion of all such fancies we have the great chapter in Gould's *History of Masonry* (vol. ii, chap. xiii). It seems a pity that so much time and labor and learning had to be expended on theories so fragile, but it was necessary; and no man was better fitted for the study than Gould. Perhaps the present writer is unkind, or at least impatient; if so he humbly begs forgiveness; but after reading tomes of conjecture about the alleged Rosicrucian origin of Masonry, he is weary of the wide-eyed wonder of mystery-mongers about things that never were, and which would be of no value if they had been. (Read *The Rosicrucian Cosmo-Conception, or Christian Occult Science,* by Max Heindel, and be instructed in matters whereof no mortal knoweth.)

Lodge which Conder, the historian of the Company, has traced back to 1620, "and were the books of the Company prior to that date in existence, we should no doubt be able to trace the custom of receiving accepted members back to pre-reformation times." [1] From an entry in the books of the Company, dated 1665, it appears that

> There was hanging up in the Hall a list of the *Accepted Masons* enclosed in a "faire frame, with a lock and key." Why was this? No doubt the Accepted Masons, or those who were initiated into the esoteric aspect of the Company, did not include the *whole* Company, and this was a list of the "enlightened ones," whose names were thus honored and kept on record, probably long after their decease. . . . This we cannot say for certain, but we can say that as early as 1620, and inferentially very much earlier, there were certain members of the Masons' Company and others who met from time to time to form a Lodge for the purpose of Speculative Masonry. [2]

Conder also mentions a copy of the *Old Charges,* or Gothic Constitutions, in the chest of the London Masons' Company, known as *The Book of the Constitutions of the Accepted Masons;* and this he seems to identify with the *Regius MS.* Another witness during this period is Randle Holme, of Chester, whose references to the Craft in his *Acadamie Armory,* 1688, are of great value, for that he writes "as a member of that society called Free-masons." The

[1] *The Hole Craft and Fellowship of Masons,* by Edward Conder.
[2] *Ibid.,* Introduction.

Harleian MS. is in his handwriting, and on the next leaf there is a remarkable list of twenty-six names, including his own. It is the only list of the kind known in England, and a careful examination of all the sources of information relative to the Chester men shows that nearly all of them were Accepted Masons. Even earlier there is the *Natural History of Staffordshire,* by Dr. Plott, 1686, in which, though in an unfriendly manner, we are told many things about Craft usages and regulations of that day. Lodges had to be formed of at least five members to make a quorum, gloves were presented to candidates, and a banquet following initiations was a custom. He states that there were several signs and passwords by which the members were able "to be known to one another all over the nation," his faith in their effectiveness surpassing that of the most credulous in our day.

Still another striking record is found in *The Natural History of Wiltshire,* by John Aubrey, the MS. of which in the Bodleian Library, Oxford, is apparently dated 1686; and on the reverse side of folio 72 of this MS. is the following note by Aubrey: "This day [May 18, 1681] is a great convention at St. Pauls Church of the fraternity of the free [then he crossed out the word Free and inserted Accepted] Masons; where Sir Christopher Wren is to be adopted a Brother: and Sir Henry Goodric of ye Tower and divers others." [1] From which we may infer that there

---

[1] Whether Sir Christopher Wren was ever Grand Master, as tradition affirms, is open to debate, and some even doubt his membership in the order (Gould, *History of Masonry*). Unfortunately,

were Assemblies before 1717, and that they were of sufficient importance to be known to a non-Mason. Other evidence might be adduced, but this is enough to show that Speculative Masonry, so far from being a novelty, was very old at the time when many suppose it was invented. With the Great Fire of London, in 1666, there came a renewed interest in Masonry, many who had abandoned it flocking to the capital to rebuild the city and especially the Cathedral of St. Paul. Old Lodges were revived, new ones were formed, and an effort was made to renew the old annual, or quarterly, Assemblies, while at the same time Accepted Masons increased both in numbers and in zeal.

Now the crux of the whole matter as regards Accepted Masons lies in the answer to such questions as these: Why did soldiers, scholars, antiquaries, clergymen, lawyers, and even members of the nobility ask to be accepted as members of the order of Free-masons? Wherefore their interest in the order

he has left no record, and the *Parentalia,* written by his son, helps us very little, containing nothing more than his theory that the order began with Gothic architecture. Ashmole, if we may trust his friend, Dr. Knipe, had planned to write a *History of Masonry* refuting the theory of Wren that Freemasonry took its rise from a Bull granted by the Pope, in the reign of Henry III, to some Italian architects, holding, and rightly so, that the Bull "was confirmatory only, and did not by any means create our fraternity, or even establish it in this kingdom" (*Life of Ashmole,* by Campbell). This item makes still more absurd the idea that Ashmole himself created Masonry, whereas he was only a student of its antiquities. Wren was probably never an Operative Mason—though an architect—but he seems to have become an Accepted member of the fraternity in his last years, since his neglect of the order, due to his age, is given as a reason for the organization of the first Grand Lodge.

at all? What attracted them to it as far back as 1600, and earlier? What held them with increasing power and an ever-deepening interest? Why did they continue to enter the Lodges until they had the rule of them? There must have been something more in their motive than a simple desire for association, for they had their clubs, societies, and learned fellowships. Still less could a mere curiosity to learn certain signs and passwords have held such men for long, even in an age of quaint conceits in the matter of association and when architecture was affected as a fad. No, there is only one explanation: that these men saw in Masonry a deposit of the high and simple wisdom of old, preserved in tradition and taught in symbols—little understood, it may be, by many members of the order—and this it was that they sought to bring to light, turning history into allegory and legend into drama, and making it a teacher of wise and beautiful truth.

GRAND LODGE OF
ENGLAND

The doctrines of Masonry are the most beautiful that it is possible to imagine. They breathe the simplicity of the earliest ages animated by the love of a martyred God. That word which the Puritans translated CHARITY, *but which is really* LOVE, *is the key-stone which supports the entire edifice of this mystic science. Love one another, teach one another, help one another. That is all our doctrine, all our science, all our law. We have no narrow-minded prejudices; we do not debar from our society this sect or that sect; it is sufficient for us that a man worships God, no matter under what name or in what manner. Ah! rail against us bigoted and ignorant men, if you will. Those who listen to the truths which Masonry inculcates can readily forgive you. It is impossible to be a good Mason without being a good man.*

—WINWOOD READE, *The Veil of Isis*

Chapter Four

GRAND LODGE OF ENGLAND

WHILE PRAYING in a little chapel one day, Francis of Assisi was exhorted by an old Byzantine crucifix: "Go now, and rebuild my Church, which is falling into ruins." In sheer loyalty he had a lamp placed; then he saw his task in a larger way, and an artist has painted him carrying stones and mortar. Finally there burst upon him the full import of the allocution—that he himself was to be the corner-stone of a renewed and purified Church. Purse and prestige he flung to the winds, and went along the highways of Umbria calling men back from the rot of luxury to the ways of purity, pity, and gladness, his life at once a poem and a power, his faith a vision of the world as love and comradeship.

That is a perfect parable of the history of Ma-

sonry. Of old the working Masons built the great
cathedrals, and we have seen them not only carrying stones, but drawing triangles, squares, and circles in such a manner as to show that they assigned
to those figures high mystical meanings. But the
real Home of the Soul cannot be built of brick and
stone; it is a house not made with hands. Slowly it
rises, fashioned of the thoughts, hopes, prayers,
dreams, and righteous acts of devout and free men;
built of their hunger for truth, their love of God,
and their loyalty to one another. There came a
day when the Masons, laying aside their stones,
became workmen of another kind, not less builders
than before, but using truths for tools and dramas
for designs, uplifting such a temple as Watts
dreamed of decorating with his visions of the august
allegory of the evolution of man.

1

From every point of view, the organization of the
Grand Lodge of England, in 1717, was a significant
and far-reaching event. Not only did it divide the
story of Masonry into before and after, giving a
new date from which to reckon, but it was a way-
mark in the intellectual and spiritual history of
mankind. One has only to study that first Grand
Lodge, the influences surrounding it, the men who
composed it, the Constitutions adopted, and its
spirit and purpose, to see that it was the beginning
of a movement of profound meaning. When we see
it in the setting of its age—as revealed, for example,

in the Journals of Fox and Wesley, which from being religious time-tables broadened into detailed panoramic pictures of the period before, and that following, the Grand Lodge—the Assembly of 1717 becomes the more remarkable. Against such a background, when religion and morals seemed to reach the nadir of degradation, the men of that Assembly stand out as prophets of liberty of faith and righteousness of life.[1]

Some imagination is needed to realize the moral declension of that time, as it is portrayed—to use a single example—in the sermon by the Bishop of Lichfield before the Society for the Reformation of Manners, in 1724. Lewdness, drunkenness, and degeneracy, he said, were well nigh universal, no class being free from the infection. Murders were common and foul, wanton and obscene books found so good a market as to encourage the publishing of them. Immorality of every kind was so hardened as to be defended, yes, justified on principle. The rich were debauched and indifferent; the poor were as miserable in their labor as they were coarse and cruel in their sport. Writing in 1713, Bishop Burnet said that those who came to be ordained as

[1] We should not forget that noble dynasty of large and liberal souls in the seventeenth century—John Hales, Chillingsworth, Whichcote, John Smith, Henry More, Jeremy Taylor—whose *Liberty of Prophesying* set the principle of toleration to stately strains of eloquence—Sir Thomas Browne, and Richard Baxter; saints, every one of them, finely poised, sweet-tempered, repelled from all extremes alike, and walking the middle path of wisdom and charity. Milton, too, taught tolerance in a bigoted and bitter age (see *Seventeenth Century Men of Latitude*, E. A. George).

clergymen were "ignorant to a degree not to be comprehended by those who are not obliged to know it." Religion seemed dying or dead, and to mention the word provoked a laugh. Wesley, then only a lad, had not yet come with his magnificent and cleansing evangel. Empty formalism on one side, a dead polemical dogmatism on the other, bigotry, bitterness, intolerance, and interminable feud everywhere, no wonder Bishop Butler sat oppressed in his castle with hardly a hope surviving.

As for Masonry, it had fallen far and fallen low betimes, but with the revival following the Great Fire of London, in 1666, it had taken on new life and a bolder spirit, and was passing through a transition—or, rather, a transfiguration. For, when we compare the Masonry of, say, 1688 with that of 1723, we discover that much more than a revival had come to pass. See the instructions of the *Old Charges*—not all of them, however, for even in earliest times some of them escaped the stamp of the Church [1]—in respect of religion alongside the same article in the *Constitutions* of 1723, and the contrast is amazing. The old charge read: "The first charge is this, that you be true to God and

[1] For instance the *Cooke MS.*, next to the oldest of all, as well as the *W. Watson* and *York No. 4* MSS. It is rather surprising, in view of the supremacy of the Church in those times, to find such evidence of what Dr. Mackey called the chief mission of primitive Masonry—the preservation of belief in the unity of God. These MSS. did not succumb to the theology of the Church, and their invocations remind us more of the God of Isaiah than of the decrees of the Council of Nicæa.

Holy Church and use no error or heresy." **Hear** now the charge in 1723:

> *A Mason is obliged by his Tenure, to obey the moral law; and if he rightly understands the Art, he will never be a stupid Atheist nor an irreligious Libertine. But though in ancient times Masons were charged in every country to be of the religion of that country or nation, whatever it was, yet it is now thought more expedient only to oblige them to that religion in which all men agree, leaving their particular Opinions to themselves: that is, to be Good men and True, or Men of Honor and Honesty, by whatever Denomination or Persuasion they may be distinguished; whereby Masonry becomes the Centre of Union and the Means of conciliating true Friendship among persons that must have remained at a perpetual distance.*

If that statement had been written yesterday, it would be remarkable enough. But when we consider that it was set forth in 1723, amidst bitter sectarian rancor and intolerance unimaginable, it rises up as forever memorable in the history of men. The man who wrote that document is entitled to be held till the end of time in the grateful and venerative memory of his race. The temper of the times was all for relentless partisanship, both in religion and in politics. The alternative offered in religion was an ecclesiastical tyranny, allowing a certain liberty of belief, or a doctrinal tyranny, allowing a slight liberty of worship; a sad choice in truth. The *Constitutions* appeared midway between George Fox, the Quaker, and John Wesley, the Methodist, in the

oddest kind of England, divided into tiny sects—
some of them small enough to be insects—when men
argued endlessly about inconsequential issues, often
pommeling each other with their Bibles. They had
forgotten the wisdom of William Penn who said
when men fight about religion, they have no
religion to fight about, since they do in the name
of religion that which religion itself forbids. It is,
then, to the everlasting honor of the century, that,
in the midst of its clashing extremes, the Masons
appeared with heads unbowed, abjuring both tyran-
nies and championing both liberties.[1] Ecclesiasti-
cally and doctrinally they stood in the open, while
Romanist and Protestant, Anglican and Puritan,
Calvinist and Arminian waged bitter war, filling the
air with angry maledictions. These men of latitude
in a cramped age felt pent up alike by narrowness
of ritual and by narrowness of creed, and they cried
out for room and air, for liberty and charity!

Though differences of creed played no part in
Masonry, nevertheless it held religion in high esteem, and was then, as now, the steadfast upholder
of the only two articles of faith that never were invented by man—the existence of God and the im-

[1] It was, perhaps, a picture of the Masonic Lodges of that era that
Toland drew in his *Socratic Society*, published in 1720, which, however, he clothed in a vesture quite un-Grecian. At least, the symposia
or brotherly feasts of his society, their give-and-take of questions
and answers, their aversion to the rule of mere physical force, to
compulsory religious belief, and to creed hatred, as well as their
mild and tolerant disposition and their brotherly regard for one
another, remind one of the spirit and habits of the Masons of that
day.

mortality of the soul. Accordingly, every Lodge was opened and closed with prayer to the "Almighty Architect of the universe"; and when a Lodge of mourning met in memory of a brother fallen asleep, the formula was: "He has passed over into the eternal East"—to that region whence cometh light and hope. Unsectarian in religion, the Masons were also non-partisan in politics: one principle being common to them all—love of country, respect for law and order, and the desire for human welfare.[1] Upon that basis the first Grand Lodge was founded, and upon that basis Masonry rests today—holding that a unity of spirit is better than a uniformity of opinion, and that beyond the great and simple "religion in which all men agree" no dogma is worth a breach of charity.

[1] Now is as good a time as another to name certain curious theories which have been put forth to account for the origin of Masonry in general, and of the organization of the Grand Lodge in particular. They are as follows: First, that it was all due to an imaginary Temple of Solomon described by Lord Bacon in a utopian romance called the *New Atlantis;* and this despite the fact that the temple in the Bacon story was not a house at all, but the name of an ideal state. Second, that the object of Freemasonry and the origin of the Third Degree was the restoration of Charles II to the throne of England; the idea being that the Masons, who called themselves "Sons of the Widow," meant thereby to express their allegiance to the Queen. Third, that Freemasonry was founded by Oliver Cromwell—he of all men!—to defeat the royalists. Fourth, that Free-masons were derived from the order of the Knights Templars. Even Lessing once held this theory, but seems later to have given it up. Which one of these theories surpasses the others in absurdity, it would be hard to say. De Quincey explodes them one by one with some detail in his "Inquiry into the Origin of the Freemasons," to which he might also have added his own pet notion of the Rosicrucian origin of the order—it being only a little less fantastic than the rest (*De Quincey's Works,* vol. xvi).

2

With honorable pride in this tradition of spiritual faith and intellectual freedom, we are all the more eager to recite such facts as are known about the organization of the first Grand Lodge. How many Lodges of Masons existed in London at that time is a matter of conjecture, but there must have been a number. What bond, if any, united them, other than their esoteric secrets and customs, is equally unknown. Nor is there any record to tell us whether all the Lodges in and about London were invited to join in the movement. Unfortunately the minutes of the Grand Lodge only commence on June 24, 1723, and our only history of the events is that found in *The New Book of Constitutions,* by Dr. James Anderson, in 1738, twenty years later! Indeed, one has the feeling that the Brethren who founded the Mother Grand Lodge, in a half playful mood, did not realize how great a movement they had initiated; and it is so that memorable things are done—not by deliberate plan, but by spontaneous impulse, moved by the spirit of the age and a deeply felt need. They kept no minutes of the proceedings! However, if not an actor in the scene, Anderson was in a position to know the facts from eye-witnesses, and his book was approved by the Grand Lodge itself. His account is so brief that it may be given as it stands:

> King George I enter'd *London* most magnificently on 20 *Sept.* 1714. And after the Rebellion was over

A. D. 1716, the few *Lodges* at *London* finding themselves neglected by Sir *Christopher Wren*, thought fit to cement under a *Grand Master* as the Centre of Union and Harmony, *viz.*, the *Lodges* that met,

1. At the *Goose* and *Gridiron* Ale house in *St. Paul's Church-Yard.*

2. At the *Crown* Ale-house in *Parker's Lane* near *Drury Lane.*

3. At the *Apple-Tree* Tavern in *Charles-street, Covent-Garden.*

4. At the *Rummer* and *Grape* Tavern in *Channel-Row, Westminster.*

They and some other old Brothers met at the said *Apple-Tree,* and having put into the chair the *oldest Master* Mason (now the *Master* of a *Lodge*) they constituted themselves a Grand Lodge pro Tempore in *Due Form,* and forthwith revived the Quarterly *Communication* of the *Officers* of Lodges (call'd the GRAND LODGE) resolv'd to hold the *Annual* Assembly *and Feast,* and then to chuse a Grand Master from among themselves, till they should have the Honor of a Noble Brother at their Head.

Accordingly, on *St. John's Baptist's* Day, in the 3d year of King George I, A. D. 1717, the ASSEMBLY and *Feast* of the *Free and Accepted Masons* was held at the foresaid *Goose* and *Gridiron* Ale-house.

Before Dinner, the *oldest Master* Mason (now the *Master* of a *Lodge*) in the Chair, proposed a List of proper Candidates; and the Brethren by a majority of Hands elected Mr. Anthony Sayer,[1] *Gentleman, Grand Master of Masons* (Mr. *Jacob Lamball,* Carpenter, Capt. *Joseph Elliot,* Grand Wardens) who being forth-

---

[1] Calvert's *The Grand Lodge of England,* p. 18, records some interesting and pathetic facts about the later years of the first Grand Master, who became Tyler of Old King's Arms Lodge, No. 28, and was assisted "out of the box of this Society."

with invested with the Badges of Office and Power by
the said *oldest Master,* and install'd, was duly con-
gratulated by the Assembly who paid him the Homage.

Sayer, *Grand Master,* commanded the *Masters* and
Wardens of Lodges to meet the *Grand* Officers every
Quarter in *Communication,* at the Place that he
should appoint in the Summons sent by the *Tyler.*

So reads the only record that has come down to us
of the founding of the Grand Lodge of England.
Preston and others had no other authority than this
passage for their descriptions of the scene, albeit
when Preston wrote, such facts as he added may have
been learned from men still living. Who were present, beyond the three officers named, has so far
eluded all research, and the only variation in the
accounts is found in a rare old book called *Multa
Paucis,* which asserts that six Lodges, not four, were
represented. Looking at this record in the light of
what we know of the Masonry of that period, a
number of things are suggested:

First, so far from being a revolution, the organization of the Grand Lodge was a revival of the old
quarterly and annual Assembly, born, doubtless, of
a felt need of community of action for the welfare
of the Craft. There was no idea of innovation, but,
as Anderson states in a note, "it should meet Quarterly *according to ancient Usage,*" tradition having
by this time become authoritative in such matters.
Hints of what the old usages were are given in the
observance of St. John's Day [1] as a feast, in the

---

[1] Of the Masonic feasts of St. John the Baptist and St. John the

ANTHONY SAYER, GENTLEMAN
The First Grand Master of Masons, 1717

democracy of the order and its manner of voting by a show of hands, in its deference to the oldest Master Mason, its use of badges of office,[1] its ceremony of installation, all in a lodge duly tyled.

Second, it is clear that, instead of being a deliberately planned effort to organize Masonry in general, the Grand Lodge was intended at first to affect only London and Westminster; [2] the desire being to weld a link of closer fellowship and coöperation be-

Evangelist much has been written, and to little account. In pre-Christian times, as we have seen, the Roman Collegia were wont to adopt pagan deities as patrons. When Christianity came, the names of its saints—some of them martyrs of the order of builders—were substituted for the old pagan gods. Why the two Saints John were chosen by Masons—rather than St. Thomas, who was the patron saint of architecture—has never been made clear. At any rate, these two feasts, coming at the time of the summer and winter solstices, are in reality older than Christianity, being reminiscences of the old Light Religion in which Masonry had its origin.

[1] The badge of office was a huge white apron, such as we see in Hogarth's picture of the *Night*. The collar was of much the same shape as that at present in use, only shorter. When the color was changed to blue, and why, is uncertain, but probably not until 1813, when we begin to see both apron and collar edged with blue. (See chapter on "Clothing and Regalia," in *Things a Freemason Ought to Know*, by J. W. Crowe.) In 1727 the officers of all private—or as we would say, subordinate—Lodges were ordered to wear "the jewels of Masonry hanging to a white apron." In 1731 we find the Grand Master wearing gold or gilt jewels pendant to blue ribbons about the neck, and a white leather apron *lined* with blue silk.

[2] This is clear from the book of *Constitutions* of 1723, which is said to be "for the use of Lodges in London." Then follow the names of the Masters and Wardens of twenty Lodges, all in London. There was no thought at the time of imposing the authority of the Grand Lodge upon the country in general, much less upon the world. Its growth we shall sketch later. For an excellent article on "The Foundation of Modern Masonry," by G. W. Speth, giving details of the organization of the Grand Lodge and its changes, see *A. Q. C.*, ii, 86. If an elaborate account is wanted, it may be found in Gould's *History of Masonry*, vol. iii.

tween the Lodges. While we do not know the names of the moving spirits—unless we may infer that the men elected to office were such—nothing is clearer than that the initiative came from the heart of the order itself, and was in no sense imposed upon it from without; and so great was the necessity for it that, when once started, link after link was added until it "put a girdle around the earth."

Third, of the four Lodges [1] known to have taken part, only one—that meeting at the Rummer and Grape Tavern—had a majority of Accepted Masons in its membership; the other three being Operative Lodges, or largely so. Obviously, then, the movement was predominantly a movement of Operative Masons—or of men who had been Operative Masons—and not, as has been so often implied, the design of men who simply made use of the remnants of Operative Masonry the better to exploit some hidden philosophy. Yet it is worthy of note that the leading men of the craft in those early years were, nearly all of them, Accepted Masons and members of the Rummer and Grape Lodge. Besides Dr. Anderson, the historian, both George Payne and Dr. Desaguliers, the second and third Grand Masters, were of that Lodge. In 1721 the Duke of Montagu was elected to the chair, and thereafter members of the nobility sat in the East until it became the cus-

---

[1] *History of the Four Lodges,* by R. F. Gould. Apparently the Goose and Gridiron Lodge—No. 1—is the only one of the four now in existence. After various changes of name it is now the Lodge of Antiquity, No. 2. (See *The Grand Lodge of England,* by A. F. Calvert.)

tom for the Prince of Wales to be Grand Master of Masons in England.[1]

Fourth, why did Masonry alone of all trades and professions live after its work was done, preserving not only its identity of organization, but its old emblems and usages, and transforming them into instruments of religion and righteousness? The cathedrals had long been finished or left incomplete; the spirit of Gothic architecture was dead and the style treated almost with contempt. The occupation of the Master Mason was gone, his place having been taken by the architect who, like Wren and Inigo Jones, was no longer a child of the Lodges as in the old days, but a man trained in books and by foreign travel. Why did not Freemasonry die, along with the Guilds, or else revert to some kind of trade union? Surely here is the best possible proof that it had never been simply an order of architects building churches, but a moral and spiritual fellowship —the keeper of great symbols and a teacher of truths that never die. So and only so may anyone ever hope to explain the story of Masonry, and those who do not see this fact have no clue to its history, much less an understanding of its genius.

Of course, these pages cannot recite in detail the history and growth of the Grand Lodge, but a few of the more salient events may be noted. As early as 1719 the *Old Charges,* or Gothic Constitutions, began to be collected and collated, a number having already been burned by scrupulous Masons to pre-

---

[1] *Royal Masons,* by G. W. Speth.

vent their falling into strange hands—albeit the
documents destroyed might have been of quite a
different kind! In 1721, Grand Master Montagu
found fault with the *Old Charges* as being inadequate, and ordered Dr. Anderson to make a digest
of them with a view to formulating a better set of
regulations for the rule of the Lodges. Anderson
obeyed—he seems to have been engaged in such a
work already, and may have suggested the idea to
the Grand Master—and a committee of fourteen
"learned brethren" was appointed to examine the
MS. and make report. They suggested a few amend-
ments, and the book was ordered published by the
Grand Master, appearing in the latter part of 1723.
This first issue, however, did not contain the account
of the organization of the Grand Lodge, which does
not seem to have been added until the edition of
1738. How much Past Grand Master Payne had to
do with this work is not certain, but the chief credit
is due to Dr. Anderson, who deserves the perpetual
gratitude of the order—the more so if he it was who
wrote the article, already quoted, setting forth the
religious attitude of the order. That article, by
whomsoever written, is one of the great documents
of mankind, and it would be an added joy to know
that it was penned by a minister.[1] The *Book of Con-*

---

[1] From a meager sketch of Dr. Anderson in the *Gentlemen's Maga-
zine,* 1783, we learn that he was a native of Scotland—the place of
his birth is not given—and that for many years he was minister of
the Scots Presbyterian Church in Swallow Street, Piccadilly, and well
known to the folk of that faith in London—called "Bishop" Anderson
by his friends. He married the widow of an army officer, who bore

stitutions, which is still the groundwork of Masonry, has been printed in many editions, and is accessible to every one.

Another event in the story of the Grand Lodge, never to be forgotten, was a plan started in 1724 of raising funds of General Charity for distressed Masons. Proposed by the Earl of Dalkeith, it at once met with enthusiastic support, and it is a curious coincidence that one of the first to petition for relief was Anthony Sayer, first Grand Master. The minutes do not state whether he was relieved at that time, but we know that sums of money were voted to him in 1730, and again in 1741. This Board of Benevolence, as it came to be called, became very important, it being unanimously agreed in 1733 that all such business as could not be conveniently despatched by the Quarterly Communication should be referred to it. Also, that all Masters of Regular Lodges, together with all present, former, and future Grand Officers should be members of the Board. Later this Board was still further empowered to hear

him a son and a daughter. Although a learned man—compiler of a book of *Royal Genealogies,* which seems to have been his hobby—he was somewhat imprudent in business, having lost most of his property in 1720. Whether he was a Mason before coming to London is unknown, but he took a great part in the work of the Grand Lodge, entering it, apparently, in 1721. Toward the close of his life he suffered many misfortunes, but of what description we are not told. He died in 1739. Perhaps his learning was exaggerated by his Masonic eulogists, but he was a noble man and manifestly a useful one (Gould's *History of Masonry,* vol. iii). For a still later account and estimate of Dr. Anderson, with much valuable material well exhibited, see *The Grand Lodge of England,* by A. F. Calvert, whose accuracy and industry of research in Grand Lodge history entitle him to the perpetual gratitude of the craft.

complaints and to report thereon to the Grand Lodge. Let it also be noted that in actual practice the Board of Charity gave free play to one of the most admirable principles of Masonry—helping the needy and unfortunate, whether within the order or without.

3

Once more we come to a much debated question, about which not a little has been written, and most of it wide of the mark—the question of the origin of the Third Degree. Here again students have gone hither and yon hunting in every cranny for the motif of this degree, and it would seem that their failure to find it would by this time have turned them back to the only place where they may ever hope to discover it—in Masonry itself. But no; they are bound to bring mystics, occultists, alchemists, Culdees or Cabalists—even the *Vehmgerichte* of Germany—into the making of Masonry somewhere, if only for the sake of glamor, and this is the last opportunity to do it.[1] Willing to give due credit to Cabalists and Rosi-

[1] Having emphasized this point so repeatedly, the writer feels it just to himself to state his own position, lest he be thought a kind of materialist, or at least an enemy of mysticism. Not so. Instead, he has long been an humble student of the great mystics; they are his best friends—as witness his two little books, *The Eternal Christ*, and *What Have the Saints to Teach Us?* (The second book was revised and republished in 1948, under the title, *Life Victorious: A Testament of Faith*.) But mysticism is one thing, and mystification is another, and the former may be stated in this way:

First, by mysticism—only another word for spirituality—is meant our sense of an Unseen World, of our citizenship in it, of God and the soul, and of all the forms of life and beauty as symbols of things higher than themselves. That is to say, if a man has any religion

crucians, the present writer rejects all such theories on the ground that there is no reason for thinking that they helped to make Masonry, *much less any fact to prove it.*

Hear now a review of the facts in the case. No one denies that the Temple of Solomon was much in the minds of men at the time of the organization of the Grand Lodge, and long before—as in the Bacon romance of the *New Atlantis* in 1597.[1] Broughton, Selden, Lightfoot, Walton, Lee, Prideaux, and other English writers were deeply interested in the Hebrew Temple, not, however, so much in its symbolical suggestion as in its form and construction— a model of which was brought to London by Judah

at all that is not mere theory or form, he is a mystic; the difference between him and Plato or St. Francis being only a matter of genius and spiritual culture—between a boy whistling a tune and Beethoven writing music.

Second, since mysticism is native to the soul of man and the common experience of all who rise above the animal, it is not an exclusive possession of any set of adepts to be held as a secret. Any man who bows in prayer, or lifts his thought heavenward, is an initiate into the eternal mysticism which is the strength and solace of human life.

Third, the old time Masons were religious men, and as such sharers in this great human experience of divine things, and did not need to go to Hidden Teachers to learn mysticism. They lived and worked in the light of it. It shone in their symbols, as it does in all symbols that have any meaning or beauty. It is, indeed, the soul of symbolism, every emblem being an effort to express a reality too great for words.

So, then, Masonry is mystical as music is mystical—like poetry, and love, and faith, and prayer, and all else that makes it worth our time to live; but its mysticism is sweet, sane, and natural, far from fantastic, and in nowise eerie, unreal, or unbalanced. Of course these words fail to describe it, as all words must, and it is therefore that Masonry uses parables, pictures, and symbols.

[1] *Seventeenth Century Descriptions of Solomon's Temple,* by Prof. S. P. Johnston (*A. Q. C.,* xii, 135).

Templo in the reign of Charles II.[1] It was much the
same on the Continent, but so far from being a new
topic of study and discussion, we may trace this interest in the Temple all through the Middle Ages.
Nor was it peculiar to the Cabalists, at least not to
such a degree that they must needs be brought in to
account for the Biblical imagery and symbolism in
Masonry. Indeed, it might with more reason be
argued that Masonry explains the interest in the
Temple than otherwise. For, as James Fergusson
remarks—and there is no higher authority than the
historian of architecture: "There is perhaps no
building of the ancient world which has excited so
much attention since the time of its destruction, as
the Temple of Solomon built in Jerusalem, and its
successor as built by Herod. *Throughout the
Middle Ages it influenced to a considerable degree
the forms of Christian churches, and its peculiarities
were the watchwords and rallying points of associations of builders.*" [2] Clearly, the notion that interest
in the Temple was new, and that its symbolical
meaning was imposed upon Masonry as something
novel, falls flat.

But we are told that there is no hint of the
Hiramic legend, still less any intimation of a tragedy
associated with the building of the Temple. No
Hiramic legend! No hint of tragedy! Why, both
were almost as old as the Temple itself, rabbinic
legend affirming that *"all the workmen were killed*

[1] *Transactions Jewish Historical Society of England,* vol. ii.
[2] Smith's *Dictionary of the Bible,* article "Temple."

*that they should not build another Temple devoted
to idolatry, Hiram himself being translated to
heaven like Enoch."* [1] The Talmud has many variations of this legend. Where would one expect the
legends of the Temple to be kept alive and be made
use of in ceremonial, if not in a religious order of
builders like the Masons? Is it surprising that we
find so few references in later literature to what was
thus held as a sacred secret? As we have seen, the
legend of Hiram was kept as a profound secret until
1841 by the French Companionage, who almost certainly learned it from the Free-masons. Naturally
it was never made a matter of record,[2] but was transmitted by oral tradition within the order; and it was
also natural, if not inevitable, that the legend of the
master-artist of the Temple should be "the Master's
Part" among Masons who were temple-builders.
How else explain the veiled allusions to the name
in the *Old Charges* as read to Entered Apprentices,
if it was not a secret reserved for a higher rank of
Mason? Why any disguise at all if it had no hidden
meaning? Manifestly the motif of the Third Degree

[1] *Jewish Encyclopedia,* art. "Freemasonry." Also *Builders' Rites,*
G. W. Speth.

[2] In the *Book of Constitutions,* 1723, Dr. Anderson dilates at length
on the building of the Temple—including a note on the meaning
of the name Abif, which, it will be remembered, was not found in
the Authorized Version of the Bible; and then he suddenly breaks
off with the words: *"But leaving what must not, indeed cannot, be
communicated in Writing."* It is incredible that he thus introduced
among Masons a name and legend unknown to them. Had he done
so, would it have met with such instant and universal acceptance
by old Masons who stood for the ancient usages of the order?

was purely Masonic, and we need not go outside the traditions of the order to account for it.

Not content to trace the evolution of Masonry, even so able a man as Albert Pike will have it that to a few men of intelligence who belonged to one of the four old lodges in 1717 "is to be ascribed the authorship of the Third Degree, and the introduction of Hermetic and other symbols into Masonry; that they framed the three degrees for the purpose of communicating their doctrines, veiled by their symbols, to those fitted to receive them, and gave to others trite moral explanations they could comprehend." [1] How gracious of them to vouchsafe even trite explanations, but why frame a set of degrees to conceal what they wished to hide? This is the same idea of something alien imposed upon Masonry from without, with the added suggestion, novel indeed, that Masonry was organized to hide the truth, rather than to teach it. But did Masonry have to go outside its own history and tradition to learn Hermetic truths and symbols? Who was Hermes? Whether man or myth no one knows, but he was a great figure in the Egyptian Mysteries, and was called the Father of Wisdom.[2] What *was* his wisdom? From such fragments of his lore as have floated down to us, impaired, it may be, but always vivid, we discover that his wisdom was only a high spiritual faith and morality taught in visions and rhapsodies, and using numbers as symbols. Was

[1] Letter to Gould "Touching Masonic Symbolism."
[2] *Hermes and Plato*, Edouard Schure.

JOHN THEOPHILUS DESAGULIERS

The father of modern Speculative Freemasonry, to whom the Fraternity is greatly indebted for the influence he wrought during the early days of the premier Grand Lodge.

such wisdom new to Masonry? Had not Hermes himself been a hero of the order from the first, of whom we read in the *Old Charges,* in which he has a place of honor alongside Euclid and Pythagoras? Wherefore go elsewhere than to Masonry itself to trace the *pure* stream of Hermetic faith through the ages? Certainly the men of the Grand Lodge were adepts, but they were *Masonic adepts seeking to bring the buried temple of Masonry to light and reveal it in a setting befitting its beauty,* not cultists making use of it to exploit a private scheme of the universe.

Who were those "men of intelligence" to whom Pike ascribed the making of the Third Degree of Masonry? Tradition has fixed upon Desaguliers as the ritualist of the Grand Lodge, and Lyon speaks of him as "the pioneer and co-fabricator of symbolical Masonry." [1] This, however, is an exaggeration, albeit Desaguliers was worthy of high eulogy, as were Anderson and Payne, who are said to have been his collaborators.[2] But the fact is that the

[1] *History of the Lodge of Edinburgh.*

[2] Steinbrenner, following Findel, speaks of the Third Degree as if it were a pure invention, quoting a passage from *Ahiman Rezon,* by Lawrence Dermott, to prove it. He further states that Anderson and Desaguliers were "publicly accused of manufacturing the degree, *which they never denied*" (*History of Masonry,* chap. vii). But inasmuch as they were not accused of it until they had been many years in their graves, their silence is hardly to be wondered at. Dr. Mackey styles Desaguliers "the Father of Modern Speculative Masonry," and attributes to him, more than to any other one man, the present existence of the order as a living institution (*Encyclopedia of Freemasonry*). Surely that is going too far, much as Desaguliers deserves to be honored by the order. Dr. J. T. Desaguliers was the son of **a**

Third Degree was not made; it grew—like the great cathedrals, no one of which can be ascribed to a single artist, but to an order of men working in unity of enterprise and aspiration. The process by which the old ritual, described in the *Sloane MS.*, was divided and developed into three degrees between 1717 and 1730 was so gradual, so imperceptible, that no exact date can be set; still less can it be attributed to any one or two men. From the minutes of the Musical Society we learn that the Lodge at the Queen's Head in Hollis Street was using three distinct degrees in 1724. As early as 1727 we come upon the custom of setting apart a separate night for the Master's Degree, the drama having evidently become more elaborate.

Further than this the Degree may not be discussed, except to say that the Masons, tiring of the endless quarrels of sects, turned for relief to the truth taught in the Ancient Mysteries as handed down in their traditions if not in their legends and ceremonies—the old, high, heroic faith in God, and

French Protestant clergyman, whose family came to England following the revocation of the Edict of Nantes. He was graduated from Christ Church College, Oxford, in 1710, succeeding Keill as lecturer in Experimental Philosophy. He was especially learned in natural philosophy, mathematics, geometry, and optics, having lectured before the King on various occasions. He was very popular in the Grand Lodge, and his power as an orator made his manner of conferring a degree impressive—which may explain his having been accused of inventing the degrees. He was a loyal and able Mason, a student of the history and ritual of the order, and was elected as the third Grand Master of Masons in England. Like Anderson, his later life is said to have been beclouded by poverty and sorrow, though some of the facts are in dispute (Gould's *History of Masonry*, vol. iii, also Calvert's *The Grand Lodge of England*, chap. i).

in the soul of man as the one unconquerable thing upon this earth. If, as Aristotle said, it be the mission of tragedy to cleanse and exalt us, leaving us subdued with a sense of pity and hope and fortified against ill fortune, it is permitted us to add that in simplicity, depth, and power, in its grasp of the realities of the life of man, its portrayal of the stupidity of evil and the splendor of virtue, its revelation of that in our humanity which leads it to defy death, giving up everything, even life itself, rather than defame, defile, or betray its moral integrity, and in its prophecy of the victory of light over shadow, there is not another drama known among men like the Third Degree of Masonry.[1] Edwin Booth, a loyal Mason, and no mean judge of the essence of tragedy, left these words:

> In all my research and study, in all my close analysis of the masterpieces of Shakespeare, in my earnest determination to make those plays appear real on the

[1] The three great dramas of the race are the Prajapati ritual of ancient Hinduism, the Third Degree of Masonry, and the Mass of the Christian Church, which, even if interpreted as revelations, are still dramas. To which might be added the Judgment Scene in the Egyptian *Book of the Dead,* which is really a ritual of the immortal life. Widely as they may differ in detail, and far apart as they may seem to be in externals, they are the supreme efforts of man to surprise in art and embody in experience the mystery, meaning and prophecy of life; portraying the ascent of the soul through time, and vicissitudes of nature, to eternity. Together they testify to the profoundest insight of the human spirit—that God becomes man that man may become God. Of the Egyptian origin of the drama of the Third Degree there is little doubt, albeit there is no trace of it, apparently, in Hebrew lore. (See my study of *The Religion of Masonry,* Chap. 7, and an interesting essay on *Freemasonry in Ancient Egypt,* by Edward Gilchrist.)

mimic stage, I have never, and nowhere, met tragedy so real, so sublime, so magnificent as the legend of Hiram. It is substance without shadow—the manifest destiny of life which requires no picture and scarcely a word to make a lasting impression upon all who can understand. To be a Worshipful Master, and to throw my whole soul into that work, with the candidate for my audience and the Lodge for my stage, would be a greater personal distinction than to receive the plaudits of people in the theaters of the world.

UNIVERSAL MASONRY

These signs and tokens are of no small value; they speak a universal language, and act as a passport to the attention and support of the initiated in all parts of the world. They cannot be lost so long as memory retains its power. Let the possessor of them be expatriated, shipwrecked, or imprisoned; let him be stripped of everything he has got in the world; still these credentials remain and are available for use as circumstances require.

The great effects which they have produced are established by the most incontestable facts of history. They have stayed the uplifted hand of the destroyer; they have softened the asperities of the tyrant; they have mitigated the horrors of captivity; they have subdued the rancor of malevolence; and broken down the barriers of political animosity and sectarian alienation.

On the field of battle, in the solitude of the uncultivated forests, or in the busy haunts of the crowded city, they have made men of the most hostile feelings, and most distant religions, and the most diversified conditions, rush to the aid of each other, and feel a social joy and satisfaction that they have been able to afford relief to a brother Mason.

—BENJAMIN FRANKLIN

Chapter Five

UNIVERSAL MASONRY

1

HENCEFORTH THE Masons of England were no longer a society of handicraftsmen, but an association of men of all orders and every vocation, as also of almost every creed, who met together on the broad basis of humanity, and recognized no standard of human worth other than morality, kindliness, and love of truth. They retained the symbolism of the old Operative Masonry,[1]

[1] Operative Masonry, it should be remembered, was not entirely dead, nor did it all at once disappear. Indeed, it still exists in some form, although there is, so far, no proof of its continuous existence from olden time, as some brethren are wont to claim in its behalf. An interesting account of its forms, degrees, symbols, usages, and traditions may be found in an article on "Operative Masonry," by C. E. Stretton (*Transactions Leicester Lodge of Research*, 1909-10, 1911-12). The second of these volumes also contains an essay on "Operative Free-masons," by Thomas Carr, with a list of lodges, and a study of their history, customs, and emblems—especially the Swastika. Speculative Masons are now said to be joining these Operative Lodges, seeking more light on what are called the Lost Symbols of Masonry.

its language, its legends, its ritual, and its oral tradition. No longer did they build churches, but the
spiritual temple of humanity; using the Square not
to measure right angles of blocks of stone, but for
evening the inequalities of human character, nor the
Compass any more to describe circles on a tracing-
board, but to draw a Circle of goodwill around all
mankind.

Howbeit, one generation of men, as Hume remarks, does not go off the stage at once, and another
succeed, like silkworms and butterflies. No more
did this metamorphosis of Masonry, so to name it,
take place suddenly or radically, as it has become
the fashion to think. It was a slow process, and like
every such period the Epoch of Transition was attended by many problems, uncertainties, and difficulties. Some of the Lodges, as we have noted,
would never agree to admit Accepted Masons, so
jealous were they of the ancient landmarks of the
Craft. Even the Grand Lodge, albeit a revival of the
old Assembly, was looked upon with suspicion by
not a few, as tending toward undue centralization;
and not without cause. From the first the Grand
Master was given more power than was ever granted
to the President of an ancient Assembly; of necessity so, perhaps, but it led to misunderstanding.
Other influences added to the confusion, and at the
same time emphasized the need of welding the order
into a more coherent unity for its wider service to
humanity.

There are hints to the effect that the new Masonry, if so it may be called, made very slow progress in the public favor at first, owing to the conditions just stated; and this despite the remark of Anderson in June, 1719: "Now several old Brothers that had neglected the Craft, visited the Lodges; some Noblemen were also made Brothers, and more new Lodges were constituted." Stuckeley, the antiquary, tells us in his *Diary* under date of January, 1721—at which time he was initiated—that he was the first person made a Mason in London for years, and that it was not easy to find men enough to perform the ceremony. Incidentally, he confides to us that he entered the order in search of the long hidden secrets of "the Ancient Mysteries." No doubt he exaggerated in the matter of numbers, though it is possible that initiations were comparatively few at the time, the Lodges being recruited, for the most part, by the adhesion of old Masons, both Operative and Speculative; and among his friends he may have had some difficulty in finding men with an adequate knowledge of the ritual. But that there was any real difficulty in gathering together seven Masons in London is, on the face of it, absurd. Immediately thereafter, Stuckeley records, Masonry "took a run, and ran itself out of breath through the folly of its members," but he does not tell us what the folly was. The "run" referred to was almost certainly due to the acceptance by the Duke of Montagu of the Grand Mastership, which gave the order a prestige it had never had before; and it was also in the same year, 1721, that the old Constitutions of the Craft were revised.

Twelve Lodges attended the June quarterly communication of the Grand Lodge in 1721, sixteen in September, twenty in December, and by April, 1723, the number had grown to thirty. All these Lodges, be it noted, were in London, a fact amply justifying the optimism of Anderson in the last paragraph of the *Book of Constitutions,* issued in that year. So far the Grand Lodge had not extended its jurisdiction beyond London and Westminster, but the very next year, 1724, there were already nine Lodges in the provinces acknowledging its obedience, the first being the Lodge at the Queen's Head, City of Bath. Within a few years Masonry extended its labors abroad, both on British and on foreign soil. The first Lodge on foreign soil was founded by the Duke of Wharton at Madrid, in 1728, and regularized the following year, by which time a Lodge had been established at the East India Arms, Bengal, and also at Gibraltar. It was not long before Lodges arose in many lands, founded by English Masons or by men who had received initiation in England; these Lodges, when sufficiently numerous, uniting under Grand Lodges—the old Lodge at York, that ancient Mecca of Masonry, had called itself a Grand Lodge as early as 1725. The Grand Lodge of Ireland was created in 1729, those of Scotland [1] and France in 1736; a Lodge at Hamburg in 1737,[2] though it was

[1] The Grand Lodges of Ireland and Scotland, it may be added, were self-constituted, without assistance or intervention from England in any form.

[2] A deputation of the Hamburg Lodge initiated Frederick—afterwards Frederick the Great of Prussia—into the order of Masons at

THOMAS SMITH WEBB

The American Preston, whose lectures exist practically unchanged in the various American workings. His first book, *The Free-Mason's Monitor,* was published at Albany, New York, in 1797.

not patented until 1740; the Unity Lodge at Frank-
fort-on-the-Main in 1742, another at Vienna the
same year; the Grand Lodge of the Three World-
spheres at Berlin in 1744; and so on, until the order
made its advent in Sweden, Switzerland, Russia,
Italy, Spain, and Portugal.

Following the footsteps of Masonry from land to
land is almost as difficult as tracing its early history,
owing to the secrecy in which it enwrapped its move-
ments. For example, in 1680 there came to South
Carolina one John Moore, a native of England, who
before the close of the century removed to Philadelphia, where, in 1703, he was Collector of the Port.
In a letter written by him in 1715, he mentions having "spent a few evenings in festivity with my Masonic brethren." This is the first vestige of Masonry
in America, unless we accept as authentic a curious
document in the early history of Rhode Island, as
follows: "This ye [day and month obliterated] 1656,
Wee mett att y House off Mordicai Campanell and

Brunswick, August 14, 1738 (*Frederick and his Times*, by Campbell,
History of Frederick, by Carlyle, Findel's *History of Masonry*). Other
noblemen followed his example, and their zeal for the order gave
a new date to the history of Masonry in Germany. When Frederick
ascended the throne, in 1740, the Craft was honored, and it flourished
in his kingdom. As to the interest of Frederick in the order in his
later years, the facts are not clear, but that he remained its friend
seems certain (Mackey, *Encyclopedia*). However, the Craft underwent
many vicissitudes in Germany, a detailed account of which Findel
recites (*History of Masonry*). Few realize through what frightful per-
secutions Masonry has passed in many lands, owing in part to its
secrecy, but in larger part to its principle of civil and religious
liberty. Whenever that story is told, as it surely will be, men everywhere will pay homage to the Ancient Free and Accepted Masons as
friends of mankind.

after synagog gave Abram Moses the degrees of Maconrie." [1] On June 5, 1730, the first authority for the assembling of Freemasons in America was issued by the Duke of Norfolk, to Daniel Coxe, of New Jersey, appointing him Provincial Grand Master of New York, New Jersey, and Pennsylvania; but he seems not to have exercised his authority until later, if indeed he ever exercised it at all. Three years later, 1733, Henry Price, of Boston, was appointed to the same office for New England, and to Price belongs the honor of being *the father of regular Masonry in America*.[2] But Masons had evidently been coming to the New World for years, for the two cases just cited date back to the Grand Lodge of 1717.

How soon Coxe acted on any authority given him is not certain, but the *Pennsylvania Gazette*, published by Benjamin Franklin, contains many references to Masonic affairs as early as July, 1730. Just when Franklin himself became interested in Masonry is not recorded—he was initiated in 1730-31 [3]

[1] *History of Freemasonry*, by Hughan and Stillson, chapter on "Early American Masonic History."

[2] *The Beginnings of Freemasonry in America*, by Melvin M. Johnson. The crux of the matter may be stated simply: *If* Daniel Coxe did not exercise authority under his deputation of 1730, then the honor of being the first *regular* Mason in America belongs to Henry Price under his deputation of 1733. *If* Coxe did exercise his authority, as David McGregor, Historian of the Grand Lodge of New Jersey, insists he did, then the honor belongs to him. When the eagles disagree about the depth of the heavens, it is idle for owls and bats to debate the issue.

[3] *Benjamin Franklin as a Free Mason*, by J. F. Sachse. Oddly enough, there is no mention of Masonry by Franklin in his *Autobiography*, or in any of his letters, with but two exceptions, so far

—but he was a leader, at that day, of everything that would advance his adopted city; and the "Junto," formed in 1725, often inaccurately called the Leathern-Apron Club, owed its origin to him. In a Masonic item in the *Gazette* of December 3, 1730, he refers to "several Lodges of Freemasons" in the Province, and on June 9, 1732, notes the organization of the Grand Lodge of Pennsylvania, of which he was appointed a Warden, at the Sun Tavern, in Water Street. Two years later Franklin was elected Grand Master, and the same year published an edition of the *Book of Constitutions*—the first Masonic book issued in America. Thus Masonry made an early advent into the new world, in which it has labored so nobly, helping to lay the foundations and building its own basic principles into the organic law of the greatest of all republics.

2

Returning to the Grand Lodge of England, we have now to make record of ridicule and opposition from without, and, alas, of disloyalty and discord within the order itself. With the publication of the *Book of Constitutions,* by Anderson, in 1723, the platform and principles of Masonry became matters of common knowledge, and its enemies were alert and vigilant. None is so blind as he who will not see,

as known; which is the more remarkable when we look at his Masonic career in France during his later years, where he was actively and intimately associated with the order, even advancing to the higher degrees. Never for a day did he abate by one jot his interest in the order, or his love for it.

and not a few, unacquainted with the spirit of Masonry, or unable to grasp its principle of liberality and tolerance, affected to detect in its secrecy some dark political design; and this despite the noble charge in the *Book of Constitutions* enjoining politics from entering the lodge—a charge hardly less memorable than the article defining its attitude toward differing religious creeds, and which it behooves Masons to keep always in mind as both true and wise, especially in our day when effort is being made to inject the religious issue into politics:

> In order to preserve peace and harmony no private piques or quarrels must be brought within the door of the Lodge, far less any quarrel about Religions or Nations or State-Policy, we being only, as Masons, of the Catholic Religion above mentioned (the religion in which all men agree); we are also of all Nations, Tongues, Kindreds and Languages, and are resolved against all Politics as what never yet conduced to the welfare of the Lodge, nor ever will. This charge has always been actively enjoined and observed; but especially ever since the Reformation in Britain or the dissent and secession of these Nations from the communion of Rome.

No sooner had these noble words been printed,[1] than there came to light a secret society calling itself

---

[1] This injunction was made doubly strong in the edition of the *Book of Constitutions*, in 1738. For example: "no quarrels about nations, families, religion or politics must by any means or under any color or pretense whatever be brought within the door of the Lodge . . . Masons being of all nations upon the square, level and plumb; and like our predecessors in all ages, we are resolved against political disputes," etc.

the "truly Ancient Noble Order of the Gormogons," alleged to have been instituted by Chin-Quaw Ky-Po, the first Emperor of China, many thousand years before Adam. Notice of a meeting of the order appeared in the *Daily Post,* September 3, 1723, in which it was stated, among other high-sounding declarations, that "no Mason will be received as a Member till he has renounced his noble order and been properly degraded." Obviously, from this notice and others of like kind—all hinting at the secrets of the Lodges—the order was aping Masonry by way of parody with intent to destroy it, if possible, by ridicule. For all that, if we may believe the *Saturday Post* of October following, "many eminent Freemasons" had by that time "degraded themselves" and gone over to the Gormogons. Not "many" perhaps, but, alas, one eminent Mason at least, none other than a Past Grand Master, the Duke of Wharton, who, piqued at an act of the Grand Lodge, had turned against it. Erratic of mind, unstable of morals, having an inordinate lust for praise, and pilloried as a "fool" by Pope in his *Moral Essays,* he betrayed his fraternity—as, later, he turned traitor to his faith, his flag, and his native land.

Simultaneously with the announcement that many eminent Masons had "degraded themselves"—words most fitly chosen—and gone over to the Gormogons, there appeared a book called the *Grand Mystery of Freemasons Discovered,* and the cat was out of the bag. Everything was plain to the Masons, and if it had not been clear, the way in which the writer emphasized his hatred of the Jesuits would have told it all. It was a Jesuit [1] plot hatched in Rome to expose the secrets of Masonry, and making use of the dissolute and degenerate Mason for that purpose—tactics often enough used in the name of Jesus! Curiously enough, this was further made evident by the fact that the order ceased to exist in 1738, the year in which Clement XII published his Bull against the Masons. Thereupon the "ancient order of Gormogons" swallowed itself, and so disappeared—not, however, without one last, futile effort to achieve its ends.[2] Naturally this episode stirred the Masons deeply. It was denounced in burning words on the floor of the Grand Lodge, which took new caution to guard its rites from treachery and vandalism, in

[1] Masons have sometimes been absurdly called "Protestant Jesuits," but the two orders are exactly opposite in spirit, principle, purpose, and method. All that they have in common is that they are both *secret* societies, which makes it plain that the opposition of the Latin church to Masonry is not on the ground of its being a secret order, else why sanction the Jesuits, to name no other? The difference has been stated in this way: "Opposite poles these two societies are, for each possesses precisely those qualities which the other lacks. The Jesuits are strongly centralized, the Freemasons only confederated. Jesuits are controlled by one man's rule, Freemasons are under majority rule. Jesuits bottom morality in expediency, Freemasons in regard for the well-being of mankind. Jesuits recognize only one creed, Freemasons hold in respect all honest convictions. Jesuits seek to break down individual independence, Freemasons to build it up" (*Mysteria*, by Otto Henne Am Rhyn). See *The Freemasons* by Eugen Lennhoff, Part III, Chap. I, "The Papal Bulls."

[2] For a detailed account of the Duke of Wharton and the true history of the Gormogons, see an essay by R. F. Gould, in his "Masonic Celebrities" series (*A. Q. C.*, viii, 144), and more recently, *The Life and Writings of Philip, Duke of Wharton*, by Lewis Melville.

which respects it had not exercised due care, admitting men to the order who were unworthy of the honor.

There were those who thought that the power of Masonry lay in its secrecy; some think so still, not knowing that its *real* power lies in the sanctity of its truth, the simplicity of its faith, the sweetness of its spirit, and its service to mankind, and that if all its rites were made public today it would still hold the hearts of men.[1] Nevertheless, of alleged exposures there were many between 1724 and 1730, both anonymous and signed, and they made much ado, especially among men who were not Masons. It will be enough to name the most famous, as well as the most elaborate, of them all, *Masonry Dissected,* by Samuel Prichard, which ran through three editions in one month, October, 1730, and called out a noble *Defence of Masonry,* written, it is thought, by Anderson, but the present writer believes by Desaguliers. Others came later, such as *Jachim and Boaz,* the *Three Distinct Knocks,* and so forth. They had their day and ceased to be, having now only an antiquarian interest to those who would know the manners and customs of a far-off time. Instead of injuring the order, they really helped it, as such things usually do, by showing that there must be something to expose since so many were trying to do

[1] Findel has a nobly eloquent passage on this point, and it tells the everlasting truth (*History of Masonry,* p. 378). His whole history, indeed, is exceedingly worth reading, the more so because it was one of the first books of the right kind, and it stimulated research.

it. But Masonry went marching on, leaving them behind in the rubbish of things forgotten, as it does all its back-stair spies and heel-snapping critics.

More serious by far was the series of schisms within the order which began in 1725, and ran on even into the next century. For the student they make the period very complex, calculated to bewilder the beginner; for when we read of four Grand Lodges in England (if not five), and for some years all of them running at once, and each one claiming to be the Grand Lodge of England, the confusion seems not a little confounded. Also, one Grand Lodge of a very limited territory, and few adherents, adopted the title of Grand Lodge of *all* England, while another which commenced in the middle of the century assumed the title of "The Ancients," and dubbed the older and parent Grand Lodge "The Moderns." Besides, there are traces of an unrecorded Grand body calling itself "The Supreme Grand Lodge," [1] as if each were trying to make up in name what was lacking in numbers. Strict search and due inquiry into the causes of these divisions would seem to show the following results:

First, there was a fear, not unjustified by facts, that the ancient democracy of the order had been infringed upon by certain acts of the Grand Lodge of

[1] A paper entitled "An Unrecorded Grand Lodge," by Sadler (*A. Q. C.*, vol. xviii, 60-90), tells practically all that is known of this movement, which merged with the Grand Lodge of London in 1776. Since Bro. Sadler's paper was written, further evidence of an Anglo-Scottish Grand Lodge has been traced, the constituent bodies of which seem to have been absorbed by the "Ancient" Grand Lodge.

1717—as, for example, giving to the Grand Master power to appoint the Wardens.[1] Second, there was a tendency, due to the influence of some clergymen active in the order, to give a distinctively Christian tinge to Masonry, first in their interpretations of its symbols, and later to the ritual itself. This fact has not been enough emphasized by our historians, for it explains much. Third, there was the further fact that Masonry in Scotland differed from Masonry in England, in details at least, and the two did not all at once harmonize, each being rather tenacious of its usage and tradition. Fourth, in one instance, if no more, pride of locality and historic memories led to independent organization. Fifth, there was the ever-present element of personal ambition with which all human societies, of whatever kind, must reckon at all times and places this side of heaven. Altogether, the situation was amply conducive to division, if not to explosion, and the wonder is that the schisms were so few.

[1] Nor was that all. In 1735 it was resolved in the Grand Lodge "that in the future all Grand Officers (except Grand Master) shall be selected out of that body"—meaning the Past Grand Stewards. This act was amazing. Already the Craft had let go its power to elect the Wardens, and now the choice of the Grand Master was narrowed to the ranks of an oligarchy in its worst form—a queer outcome of Masonic equality. Three months later the Grand Stewards presented a memorial asking that they "might form themselves into a special lodge," with special jewels, etc. Naturally this bred discontent and apprehension, and justly so. For a more recent investigation of this whole matter, see *The Grand Stewards and Red Apron Lodges,* by A. F. Calvert.

3

Time out of mind the ancient city of York had been a seat of the Masonic Craft, tradition tracing it back to the days of Athelstan, in 926 A. D. Be that as it may, the Lodge minutes of York are the oldest in the country, and the relics of the Craft now preserved in that city entitle it to be called the Mecca of Masonry. Whether the old society was a Private or a Grand Lodge is not plain; but in 1725 it assumed the title of the "Grand Lodge of All England,"—feeling, it would seem, that its inherent right by virtue of antiquity had in some way been usurped by the Grand Lodge of London. After ten or fifteen years the minutes cease, but the records of other Grand bodies speak of it as still working. In 1761 six of its surviving members revived the Grand Lodge, which continued with varying success until its final extinction in 1791, having only a few subordinate Lodges, chiefly in Yorkshire. Never antagonistic, it chose to remain independent, and its history is a noble tradition. York Masonry was acknowledged by all parties to be both ancient and orthodox, and even to this day, in England and over the seas, a certain mellow, magic charm clings to the city which was for so long a meeting place of Masons.[1]

---

[1] Often we speak of "the York Rite," as though it were the oldest and truest form of Masonry, but, while it serves to distinguish one branch of Masonry from another, it is not accurate; for, strictly speaking, there is no such thing as a York Rite. The name is more a tribute of reverence than a description of fact.

Far more formidable was the cleavage of 1752, which had its origin, as is now thought, in a group of Irish Masons in London who were not recognized by the premier Grand Lodge,[1] and, indeed, had not sought affiliation with it. Whereupon they denounced the Grand Lodge, averring that it had adopted "new plans" and departed from the old landmarks, reverted, as they alleged, to the old forms, and set themselves up as *Ancient* Masons—bestowing upon their rivals the odious name of *Moderns*. Later the two were further distinguished from each other by the names of their respective Grand Masters, one called Prince of Wales' Masons, the other the Atholl Masons.[2] (It need hardly be added that the doctrine of "exclusive jurisdiction," now so widely accepted, had not been formulated.) The great figure in the Atholl Grand body was Laurence Dermott, to whose keen pen and indefatigable industry as its secretary for more than thirty years was due, in large measure, its success.

Dermott was born in Ireland in 1720, was initiated a Mason in 1740, and installed a Master of Lodge No. 26, in Dublin, in 1746; the same year he became a Royal Arch Mason. He came to London as a journeyman painter in 1748, and while he was "introduced to the society," as he tells us, as a visitor, there is no record that he *affiliated* with any lodge under the obedience of the Grand Lodge of England. He was not one of the organizers of the

[1] *Masonic Facts and Fictions,* by Henry Sadler.
[2] *Atholl Lodges,* by R. F. Gould.

"Ancient" Grand Lodge, as he seems not to have joined a London lodge until after the organization was completed, when he demitted to "Lodge No. 9" of the "Ancients," in 1752.

Unfortunately, no likeness of Dermott has come down to us. Yet, such was his charm of personality —his vivacity, his versatility, his sparkle of spirit— his aggressive enthusiasm for Masonry, his alert and resourceful ability—perhaps, also, his Irish feeling about Royalty—that he became, and remained, the outstanding leader of the "Ancient" Grand Lodge, outwitting the "Moderns" at every turn by his wily strategy.

In 1756 he published its first book of laws, entitled *Ahiman Rezon, or, Help to a Brother,* much of which was taken from the *Irish Constitutions* of 1751, by Pratt, and the rest from the *Book of Constitutions,* by Anderson—whom he did not fail to criticize with stinging satire, of which he was a master. Among other things, the office of Deacon seems to have had its origin with this body. Atholl Masons were presided over by the Masters of affiliated Lodges until 1756, when Lord Blessington, their first titled Grand Master, was induced to accept the honor—their warrants having been left blank betimes, awaiting the coming of a nobleman to that office. Later the fourth Duke of Atholl was Grand Master at the same time of Scotland and of the Atholl Grand Lodge, the Grand Lodges of Scotland and Ireland being represented at his installation in London.

More recent research makes it clear that what has so long been called "the Great Schism" in the mother Grand Lodge, was in reality not a schism at all, because the two factions had never been united. The rival Grand Lodge of the "Ancients" was made up, almost entirely, of lodges which had not entered into the Grand Lodge of 1717. In fact, they resented the authority assumed by the Grand Lodge and refused to submit to it; naturally, they refused to be excommunicated by it. They were not rebellious members of the Grand Lodge, but independent Masons, mostly Irish, who, under the usages of the period, had a perfect right to organize lodges. Why they should have preferred to work outside the Grand Lodge of England is easily understood when we realize that the Grand Lodge was composed of the aristocratic element, while the Anglo-Irish brethren were mostly men of humbler walks of life—painters, tailors, and other artisans—working in London. Even thus early the old irritation between the Irish and the English was keen, and Irish Masons felt—indeed, were made to feel—the sting of it, and were irked by it.

It is not possible to exhibit here all the evidence to this effect, but there is little doubt that here lay the *real* reason for the setting up of a second and rival Grand Lodge—a difference of social status of the brethren who, on February 5th, 1751, formed the "Grand Lodge of England According to the Old Institutions," in Griffin Tavern in Holborn.

Of course, the reasons *assigned* for the rival Grand Lodge were very different; first, very cleverly

Dermott—who was no scholar, and often mistook fantastic legends for history—traced the new Grand Lodge back to the alleged first Constitutions of the Anglo-Saxon Prince Edwin of 926, and derived therefrom the right to describe the new Grand Lodge as the "Ancients" and the other as the "Moderns." It was good psychology, since antiquity is authority among Masons, and the phrase "from time immemorial" works like magic. Also, the "Moderns" were accused of having departed from the ancient Landmarks of the Craft, and Masons want things done as in the beginning, world without end. Some changes in laws and usages had been made by the Grand Lodge of England, but these had been adopted in Ireland without question; why, then, should later changes have been deemed an apostasy? A number of spurious rituals were afloat which caused Grand Lodge to make certain changes alluded to but not described in the minutes; changes of ritual, no doubt, as otherwise the resolution itself would have been given and not a mere reference to it.

The intention of these changes was to prevent spurious Masons from gaining admission to lodges, but the real effect was to make it difficult, if not impossible, for regular Masons, owing allegiance to the Grand Lodges of Ireland and Scotland, to visit English lodges. This may explain why the Grand Lodges of Ireland and Scotland were more friendly with the "Ancients" than with the "Moderns." Had there been no air of irritation, all these matters could have been easily ironed out without friction; instead they were used as clubs.

As if the situation were not tense enough, the religious issue, always explosive, was injected into it. The Article on "God and Religion" in the Constitutions of 1723, it was said, tended to make Masonry un-Christian, if not anti-Christian, in behalf of a vague blur of naturalism and Deism; whereas its intent was to keep the Craft religious and make it unsectarian. In those days—alas, as too much in our day—Christianity was narrowly, even bitterly, sectarian, and it was to avoid a chilly, critical Deism on the one side and a petty, rabid sectarianism on the other, that the Article was written.

So far from abandoning Christian faith, the two men who had most to do with the Article were Christian ministers—Anderson, a Presbyterian, and Desaguliers, an Anglican—and to their wisdom, tact, and vision we owe the fact that if Freemasonry began in a Tavern, it ended in a Temple. Both had gone to their graves, followed by leaders of a different caliber. Dermott had but slight knowledge of the early days of Grand Lodge, and it suited his purpose to play-up the charge that "Moderns" had abandoned the Christian faith with every art of propaganda. Some have seen in this flare-up of bigotry a hint of anti-Semitism, but that is hardly probable—there was very little of that poison in England, at least since the days of Cromwell, as we may read in the *History of the Jews in England,* by Hyamson. In any case, the "religious" issue proved to be less effective than was expected, and time and change made men weary of old debates.

As we shall see in the sequel, the "Ancients," albeit the stronger of the two Grand Lodges, suddenly receded from nearly everything they had fought for. In an air of mystery and urgency, all was forgiven, and issues which had torn the Craft into rival and contending camps were either compromised or forgotten, never to be revived. At the time, a major cleavage in Masonry, continuing for fifty years, was deeply regretted, making the Craft itself sectarian; but in the end it made for good, and the fraternity advanced in its benign labors.[1]

Still another "schism," not serious but significant, came in 1778, led by William Preston,[2] who after-

[1] *The Birth and Growth of the Grand Lodge of England, 1717-1926,* by Gilbert W. Daynes, gives a colorless but accurate account of the facts. Also *The Freemasons,* by Eugen Lennhoff; for further details as to the workings of the rival Grand Lodges in America, see my short story of *Modern Masonry.* In regard to the "religious issue," there is a brief, scholarly, carefully documented essay, the more objective because written by a non-Mason, entitled "The Religion of Early Freemasonry," by Charles H. Lyttle, in *Environmental Factors in Christian History.* (Univ. of Chicago Press.) The essay ends by asking:—"Was the grand design of Anderson, Desaguliers, and their colleagues justified by its spiritual as well as institutional success? Are we entitled to trace the ebb of critical Deism, of sceptical libertinism, of attacks upon the Church of England and clericalism in general, of doubts concerning the religious and moral effects of science to the influence of Freemasonry in the eighteenth century? *It is a well-founded surmise that we are.*"

[2] William Preston was born in Edinburgh in 1742, and came as a journeyman printer to London in 1760, where he made himself conversant with the history, laws, and rites of the Craft, being much in demand as a lecturer. He was a good speaker, and frequently addressed the lodges of the city. After his blunder of seceding had been forgiven, he was honored with many offices, especially the Deputy

WILLIAM PRESTON

A distinguished instructor in Masonic Ritual and the founder of the lectures which still bear his name. To Preston more than any one else the Fraternity is indebted for the Middle Chamber lecture. His *Illustrations of Masonry* was first published at London in 1772.

wards became a shining light in the order. On St. John's Day, December 27, 1777, the Antiquity Lodge of London, of which Preston was Master— one of the four original Lodges forming the Grand Lodge—attended church in a body, to hear a sermon by its Chaplain. They robed in the vestry, and then marched into the church, but after the service they walked back to the Hall wearing their Masonic clothing. Difference of opinion arose as to the regularity of the act, Preston holding it to be valid, if for no other reason, by virtue of the inherent right of Antiquity Lodge itself. Three members objected to his ruling and appealed to the Grand Lodge, he foolishly striking their names off the Lodge roll for so doing. Eventually the Grand Lodge took the matter up, decided against Preston, and ordered the reinstatement of the three protesting members. At its next meeting the Antiquity Lodge voted not to comply with the order of the Grand Lodge, and, instead, to withdraw from that body and form an alliance with the "Old Grand Lodge of All England at York City," as they called it. They were received by the York Grand Lodge, and soon thereafter obtained a constitution for a "Grand Lodge of England South of the Trent." Although much vitality was shown at the outset, this body only constituted

Grand Secretaryship, which gave him time to pursue his studies. Later he wrote the *Freemason's Callender*, an appendix to the *Book of Constitutions*, a *History of Masonry*, and, most famous of all, *Illustrations of Masonry*, which passed through a score of editions. Besides, he had much to do with the development of the Ritual (see *The Grand Lodge of England*, by A. F. Calvert, chap. iii).

two subordinate Lodges, and ceased to exist. Having failed, in 1789 Preston and his friends recanted their folly, apologized to the Grand Lodge, reunited with the men whom they had expelled, and were received back into the fold; and so the matter ended.

These divisions, while they were in some ways unhappy, really made for the good of the order in the sequel—the activity of contending Grand Lodges, often keen, seldom bitter, promoting the spread of its principles to which all were alike loyal, and to the enrichment of its Ritual [1] to which each contributed. It was rivalry without rancor and contest without conflict, as it ought always to be among Masons. Dermott, an able executive and audacious antagonist, albeit fighting with gay fantastic humor, salted with sarcasm, had left no stone unturned to

[1] The history of the Ritual is most interesting, and should be written in more detail (History of Masonry, by Steinbrenner, chap. vii, "The Ritual"). An article giving a brief story of it appeared in the Masonic Monthly, of Boston, November, 1863 (reprinted in the New England Craftsman, vol. vii, and still later in the Bulletin of Iowa Masonic Library, vol. xv, April, 1914). This article is valuable as showing the growth of the Ritual—as much by subtraction as by addition—and especially the introduction into it of Christian imagery and interpretation, first by Martin Clare in 1732, and by Duckerley and Hutchinson later. One need only turn to The Spirit of Masonry, by Hutchinson (1802), to see how far this tendency had gone when at last checked in 1813. At that time a committee made a careful comparative study of all rituals in use among Masons, and the ultimate result was the Preston-Webb lectures now generally in use in this country. (See a valuable article by Dr. Mackey on "The Lectures of Freemasonry," American Quarterly Review of Freemasonry, vol. ii, p. 297. What a pity that this Review died of too much excellence! Also the lecture of Prof. Pound on "Divergences in the Ritual," delivered before the Grand Lodge of Massachusetts.)

It should be added that the Grand Lodge of England has never authorized any lecture, although it has authorized the ceremonies.

advance the interests of Atholl Masonry, inducing its Grand Lodge to grant warrants to army Lodges, which bore fruit in making Masons in every part of the world where the English army went,[1] while the "Modern" Grand Lodge made a like use of the navy. Howbeit, when that resourceful secretary and uncompromising fighter had gone to his long rest, a better mood began to make itself felt, especially among Masons in America, who were weary of old-world divisions, and a desire to heal the feud and unite all the Grand Lodges—the way having been cleared, meanwhile, by the demise of the old York Grand Lodge and the "Grand Lodge South of the Trent." Overtures to that end were made in 1802 without avail, but by 1809 committees were meeting and reporting on the "propriety and practicability of union." Fraternal letters were exchanged, and at last a joint committee met, canvassed all differences, and found a way to heal the breach.[2]

[1] *Military Lodges,* by Gould; also Kipling's poem, *The Mother Lodge.*

[2] Among the articles of union, it was agreed that Freemasonry should consist of the three symbolic degrees, *"including the Holy Royal Arch."* The present study does not contemplate a detailed study of Capitular Masonry, which has its own history and historians (*Origin of the English Rite,* Hughan), except to say that it seems to have begun about 1738-40, the concensus of opinion differing as to whether it began in England or on the Continent ("Royal Arch Masonry," by C. P. Noar, *Manchester Lodge of Research,* vol. iii, 1911-12). Laurence Dermott, always alert, had it adopted by the Atholl Grand Lodge about thirty years before the Grand Lodge of England took it up in 1770-76, when Thomas Dunckerley was appointed to arrange and introduce it. Dermott held it to be "the very essence of Masonry," and he was not slow in using it as a club with which to belabor the Moderns; but he did not originate it, as some imagine, having received the degrees before he came to London, perhaps in an

Union came at length, in a great Lodge of Reconciliation held in Freemason's Hall, London, on St. John's Day, December 27, 1813. It was a memorable and inspiring scene as the two Grand Lodges, so long estranged, filed into the Hall—delegates of 641 Modern and 359 Ancient or Atholl Lodges—so mixed as to be indistinguishable the one from the other. Both Grand Masters had seats of honor in the East. The hour was fraternal, each side willing to sacrifice prejudice in behalf of principles held by all in common, and all equally anxious to preserve the ancient landmarks of the Craft—a most significant fact being that the Atholl Masons had insisted that Masonry erase such distinctively Christian color as had crept into it, and return to its first platform.[1] Once united, free of feud, cleansed of

unsystemized form. Dunckerley was accused of shifting the original Grand Masonic word from the Third Degree to the Royal Arch, and of substituting another in its stead. Enough to say that Royal Arch Masonry is authentic Masonry, being a further elaboration in drama, following the Third Degree, of the spirit and motif of old Craft Masonry (*History of Freemasonry and Concordant Orders*, by Hughan and Stillson, and *The Grand Lodge of England*, by Calvert).

[1] It is interesting to note that the writer of the article on "Masonry" in the *Catholic Encyclopedia*—an article admirable in many ways, and for the most part fair—makes much of this point, and rightly so, albeit his interpretation of it is altogether wrong. He imagines that the objection to Christian imagery in the ritual was due to enmity to Christianity. Not so. Masonry was not then, and has never at any time been, opposed to Christianity, or to any other religion. Far from it. But Christianity in those days—as, alas, too often now—was another name for a petty and bigoted sectarianism; and Masonry by its very genius was, and is, *unsectarian*. Many Masons then were devout Christians, as they are now—not a few clergymen—but the order itself is open to men of all faiths, Catholic and Protestant, Hebrew and Hindu, who confess faith in God; and so it will always remain if it is true to its principles and history.

rancor, and holding high its unsectarian, non-partisan flag, Masonry moved forward to her great ministry. If we would learn the lesson of those long dead debates, we must be vigilant, correcting our judgments, improving our regulations, and cultivating that spirit of Love which is the fountain whence issue all our voluntary efforts for what is right and true: union in essential matters, liberty in everything unimportant and doubtful; Love always—one bond, one universal law, one fellowship in spirit and in truth!

4

Remains now to give a glimpse—and, alas, only a glimpse—of the growth and influence of Masonry in America; and a great story it is, needing many volumes to tell it aright. As we have seen, it came early to the shores of the New World, long before the name of our great republic had been uttered, and with its gospel of Liberty, Equality, and Fraternity it helped to shape the institutions of this Continent. Down the Atlantic Coast, along the Great Lakes, into the wilderness of the Middle West and the forests of the far South—westward it marched as "the star of empire" led, setting up its altar on remote frontiers, a symbol of civilization, of loyalty to law and order, of friendship with school-house and church. If history recorded the unseen influences which go to the making of a nation, those forces for good which never stop, never tarry, never tire, and of which our social order is the outward and visible sign, then might the real story of Masonry in America be told.

Instead of a dry chronicle,[1] let us make effort to capture and portray the spirit of Masonry in American history, so that all may see how this great order actually presided over the birth of the republic, with whose growth it has had so much to do.[2]

[1] As for the chronicle, the one indispensable book to the student of American Masonry is the *History of Freemasonry and Concordant Orders*, by W. J. Hughan and H. L. Stillson, aided by one of the ablest board of contributors ever assembled. It includes a history of Masonry in all its Rites in North, Central, and South America, with accurate accounts of the origin and growth of every Grand Lodge in the United States and British America; also admirable chapters on Early American Masonic History, the Morgan Excitement, Masonic Jurisprudence, and statistics up to date of 1891—all carefully prepared and well written. Among other books too many to name, there are the *History of Symbolic Masonry in the United States,* by J. H. Drummond, and "The American Addenda" to Gould's massive and magnificent *History of Masonry,* vol. iv. What the present pages seek is the spirit behind this forest of facts.

[2] A history of American Masonry, written by weaving together the records of a mother lodge in each state, and in the Colonies earlier, would be a romance. In every State there was such a lodge, strategic and influential, to which the men who carved out the Commonwealth belonged. For example: St. John's Lodge and the Lodge of St. Andrew in Boston; St. John's Lodge in Providence; "Old Hiram, Number One," in Connecticut; St. John's Lodge in New York; St. John's Lodge—old "First"—in Philadelphia, to which Franklin belonged; Fredericksburg Lodge, Virginia, where Washington was made a Mason; Solomon's Lodge, South Carolina; Solomon's Lodge, Savannah, Georgia, of which Oglethorpe, founder of the Colony, was Master, to which John Wesley preached, which founded the first Orphanage in America, aided by Whitfield—all these old lodges, to name no others, are fabulously rich in history and legend. Then, following the great trek westward, Lexington Lodge, in Kentucky, spreading out fan-wise; American Union Lodge, Marietta, Ohio, a revival of the Revolutionary military lodge of the same name, of which Rufus Putnam and Lewis Cass were members; Stoney Creek Lodge, Michigan, whose story is an epic; Holland Lodge, Houston, Texas—my native State—to which Houston, Austin, and the founders

For example, no one need be told what patriotic memories cluster about the old Green Dragon Tavern, in Boston, which Webster, speaking at Andover in 1823, called *"the headquarters of the Revolution."* Even so, but it was also a *Masonic Hall,* in the "Long Room" of which the Grand Lodge of Massachusetts —an offshoot of St. Andrew's Lodge—was organized on St. John's Day, 1767, with Joseph Warren, who afterwards fell at Bunker Hill, as Grand Master. There Samuel Adams, Paul Revere, Warren, Hancock, Otis and others met and passed resolutions, and then laid schemes to make them come true. There the Boston Tea Party was planned, and executed by Masons disguised as Mohawk Indians—not by the Lodge as such, but by a club formed within the Lodge, calling itself the *Caucus Pro Bono Publico,* of which Warren was the leading spirit, and in which, says Elliott, "the plans of the Sons of Liberty were matured." As Henry Purkett used to say, he was present at the famous Tea Party as a spectator, and in disobedience to the order of the Master of the Lodge, who was *actively* present.[1]

As in Massachusetts, so throughout the Colonies

of the Republic belonged; and Trinity Lodge, Dallas, which operated the first public free school in the State—and so on, across prairies, and over mountains, to the Golden Gate; the Masonic Lodge journeying alongside the Church and the School, conquering, settling, building our country. It is a thrilling history, to make the heart of every Mason beat high. (See a Digest, a preview, of *Famous American Lodges,* prepared by the Masonic Service Association of the United States.)

[1] For the full story, see "Reminiscences of the Green Dragon Tavern," in *Centennial Memorial of St. Andrew's Lodge,* 1870.

—the Masons were everywhere active in behalf of a nation "conceived in liberty and dedicated to the proposition that all men are created equal," and so it has ever been in this our Brotherland. Of the men who signed the Declaration of Independence, the following are known to have been members of the order: William Hooper, Benjamin Franklin, Matthew Thornton, William Whipple, John Hancock, Philip Livingston, Thomas Nelson; and no doubt others, if we had the Masonic records destroyed during the war. Indeed, it has been said that, with four men out of the room, the assembly could have been opened in form as a Masonic Lodge, on the Third Degree. Not only Washington,[1] but nearly all of his generals, were Masons; such at least as Greene, Lee, Marion, Sullivan, Rufus and Israel Putnam, Edwards, Jackson, Gist, Baron Steuben, Baron De Kalb, and the Marquis de Lafayette. If the history of the old camp-lodges could be written, what a story it would tell. Not only did they initiate such men as Alexander Hamilton and John Marshall, the immortal Chief Justice, but they made the spirit of Masonry felt in "times that try men's souls" [2]—a

[1] *Washington, the Man and the Mason,* by C. H. Callahan. Jackson, Polk, Fillmore, Buchanan, Johnson, Garfield, McKinley, T. Roosevelt, Taft, Harding, F. Roosevelt, and Truman, all were Masons. A long list may be found in *Cyclopedia of Fraternities,* by Stevens, article on "Freemasonry: Distinguished Americans."

[2] Thomas Paine, whose words these are, though not a Mason, has left us an essay on *The Origin of Freemasonry.* Few men have ever been more unjustly and cruelly maligned than this great patriot, who was the first to utter the name "United States," and who, instead of being a sceptic, believed in "the religion in which all men agree"—

spirit passing through picket-lines, eluding sentinels, and softening the horrors of war.

To the glory of Freemasonry, be it said, that, while the War of the Revolution suspended Masonic fellowship, it did not sever the Masonic tie between brethren of the Motherland and our new Republic —a fact which ought to be known and never forgotten! American Masonry won its independence too, and when peace arrived all necessary adjustments were easily made without the slightest friction. However, the War did affect American Masonry deeply, even radically, due to the fact that, with notable exceptions, the "Ancient" lodges ardently supported the cause of the Colonists, while the "Modern" lodges wavered, and often took the Tory side.

Naturally, "Modern" lodges everywhere declined, and in the Province of Pennsylvania they disappeared entirely—so that, to this day, the Grand Lodge of Pennsylvania preserves intact the Constitutions, rules and rituals of the "Ancients." (Some English lodges do the same, for example, old British Lodge No. 8, in London; our British brethren prize such varieties of ritual, as adding to the charm of the Craft.) As has been said, there were exceptions, as in the case of the most famous of the Military Lodges, the "American Union,"—prophetic name—which

that is, in God, Duty, and the immortality of the soul. Yet, an American President called him a "filthy little atheist,"—for shame! (*Life of Paine*, by Monicure Conway.)

was chartered under "Modern" auspices, and attached to the "Connecticut line."

There is record of a great St. John's Day festival at Morristown, New Jersey, December 27th, 1779, which General Washington attended, when a petition was approved asking for the appointment of a Grand Master of the United States. A convention lodge, formed of different lines of the Army, was held in due form, under the authority of American Union Lodge, in Morristown, "the sixth day of March, in the year of Salvation, 1780."

Of course, Washington was named for the office of General Grand Master, and it was hoped that such a United Grand Lodge would heal the feud between the "Ancients" and the "Moderns." Alas, the project fell through and was abandoned, as every such attempt since has failed, long after the feud was reconciled. Albeit free politically and Masonically, our American Masonry has kept its organization of the Colonial period down to our time.

Laying aside their swords, these Masons helped to lay wide and deep the foundations of that liberty under the law which has made this nation, of a truth, "the last great hope of man." Nor was it an accident, but a scene in accord with the fitness of things, that George Washington was sworn into office as the first President of the Republic by the Grand Master of New York, taking his oath on a Masonic Bible. It was a parable of the whole period. If the Magna Charta demanded rights which government can grant, Masonry from the first asserted those inalienable rights which man derives from God the Father of men. Never did this truth find sweeter voice than in the tones of the old Scotch fiddle on which Robert Burns, a Master Mason, sang, in lyric glee, of the sacredness of the soul, and the native dignity of humanity as the only basis of society and the state. That music went marching on, striding over continents and seas, until it found embodiment in the Constitution and laws of this nation, where today more than two million Masons are citizens.

How strange, then, that Masonry should have been made the victim of the most bitter and baseless persecution, for it was nothing else, in the annals of the Republic. Yet so it came to pass between 1826 and 1845, in connection with the Morgan [1]

[1] William Morgan was a dissolute, nondescript printer in Batavia, New York, who, having failed in everything else, thought to make money by betraying the secrets of an order which his presence polluted. Foolishly misled, a few Masons had him arrested on a petty charge, got him out of the country, and apparently paid him to stay out. Had no attention been paid to his alleged exposure it would have fallen still-born from the press, like many another before it. Rumors of abduction started, then Morgan was said to have been thrown into Niagara River, whereas there is no proof that he was ever killed, much less murdered by Masons. Thurlow Weed and a pack of unscrupulous politicians took it up, and the rest was easy. One year later a body was found on the shore of Lake Ontario which Weed and the wife of Morgan identified—a *year afterward!*—she, no doubt, having been paid to do so; albeit the wife of a fisherman named Munroe identified the same body as that of her husband drowned a week or so before. No matter; as Weed said, *"It's good enough Morgan until after the election"*—a characteristic remark, if we may judge by his own portrait as drawn in his *Autobiography*. Politically, he was capable of anything, if he could make it win, and here he saw a chance of stirring up every vile and slimy thing in human nature for sake of office. (See a splen-

Affair, of which so much has been written, and so
little truth told.[1] Alas, it was an evil hour when, as
Galsworthy would say, "men just feel something big
and religious, and go blind to justice, fact, and
reason." Although Lodges everywhere repudiated
and denounced the crime, if crime it was, and the
Governor of New York, himself a Mason, made
every effort to detect and punish those involved, the
fanaticism would not be stayed: the mob-mood
ruled. An Anti-Masonic political party[2] was
formed, fed on frenzy, and the land was stirred from
end to end. Even such a man as John Quincy
Adams, of great credulity and strong prejudice, was
drawn into the fray, and in a series of letters flayed
Masonry as an enemy of society and a free state—
forgetting that Washington, Franklin, Marshall, and
Warren were members of the order! Meanwhile—
and, verily, it was a mean while—Weed, Seward,
Thaddeus Stevens, and others of their ilk, rode into
power on the strength of it, as they had planned to
do, defeating Henry Clay for President, because he
was a Mason—and, incidentally, electing Andrew
Jackson, another Mason! Let it be said that, if the
Masons found it hard to keep within the Compasses,
they at least acted on the Square. Finally the fury

did review of the whole matter in *History of Masonry*, by Hughan and
Stillson, also by Gould in vol. iv of his *History*.)

[1] See "Bibliography of Anti-Masonry with a Sketch of the Morgan
Affair," by Dr. William L. Cummings. *Nocalore*, vol. iv.

[2] *Cyclopedia of Fraternities*, by Stevens, article, "Anti-Masonry,"
gives detailed account with many interesting facts. Also, *The Free-
masons*, by Eugen Lennhoff, chap. xiv.

spent itself, leaving the order purged of feeble men who were Masons only in form, and a revival of Masonry followed, slowly at first, and then with great rapidity.

No sooner had Masonry recovered from this ordeal than the dark clouds of Civil War covered the land like a pall—the saddest of all wars, dividing a nation one in arts and arms and historic memories, and leaving an entail of blood and fire and tears. Let it be forever remembered that, while churches were severed and states were seceding, *the Masonic order remained unbroken* in that wild and fateful hour. An effort was made to involve Masonry in the strife, but the wise counsel of its leaders, North and South, prevented the mixing of Masonry with politics; and while it could not avert the tragedy, it did much to mitigate the woe of it—building rainbow bridges of mercy and goodwill from army to army. Though passion may have strained, it could not break the tie of Masonic love, which found a ministry on red fields, among the sick, the wounded, and those in prison; and many a man in gray planted a Sprig of Acacia on the grave of a man who wore the blue. Some day the writer hopes to tell that story, or a part of it, and then men will understand what Masonry is, what it means, and what it can do to heal the hurts of humanity.[1]

[1] Following the first day of the battle of Gettysburg, there was a Lodge meeting in town, and "Yanks" and "Johnny Rebs" met and mingled as friends under the Square and Compasses. Where else could they have done so? (*Tennessee Mason*). When the Union army attacked Little Rock. Ark., the commanding officer, Thomas H. Benton—Grand

Even so it has been, all through our national history, and today Masonry is worth more for the sanctity and safety of this republic than both its army and its navy. At every turn of events, when the rights of man have been threatened by enemies obvious or insidious, it has stood guard—its altar lights like signal fires along the heights of liberty, keeping watch. Not only in our own land, but everywhere over the broad earth, when men have thrown off the yoke of tyranny, whether political or spiritual, and demanded the rights that belong to manhood, they have found a friend in the Masonic order—as did Mazzini and Garibaldi in Italy. Nor must we be less alert and vigilant today, when, free of danger of foes from without, our republic is imperiled by the negligence of indifference, the seduction of luxury, the machinations of politicians, and the shadow of a passion-clouded, impatient discontent, whose end is madness and folly; lest the most hallowed of

Master of the Grand Lodge of Iowa—threw a guard about the home of General Albert Pike, *to protect his Masonic library*. Marching through burning Richmond, a Union officer saw the familiar emblems over a hall. He put a guard about the Lodge room, and that night, together with a number of Confederate Masons, organized a society for the relief of widows and orphans left destitute by the war (*Washington, the Man and the Mason*, Callahan). But for the kindness of a brother Mason, who saved the life of a young soldier of the South, who was a prisoner of war at Rock Island, Ill., the present writer would never have been born, much less have written this book. That young soldier was my father! Volumes of such facts might be gathered in proof of the gracious ministry of Masonry in those awful years.

Abraham Lincoln was not a Mason. As a young man, he wanted to join the Order, but his Masonic friends advised against it, owing to the anti-Masonic fanaticism still raging, which, it was feared, might imperil his political future.

all liberties be lost. Liberty is new; humanity has
known very little of it. Tyranny is old, gray, ghastly
—in our age, before our eyes, a hoary tyranny in a
new guise has spread over vast areas of the earth.
Only in liberty can fraternity flourish; only in fraternity can liberty endure.

> Love thou thy land, with love far-brought
> From out the storied past, and used
> Within the present, but transfused
> Through future time by power of thought.

5

Truly, the very existence of such a great historic
fellowship in the quest and service of the Ideal is
a fact eloquent beyond all words, and to be counted
among the precious assets of humanity. Forming
one vast society of free men, held together by voluntary obligations, it covers the whole globe from
Egypt to India, from Italy to England, from America
to Australia, and the isles of the sea; from London
to Sidney, from Chicago to Calcutta. In all civilized
lands, and among folk of every creed worthy of the
name, Masonry is found—and everywhere it upholds
all the redeeming ideals of humanity, making all
good things better by its presence, like a stream un-
derflowing a meadow.[1] Also, wherever Masonry
flourishes and is allowed to build freely after its
divine design, liberty, justice, education, and true

[1] *Cyclopedia of Fraternities,* by Stevens (last edition), article, "Free
Masonry," pictures the extent of the order, with maps and diagrams
showing its world-wide influence.

religion flourish; and where it is hindered, they suffer. Indeed, he who would reckon the spiritual possessions of the race, and estimate the forces that make for social beauty, national greatness, and human welfare, must take account of the genius of Masonry and its ministry to the higher life of the race.

Small wonder that such an order has won to its fellowship men of the first order of intellect, men of thought and action in many lands, and every walk and work of life: soldiers like Wellington, Blücher, and Garibaldi; philosophers like Krause, Fichte, and John Locke; patriots like Washington and Mazzini; writers like Walter Scott, Voltaire, Steele, Lessing, Tolstoi; poets like Goethe, Burns, Pope, Kipling, Pike; musicians like Haydn and Mozart—whose opera, *The Magic Flute,* has a Masonic motif; masters of drama like Forrest and Edwin Booth; editors such as Bowles, Prentice, Childs, Grady; ministers of many communions, from Bishop Potter to Robert Collyer; statesmen, philanthropists, educators, jurists, men of science—Masons many,[1] whose

[1] Space does not permit a survey of the literature of Masonry, still less of Masonry in literature. (Findel has two fine chapters on the literature of the order, but he wrote, in 1865, *History of Masonry*.) For traces of Masonry in literature, there is the famous chapter in *War and Peace,* by Tolstoi; *Mon Oncle Sosthenes,* by Maupassant; *Nathan the Wise,* and *Ernst and Falk,* by Lessing; the Masonic poems of Goethe, and many hints in *Wilhelm Meister;* the writings of Herder (*Classic Period of German Letters,* Findel), *The Lost Word,* by Henry Van Dyke; and, of course, the poetry of Burns.

Masonic phrases and allusions—often almost too revealing—are found all through the poems and stories of Kipling. Besides the poem, *The Mother Lodge,* so much admired, there is *The Widow of Windsor,* such

SIR ALFRED ROBBINS, PAST GRAND WARDEN

As President from 1913 to his death in 1931, of the Board
of General Purposes, United Grand Lodge of England, he
was *de facto* Prime Minister of the British Craft. His offi-
cial travels in foreign countries contributed in vast measure
to the closely knit relationships of English-speaking Freemasonry.

names shine like stars in the great world's crown of intellectual and spiritual glory. What other order has ever brought together men of such diverse types, tempers, training, interests, religions, and achievements, uniting them at an altar of prayer in the worship of God and the service of man?

In 1918, at the invitation of a charming French officer, it was my joy to attend a lodge meeting in London, in which were gathered men of nearly every living religion of the race, except Confucianism—if Confucianism is a religion, and not a code of ethics, using more proverbs than prayers. About a Masonic Altar Hindu, Hebrew, Parsee, Mohammedan, Christians of many kinds—Catholic, Anglican, Free Churchmen—met not in mere toleration, but in goodwill, appreciation, fellowship. It was a scene no one could ever forget, a vision-hour deeply moving, at once a picture and a prophecy; many races without rancor, many faiths without feud. At the close of the lodge, each man was asked to repeat the benediction of his religion in his native tongue, and translate it into English. Then, clasping hands about the Altar, they joined in the Lord's Prayer, the one prayer in which men of every race and rite can unite. It was most impressive, as if one were listening-in on the future. It made me think of the

stories as *With the Main Guard, The Winged Hats, Hal o' the Draft, The City Walls, On the Great Wall,* many examples in *Kim,* also in *Traffics and Discoveries, Puck of Pook's Hill, The Man Who Would be King,* one of the great short stories of the world, and by no means least, *In the Interests of the Brethren,* a story to break the heart—and mend it.

words of a seer in a sacred book of China: "The broad-minded see the truth in different religions; the narrow-minded see only the differences." Also, the saying of one of our own seers: "Humble, merciful, just, and devout souls are everywhere of one religion; and when death hath taken off the mask, they will know one another." Where else, except in a Masonic lodge, could men of many religions meet, each praying for all and all for each one? It taught me one lesson: If ever there is to be a Religion of Brotherhood on earth, it must begin with a Brotherhood of Religions.

For the rest, if by some art one could trace those invisible influences which move to and fro like shuttles in a loom, weaving the network of laws, reverences, sanctities which make the warp and woof of society—giving to statutes their dignity and power, to the gospel its opportunity, to the home its canopy of peace and beauty, to the young an enshrinement of inspiration, and to the old a mantle of protection; if one had such art, then he might tell the true story of Masonry. Older than any living religion, the most widespread of all orders of men, it toils for liberty, friendship, and righteousness; binding men with solemn vows to the right, uniting them upon the only basis upon which they can meet without reproach—like those fibers running through the glaciers, along which sunbeams journey, melting the frozen mass and sending it to the valleys below in streams of blessing. Other fibers are there, but none is more far-ramifying, none more tender, none more responsive to the Light than the mystical tie of Masonic love.

Truth will triumph; God's dreams will come true. Justice will yet reign from sun to sun, victorious over cruelty and evil. Finally Love will rule the race, as it rules "the sun and all the stars," casting out fear, hatred, and all unkindness, and pity will heal the old hurt and heart-ache of humanity, the whisper of grief which follows the evening sun around the world. There is nothing in history, dark as much of it is, against the ultimate fulfilment of the prophetic vision of Robert Burns—a Poet Laureate of Masonry:

> Then let us pray, that come it may—
> As come it will, for a' that—
>
> . . . . .
>
> That man to man, the world o'er
> Shall brothers be, for a' that.

Part 3

INTERPRETATION

WHAT IS MASONRY

I am afraid you may not consider it an altogether substantial concern. It has to be seen in a certain way, under certain conditions. Some people never see it at all. You must understand, this is no dead pile of stones and unmeaning timber. It is a LIVING *thing.*

When you enter it you hear a sound—a sound as of some mighty poem chanted. Listen long enough, and you will learn that it is made up of the beating of human hearts, of the nameless music of men's souls—that is, if you have ears to hear. If you have eyes, you will presently see the church itself—a looming mystery of many shapes and shadows, leaping sheer from floor to dome. The work of no ordinary builder!

The pillars of it go up like the brawny trunks of heroes; the sweet flesh of men and women is molded about its bulwarks, strong, impregnable; the faces of little children laugh out from every corner stone; the terrible spans and arches of it are the joined hands of comrades; and up in the heights and spaces are inscribed the numberless musings of all the dreamers of the world. It is yet building—building and built upon.

Sometimes the work goes on in deep darkness; sometimes in blinding light; now under the burden of unutterable anguish; now to the tune of great laughter and heroic shoutings like the cry of thunder. Sometimes, in the silence of the night-time, one may hear the tiny hammerings of the comrades at work up in the dome—the comrades that have climbed ahead.

—C. R. KENNEDY, *The Servant in the House*

Chapter One

WHAT IS MASONRY

1

HAT, THEN, is Masonry, and what is it trying to do in the world? According to one of the *Old Charges,* Masonry is declared to be an "ancient and honorable institution: ancient no doubt it is, as having subsisted from time immemorial; and honorable it must be acknowledged to be, as by natural tendency it conduces to make those so who are obedient to its precepts. To so high an eminence has its credit been advanced that in every age monarchs themselves have been promoters of the art, have not thought it derogatory from their dignity to exchange the scepter for the trowel, have patronized our mysteries and joined in our Assemblies."

While that eulogy is more than justified by sober facts, it does not tell us what Masonry is, much less its mission and ministry to mankind. If now we turn to the old, oft-quoted definition, we learn that

Masonry is "a system of morality veiled in allegory and illustrated by symbols." That is, in so far, true enough, but it is obviously inadequate, the more so when it uses the word "peculiar" as describing the morality of Masonry; and it gives no hint of a world-encircling fellowship and its far-ramifying influence. Another definition has it that Masonry is "a science which is engaged in the search after divine truth;" [1] but that is vague, indefinite, and unsatisfactory, lacking any sense of the uniqueness of the Order, and as applicable to one science as to another. For surely all science, of whatever kind, is a search after divine truth,—thinking the thoughts of God after Him, which is all our minds can do—and a physical fact, as Agassiz said, is as sacred as a moral truth—every fact being the presence of God.

Still another writer defines Masonry as "Friendship, Love, and Integrity—Friendship which rises superior to the fictitious distinctions of society, the prejudices of religion, and the pecuniary conditions of life; Love which knows no limit, nor inequality, nor decay; Integrity which binds man to the eternal law of duty." [2] Such is indeed the very essence and spirit of Masonry, but Masonry has no monopoly of that spirit, and its uniqueness consists, rather, in the form in which it seeks to embody and express the

[1] *Symbolism of Freemasonry*, by Dr. Mackey.
[2] *History and Philosophy of Masonry*, by A. C. L. Arnold, chap. xvi. To say of any man—of Socrates, for example—who had the spirit of Friendship and Integrity, that he was a Mason, is in a sense true, but it is misleading. Nevertheless, if a man have not that spirit, he is not a Mason, though he may have received the thirty-third degree.

gracious and benign spirit which is the genius of all the higher life of humanity. Masonry is not everything; it is a thing as distinctly featured as a statue by Phidias or a painting by Angelo. Definitions, like delays, may be dangerous, but perhaps we can do no better than to adopt the words of the German *Handbuch* [1] as the best description of it so far given:

> *Masonry is the activity of closely united men who, employing symbolical forms borrowed principally from the mason's trade and from architecture, work for the welfare of mankind, striving morally to ennoble themselves and others, and thereby to bring about a universal league of mankind, which they aspire to exhibit even now on a small scale.* [2]

Civilization could hardly begin until man had learned to fashion for himself a settled habitation, and thus the earliest of all human arts and crafts, and perhaps also the noblest, is that of the builder. Religion took outward shape when men first reared an altar for their offerings, and surrounded it with a sanctuary of faith and awe, of pity and consolation, and piled a cairn to mark the graves where their dead lay asleep. History is no older than architecture. How fitting, then, that the idea and art of building should be made the basis of a great order

[1] Vol. i, p. 320. The *Handbuch* is an encyclopedia of Masonry, published in 1900. See admirable review of it, *A. Q. C.*, xi, 64.

[2] Masonry is as difficult to define as religion; it breaks through language and escapes. Elsewhere I have assembled some famous definitions—if they may not be called descriptions. *The Religion of Masonry*, chapter 1, sec. 2.

of men which has no other aim than the upbuilding of humanity in Faith, Freedom, and Friendship. Seeking to ennoble and beautify life, it finds in the common task and constant labor of man its sense of human unity, its vision of life as a temple "building and built upon," and its emblems of those truths which make for purity of character and the stability of society. Thus Masonry labors, linked with the constructive genius of mankind, and so long as it remains true to its Ideal no weapon formed against it can prosper.

One of the most impressive and touching things in human history is that certain ideal interests have been set apart as especially venerated among all peoples. Guilds have arisen to cultivate the interests embodied in art, science, philosophy, fraternity, and religion; to conserve the precious, hard-won inheritances of humanity; to train men in their service; to bring their power to bear upon the common life of mortals, and send through that common life the light and glory of the Ideal—as the sun shoots its transfiguring rays through a great dull cloud, evoking beauty from the brown earth. Such is Masonry, which unites all these high interests and brings to their service a vast, world-wide fraternity of free and devout men, built upon a foundation of spiritual faith and moral idealism, whose mission it is to make men friends, to refine and exalt their lives, to deepen their faith and purify their dream, to turn them from the semblance of life to homage for truth, beauty, righteousness, and character.

More than an institution, more than a tradition, more than a society, Masonry is one of the forms of the Divine Life upon earth. No one may ever hope to define a spirit so gracious, an order so benign, an influence so prophetic of the present and future up-building of the race.

There is a common notion that Masonry is a secret society, and this idea is based on the secret rites used in its initiations, and the signs and grips by which its members recognize each other. Thus it has come to pass that the main aims of the Order are assumed to be a secret policy or teaching,[1] whereas *its one great secret is that it has no secret.* Its principles are published abroad in its writings; its purposes and laws are known, and the times and places of its meetings. Having come down from dark days of persecution, when all the finer things sought the protection of seclusion, if it still adheres to secret rites, it is not in order to hide the truth, but the better to teach it more impressively, to train men in its pure service, and to promote union and amity upon earth. Its signs and grips serve as a

[1] Much has been written about the secrecy of Masonry. Hutchinson, in his lecture on "The Secrecy of Masons," lays all the stress upon its privacy as a shelter for the gentle ministry of Charity (*Spirit of Masonry*, lecture x). Arnold is more satisfactory in his essay on "The Philosophy of Mystery," quoting the words of Carlyle in *Sartor Resartus:* "Bees will not work except in darkness; thoughts will not work except in silence; neither will virtue work except in secrecy" (*History and Philosophy of Masonry*, chap. xxi). But neither writer seems to realize the psychology and pedagogy of secrecy—the value of curiosity, of wonder and expectation, in the teaching of great truths deemed commonplace because old. Even in that atmosphere, the real secret of Masonry remains hidden to many—as sunlight hides the depths of heaven.

kind of universal language, and still more as a gracious cover for the practice of sweet charity—making it easier to help a fellow-man in dire plight without hurting his self-respect. If a few are attracted to it by curiosity, all remain to pray, finding themselves members of a great historic fellowship of the seekers and finders of God.[1] It is old because it is true; had it been false it would have perished long ago. When all men practice its simple precepts, the innocent secrets of Masonry will be laid bare, its mission accomplished, and its labor done.

2

Recalling the emphasis of the foregoing pages, it need hardly be added that Masonry is in no sense a political party, still less a society organized for social agitation. Indeed, because Masonry stands apart from partisan feud and particular plans of social reform, she has been held up to ridicule equally by the unthinking, the ambitious, and the impatient. Her critics on this side are of two kinds. There are those who hold that the humanitarian ideal is an error, maintaining that human nature has no moral aptitude, and can be saved only by submission to a definite system of dogma. Then there are those who look for salvation solely in political action and social agitation, who live in the delusion that man can be

[1] Read the noble chapter on "Prayer as a Masonic Obligation," in *Practical Masonic Lectures*, by Samuel Lawrence (lecture x); also, my study of *The Religion of Masonry*, so widely read and translated into Dutch and Spanish.

made better by passing laws and counting votes, and to whom Masonry has nothing to offer because in its ranks it permits no politics, much less party rancor. Advocates of the first view have fought Masonry from the beginning with the sharpest weapons, while those who hold the second view regard it with contempt, as a thing useless and not worth fighting.[1]

Neither adversary understands Masonry and its cult of the creative love for humanity, and of each man for his fellow, without which no dogma is of any worth; lacking which, the best laid plans of social seers "gang aft aglee." Let us look at things as they are. That we must press forward towards righteousness—that we must hunger and thirst after a social life that is true and pure, just and merciful —all will agree; but they are blind who do not see that the way is long and the process slow. What is it that so tragically delays the march of man toward the better and wiser social order whereof our prophets dream? Our age, like the ages gone before, is full of schemes of every kind for the reform and betterment of mankind. Why do they not succeed? Some fail, perhaps, because they are imprudent and ill-considered, in that they expect too much of human nature and do not take into account the stubborn facts of life. But why does not the wisest and noblest plan do more than half what its advocates hope and pray and labor so heroically to bring about? Because there are not enough men fine

[1] Read a thoughtful "Exposition of Freemasonry," by Dr. Paul Carus, *Open Court*, May, 1914.

enough of soul, large enough of sympathy, sweet enough of spirit, and noble enough of nature to make the dream come true! Because, to say it all at once, the Brotherhood of Man depends on the Manhood of the Brother.

There are no valid arguments against a great-spirited social justice but this—that men will not. Indolence, impurity, greed, injustice, meanness of spirit, the aggressiveness of authority, and above all jealousy—these are the real obstacles that thwart the nobler social aspiration of humanity. There are too many men like *The Master Builder,* in the Ibsen drama, who tried to build higher than any one else, without regard to others, all for his own selfish glory. Ibsen has also shown us how *The Pillars of Society,* resting on rotten foundations, came crashing down, wounding the innocent in their wreck. Long ago it was said that "through wisdom is an house builded, and by understanding it is established; and by knowledge shall the chambers be filled with pleasant and precious riches." [1] Time has shown that the House of Wisdom must be founded upon righteousness, justice, purity, character, faith in God and love of man, else it will fall when the floods descend and the winds beat upon it. What we need to make our social dreams come true is not more laws, not more dogmas, not less liberty, but better men, cleaner minded, more faithful, with loftier ideals and more heroic integrity; men who love the right, honor the

[1] Proverbs 24:3, 4.

truth, worship purity, and prize liberty—upright men who meet all horizontals at a perfect angle, assuring the virtue and stability of the social order.

Therefore, when Masonry, instead of identifying itself with particular schemes of reform, and thus becoming involved in endless turmoil and dispute, estranging men whom she seeks to bless, devotes all her benign energy and influence *to ennobling the souls of men,* she is doing fundamental work in behalf of all high enterprises. By as much as she succeeds, every noble cause succeeds; by as much as she fails, everything fails! By its ministry to the individual man—drawing him into the circle of a great friendship, exalting his faith, refining his ideals, enlarging his sympathies, and setting his feet in the long white path—Masonry best serves society and the state.[1] While it is not a reformatory, it is a center of moral and spiritual power, and its power is used, not only to protect the widow and orphan, but also, and still more important, to remove the cause of their woe and need by making men just, gentle, and generous to all their fellow-mortals. Who can measure such a silent, persistent, unresting

[1] While Masonry abjures political questions and disputes in its Lodges, it is all the while training good citizens, and through the quality of its men it influences public life—as Washington, Franklin, and Marshall carried the spirit of Masonry into the organic law of this republic. It is not politics that corrupts character; it is bad character that corrupts politics—and by building men up to spiritual faith and character, Masonry is helping to build up a state that will endure the shocks of time; a nobler structure than ever was wrought of mortar and marble (*The Principles of Freemasonry in the Life of Nations,* by Findel).

labor; who can describe its worth in a world of feud, of bitterness, of sorrow!

No one needs to be told that we are on the eve, if not in the midst, of a most stupendous and bewildering revolution of social and industrial life. It shakes England today. It makes France tremble tomorrow. It alarms America next week. Men want shorter hours, higher wages, and better homes—of course they do—but they need, more than these things, to know and love each other; for the questions in dispute can never be settled in an air of hostility, hatred, and ruthless class-war, as taught by Karl Marx in his *Manifesto* a century ago (1848), implemented in our day by the police-state, sacrificing liberty to the illusion of security, and losing both. If they are ever settled at all, and settled right, it must be in an atmosphere of mutual recognition and respect, such as Masonry seeks to create and make prevail,—a self-helpful, self-governing, "live and let live" philosophy of life. Whether it be a conflict of nations, or a clash of class with class, appeal must be made to intelligence and the moral sense, as befits the dignity of man. Amidst bitterness and strife Masonry brings men of every rank and walk of life together as men, and nothing else, at an altar where they can talk and not fight, discuss and not dispute, and each may learn the point of view of his fellow. Other hope there is none save in this spirit of friendship and fairness, of democracy and the fellowship of man with man. Once this spirit has its way with mankind, it will bring those brave, large reconstructions, those profitable abnegations and brotherly feats of generosity that will yet turn human life into a glad, beautiful, and triumphant coöperation all round this sunlit world.

Surely the way of Masonry is wise. Instead of becoming only one more factor in a world of factional feud, it seeks to remove all hostility which may arise from social, national, or religious differences. It helps to heal the haughtiness of the rich and the envy of the poor, and tends to establish peace on earth by allaying all fanaticism and hatred on account of varieties of language, race, creed, and even color, while striving to make the wisdom of the past available for the culture of men in faith and purity. Not a party, not a sect, not a cult, it is a great order of men selected, initiated, sworn, and trained to make sweet reason and the will of God prevail! Against the ancient enmities and inhumanities of the world it wages eternal war, without vengeance, without violence, but by softening the hearts of men and inducing a better spirit. Apparitions of a day, here for an hour and tomorrow gone, what is our puny warfare against evil and ignorance compared with the warfare which this venerable Order has been waging against them for ages, and will continue to wage after we have fallen into dust!

3

Masonry, as it is much more than a political party or a social cult, is also more than a church—unless we use the word "church" as Ruskin used it when he said: "There is a true church wherever one hand meets another helpfully, the only holy or mother church that ever was or ever shall be." It is true that Masonry is not *a* religion, but it is Religion, a worship in which all good men may unite, that each may share the faith of all. Often it has been objected that some men leave the Church and enter the Masonic Lodge, finding there a religious home. Even so, but that may be the fault, not of Masonry, but of the Church so long defamed by bigotry and distracted by sectarian feud, and which has too often made acceptance of abstract dogmas a test of its fellowship.[1] Naturally many fine minds have been

---

[1] Not a little confusion has existed, and still exists, in regard to the relation of Masonry to religion. Dr. Mackey said that old Craft-masonry was sectarian (*Symbolism of Masonry*); but it was not more so than Dr. Mackey himself, who held the curious theory that the religion of the Hebrews was genuine and that of the Egyptians spurious. Nor is there any evidence that Craft-masonry was sectarian, but much to the contrary, as has been shown in reference to the invocations in the *Old Charges*. At any rate, if it was ever sectarian, it ceased to be so with the organization of the Grand Lodge of England. Later, some of the chaplains of the order sought to identify Masonry with Christianity, as Hutchinson did—and even Arnold in his chapter on "Christianity and Freemasonry" (*History and Philosophy of Masonry*). All this confusion results from a misunderstanding of what religion is. Religions are many; religion is one—perhaps we may say one thing, but that one thing includes everything—the life of God in the soul of man, which finds expression in all the forms which life and love and duty take. This conception of religion shakes the poison out of all our wild flowers, and shows us that it is the inspiration of all scientific inquiry, all striving for liberty, all virtue and charity; the spirit of all thought, the motif of all great music, the soul of all sublime literature. The church has no monopoly of religion, nor did the Bible create it. Instead, it was religion—the natural and simple trust of the soul in a Power above and within it, and its quest of a right relation to that Power—that created the Bible and the Church, and, indeed, all our higher human life. The soul of man is greater than all books, deeper

estranged from the Church, not because they were irreligious, but because they were required to believe what it was impossible for them to believe; and, rather than sacrifice their integrity of soul, they have turned away from the last place from which a man should ever turn away. No part of the ministry of Masonry is more beautiful and wise than its appeal, not for tolerance, but for fraternity; not for uniformity, but for unity of spirit amidst varieties of outlook and opinion. Instead of criticizing Masonry, let us thank God for one altar where no man is asked to surrender his liberty of thought and become an indistinguishable atom in a mass of sectarian agglomeration. What a witness to the worth of an Order that it brings together men of all creeds in behalf of those truths which are greater than all sects, deeper than all doctrines—the glory and the hope of man!

While Masonry is not a church, it has religiously preserved some things of highest importance to the Church—among them the right of each individual soul to its own religious faith. Holding aloof from separate sects and creeds, it has taught all of them how to respect and tolerate each other; asserting a principle broader than any of them—the sanctity

than all dogmas, and more enduring than all institutions. Masonry seeks to free men from a limiting conception of religion, and thus to remove one of the chief causes of sectarianism. It is itself one of the forms of beauty wrought by the human soul under the inspiration of the Eternal Beauty, and as such is religious. (For a fuller discussion, see my two books, *The Religion of Masonry* and *The Great Light in Masonry*.)

of the soul and the duty of every man to revere, or at least to regard with charity, what is sacred to his fellows. It is like the crypts underneath the old cathedrals—a place where men of every creed who long for something deeper and truer, older and newer than they have hitherto known, meet and unite. Having put away childish things, they find themselves made one by a profound and childlike faith, each bringing down into that quiet crypt his own pearl of great price—

> the Hindu his innate disbelief in this world, and his un-hesitating belief in another world; the Buddhist his perception of an eternal law, his submission to it, his gentleness, his pity; the Mohammedan, if nothing else, his sobriety; the Jew his clinging, through good and evil days, to the one God who loveth righteousness, and whose name is "I AM;" the Christian, that which is better than all, if those who doubt it would try it—our love of God, call Him what you will, manifested in our love of man, our love of the living, our love of the dead, our living and undying love. Who knows but that the crypt of the past may become the church of the future? [1]

Of no one age, Masonry belongs to all ages; of no one religion, it finds great truths in all religions. Indeed, it holds that truth which is common to all elevating and benign religions, and is the basis of each; that faith which underlies all sects and over-arches all creeds, like the sky above and the river bed below the flow of mortal years. It does not under-

---

[1] *Hibbert Lectures,* by Max Müller.

take to explain or dogmatically to settle those questions or solve those dark mysteries which out-top human knowledge. Beyond the facts of faith it does not go. Indeed, it has been defined as "a factual religion with a simple creed." For the same reason, we are justified in calling it a Science, since it deals with facts of the moral and spiritual life.[1] With the subtleties of speculation concerning those truths, and the unworldly envies growing out of them, it has not to do. There divisions begin, and Masonry was not made to divide men, but to unite them, leaving each man free to think his own thought and fashion his own system of ultimate truth. All its emphasis rests upon two extremely simple and profound principles—love of God and love of man. Therefore, all through the ages it has been, and is today, a meeting-place of differing minds, and a prophecy of the final union of all reverent and devout souls.

Time was when one man framed a dogma and declared it to be the eternal truth. Another man did the same thing, with a different dogma; then the two began to hate each other with an unholy hatred, each seeking to impose his dogma upon the other—and that is an epitome of some of the blackest pages of history. Against those old sectarians who substituted intolerance for charity, persecution for friendship, and did not love God because they hated their neighbors, Masonry made eloquent protest, putting

[1] *Builders of Men,* by John C. Gibson.

their bigotry to shame by its simple insight, and the dignity of its golden voice. A vast change of heart is now taking place in the religious world, by reason of an exchange of thought and courtesy, and a closer personal touch, and the various sects, so long estranged, are learning to unite upon the things most worth while and the least open to debate.[1] That is to say, they are moving toward the Masonic position, and when they arrive Masonry will witness a scene which she has prophesied for ages.

At last, in the not distant future, the old feuds of the sects will come to an end,—even now their walls, once sky-high, are falling down—forgotten in the discovery that the just, the brave, the true-hearted are everywhere of one religion, and that when the masks of misunderstanding are taken off they know and love one another. Our little dogmas will have their day and cease to be, lost in the vision of a truth so great that all men are one in their little-ness; one also in their assurance of the divinity of the soul and "the kindness of the veiled Father of men." Then men of every name will ask, when they meet:

Not what is your creed?
But what is your need?

High above all dogmas that divide, all bigotries that blind, all bitterness that beclouds, will be written

[1] For a more detailed story of the rapid movement, like a tide flow-ing in the heart of the Christian churches, toward unity of faith and fellowship—unity, not uniformity—and the formation of a World Coun-cil of Churches, see my work of essays, *The One Great Church* (1948).

the simple words of the one eternal religion—the Fatherhood of God, the brotherhood of man, the moral law, the golden rule, and the hope of a life everlasting!

NOTE.—It has not been deemed necessary to enter here into the much-debated question of the Landmarks of Freemasonry, about which the literature is more voluminous than luminous. Whether we say, with Findel, that there are four Landmarks (*The Spirit and Form of Freemasonry*), or with Dr. Mackey that there are twenty-five (*Lexicon of Freemasonry*), or with some one else that there are sixty, depends on the point of view from which we regard the Craft. Obviously, a landmark must mean a limit set beyond which Masonry cannot go, some boundary within which it must labor; a line drawn against any innovation subversive of the spirit and purpose of the Fraternity. Surely the Landmarks of Freemasonry are its great fundamental principles, not any usage or custom, much less mere details of organization, save in so far as these are identical with and indispensible to the spread of its spirit and the fulfilment of its mission. Too often a tradition or custom of comparatively recent date has been elevated to the rank of a Landmark, and used as a barrier with which to exclude our Brethren—hence the sad spectacle of Masons in one part of the world refusing to recognize their fellows because, forsooth, they do not use exactly the same words. Surely this is a queer outcome of the gracious and free spirit of Masonry, whose genius it is, or should be, to make men friends and fellow-workers. As to the literature of the subject, from a legal point of view there is nothing better than the treatment of Landmarks by Brother Roscoe Pound in his lectures. (*Masonic Jurisprudence*); and, in a general way, the chapter in *Speculative Masonry*, by Brother A. S. MacBride, of Lodge Progress, Glasgow, one of the noblest and wisest teachers of this generation, whose book is one of the gems of our literature.

THE MASONIC
PHILOSOPHY

Masonry directs us to divest ourselves of confined and bigoted notions, and teaches us, that Humanity is the soul of Religion. We never suffer any religious disputes in our Lodges, and, as Masons, we only pursue the universal religion, the Religion of Nature. Worshipers of the God of Mercy, we believe that in every nation, he that feareth Him and worketh righteousness is accepted of Him. All Masons, therefore, whether Christians, Jews, or Mohammedans, who violate not the rule of right, written by the Almighty upon the tables of the heart, who DO *fear Him, and* WORK *righteousness, we are to acknowledge as brethren; and, though we take different roads, we are not to be angry with, or persecute each other on that account. We mean to travel to the same place; we know that the end of our journey is the same; and we affectionately hope to meet in the Lodge of perfect happiness. How lovely is an institution fraught with sentiments like these! How agreeable must it be to Him who is seated on a throne of Everlasting Mercy, to the God who is no respecter of persons!*

—WM. HUTCHINSON, *The Spirit of Masonry*

Chapter Two

THE MASONIC
PHILOSOPHY

AST ANY philosophy in thee, Shepherd?" [1] was the question of Touchstone in the Shakespeare play; and that is the question we must always ask ourselves. Long ago Kant said it is the mission of philosophy, not to discover truth, but to set it in order, to seek out the rhythm of things and their reason for being. Beginning in

---

[1] *As You Like It* (act ii, scene ii). Shakespeare makes no reference to any secret society, but some of his allusions suggest that he knew more than he wrote. He describes "The singing Masons building roofs of gold" (*Henry V*, act i, scene ii), and compares them to a swarm of bees at work. Did he know what the bee hive means in the symbolism of Masonry? (Read an interesting article on "Shakespeare and Freemasonry," *American Freemason*, January, 1912.) It reminds one of the passage in the *Complete Angler*, by Izaak Walton, in which the gentle fisherman talks about the meaning of Pillars in language very like that used in the *Old Charges*. But Hawkins in his edition of the *Angler* recalls that Walton was a friend of Elias Ashmole, and may have learned of Masonry from him. (*A Short Masonic History*, by F. Armitage, vol. ii, chap. 3.)

wonder, it sees the familiar as if it were strange, and its mind is full of the air that plays round every subject. Spacious, humane, eloquent, it is "a blend of science, poetry, religion and logic" [1]—a softening, enlarging, ennobling influence, giving us a wider and clearer outlook, more air, more room, more light, and more background.

When we look at Masonry in this large and mellow light, it is like a stately old cathedral, gray with age, rich in associations, its steps worn by innumerable feet of the living and the dead—not piteous, but strong and enduring. Entering its doors, we wonder at its lofty spaces, its windows with the dimness and glory of the Infinite behind them, the spring of its pillars, the leap of its arches, and its roof inlaid with stars. Inevitably we ask, whence came this temple of faith and friendship, and what does it mean—rising lightly as a lyric, uplifted by the hunger for truth and the love for beauty, and exempt from the shock of years and the ravages of decay? What faith builded this home of the soul, what philosophy underlies and upholds it? Truly did Longfellow sing of *The Builders*:

> In the elder years of art,
>   Builders wrought with greatest care
> Each minute and hidden part,
>   For the gods see everywhere.

[1] *Some Problems of Philosophy,* by William James.

1

If we examine the foundations of Masonry, we find
that it rests upon the most fundamental of all truths,
the first truth and the last, the sovereign and supreme
Reality. Upon the threshold of its Lodges every man,
whether prince or peasant, is asked to confess his
faith in God the Father Almighty, the Architect and
Master-builder of the Universe.[1] That is not a mere
form of words, but the deepest and most solemn af-

[1] In 1877 the Grand Orient of France removed the Bible from its
altar and erased from its ritual all reference to Deity; and for so doing
it was disfellowshipped by nearly every Grand Lodge in the world.
The writer of the article on "Masonry" in the *Catholic Encyclopedia*
recalls this fact with emphasis; but he is much fairer to the Grand
Orient than many Masonic writers have been. He understands that
this does not mean that the Masons of France are atheistic, as that
word is ordinarily used, but that *they do not believe that there exist
Atheists in the absolute sense of the word*; and he quotes the words
of Albert Pike: "A man who has a higher conception of God than
those about him, and who denies that their conception *is* God, is very
likely to be called an Atheist by men who are really far less believers
in God than he" (*Morals and Dogma*, p. 643). Thus, as Pike goes on
to say, the early Christians, who said the heathen idols were no Gods,
were accounted Atheists, and accordingly put to death. We need not
hold a brief for the Grand Orient, but it behooves us to understand its
position and point of view, lest we be found guilty of a petty bigotry
in regard to a word when the *reality* is a common treasure. First, it
was felt that France needed the aid of every man who was an enemy
of Latin ecclesiasticism, in order to bring about a separation of Church
and State; hence the attitude of the Grand Orient. Second, the Masons
of France agree with Plutarch that no conception of God at all is better than a dark, distorted superstition which wraps men in terror; and
they erased a word which, for many, was associated with an unworthy
faith—the better to seek a unity of effort in behalf of liberty of thought
and a loftier faith. (*The Religion of Plutarch*, by Oakesmith; also the
Bacon essay on *Superstition*.) We may deem this unwise, but we ought
at least to understand its spirit and purpose; the man who made the
motion was a Christian minister.

firmation that human lips can make. To be indifferent to God is to be indifferent to the greatest of all realities, that upon which the aspiration of humanity rests for its uprising passion of desire. No institution that is dumb concerning the meaning of life and the character of the universe can last. It is a house built upon the sand, doomed to fall when the winds blow and floods beat upon it, lacking a sure foundation. No human fraternity that has not its inspiration in the Fatherhood of God, confessed or unconfessed, can long endure; it is a rope of sand, weak as water, and its fine sentiment quickly evaporates. Life leads, if we follow its meanings and think in the drift of its deeper conclusions, to one God as the ground of the world, and upon that ground Masonry lays her corner-stone. Therefore, it endures and grows, and the gates of hell cannot prevail against it!

While Masonry is theocratic in its faith and philosophy,[1] it does not limit its conception of the Divine, much less insist upon any one name for "the Nameless One of a hundred names." Indeed, no feature of Masonry is more fascinating than its age-long quest of the Lost Word,[2] the Ineffable Name; a quest that never tires, never tarries, knowing the while that every name is inadequate, and all words are but symbols of a Truth too great for words—

[1] *Theocratic Philosophy of Freemasonry*, by Oliver.
[2] "History of the Lost Word," by J. F. Garrison, appendix to *Early History and Antiquities of Freemasonry*, by G. F. Fort—one of the most brilliant Masonic books, both in scholarship and literary style.

every letter of the alphabet, in fact, having been
evolved from some primeval sign or signal of the
faith and hope of humanity. Thus Masonry, so far
from limiting the thought of God, is evermore in
search of a more satisfying and revealing vision of
the meaning of the universe, now luminous and
lovely, now dark and terrible; and it invites all men
to unite in the quest—

> One in the freedom of the Truth,
> One in the joy of paths untrod,
> One in the soul's perennial Youth,
> One in the larger thought of God.

Truly the human consciousness of fellowship with
the Eternal, under whatever name, may well hush
all words, still more hush argument and anathema.
Possession, not recognition, is the only thing important; and if it is not recognized, the fault must
surely be, in large part, our own. Given the one
great experience, and before long kindred spirits
will join in the *Universal Prayer* of Alexander Pope,
himself a Mason:

> Father of all! in every age,
> In every clime adored,
> By Saint, by Savage, and by Sage,
> Jehovah, Jove, or Lord!

With eloquent unanimity our Masonic thinkers proclaim the unity and love of God—whence their
vision of the ultimate unity and love of mankind—
to be the great truth of the Masonic philosophy; the

unity of God and the immortality of the soul.[1]
Amidst polytheisms, dualisms, and endless confusions, they hold it to have been the great mission of
Masonry to preserve these precious truths, beside
which, in the long result of thought and faith, all
else fades and grows dim. Of this there is no doubt;
and science has come at last to vindicate this wise
insight, by unveiling the unity of the universe with
overwhelming emphasis. Unquestionably the universe is an inexhaustible wonder. Still, it is a wonder, not a contradiction, and we can never find its
rhythm save in the truth of the unity of all things
in God. Other clue there is none. Down to this
deep foundation Masonry digs for a basis of its
temple, and builds securely. If this be false or unstable, then is

> The pillar'd firmament rottenness,
> And earth's base built on stubble.

Upon the altar of Masonry lies the open Bible which,

[1] *Symbolism of Masonry,* by Dr. Mackey (chap. i) and other books
too many to name. It need hardly be said that the truth of the trinity,
whereof the triangle is an emblem—though with Pythagoras it was a
symbol of holiness, of health—was never meant to contradict the unity
of God, but to make it more vivid. As too often interpreted, it is little
more than a crude tri-theism, but at its best it is not so. "God thrice,
not three Gods," was the word of St. Augustine (*Essay on the Trinity*),
meaning three aspects of God—not the mathematics of His nature, but
its manifoldness, its variety in unity. The late W. N. Clarke—who put
more common sense into theology than any other man of his day—
pointed out that, in our time, the old debate about the trinity is as
dead as Caesar; the truth of God as a Father having taken up into itself the warmth, color, and tenderness of the truth of the trinity—
which, as said on an earlier page, was a vision of God through the
family (*Christian Doctrine of God*).

despite the changes and advances of the ages, remains the greatest Modern Book—the moral manual of civilization.[1] All through its pages, through the smoke of Sinai, through "the forest of the Psalms," through proverbs and parables, along the dreamy ways of prophecy, in gospels and epistles is heard the everlasting truth of one God who is love, and who requires of men that they love one another, do justly, be merciful, keep themselves unspotted by evil, and walk humbly before Him in whose great hand they stand. There we read of the Man of Galilee who taught that, in the far distances of the divine Fatherhood, all men were conceived in love, and so are akin—united in origin, duty, and destiny; so men learned, in lyric words when Jesus lodged with the fishermen by the sea. Therefore we are to relieve the distressed, put the wanderer into his way, and divide our bread with the hungry, which is but the way of doing good to ourselves; for we are all members of one great family, and the hurt of one means the injury of all.

This profound and reverent faith from which, as from a never-failing spring, flow heroic devotedness, moral self-respect, authentic sentiments of fraternity, inflexible fidelity in life and effectual consolation in death, Masonry has at all times religiously taught. Perseveringly it has propagated it through

[1] *The Bible, the Great Source of Masonic Secrets and Observances,* by Dr. Oliver. No Mason need be told what a large place the Bible has in the symbolism, ritual, and teaching of the Order, and it has an equally large place in its literature. (See my book, *The Great Light in Masonry,* in the "Little Masonic Library.")

the centuries, and never more zealously than in our age. Scarcely a Masonic discourse is pronounced, or a Masonic lesson read, by the highest officer or the humblest lecturer, that does not earnestly teach this one true religion which is the very soul of Masonry, its basis and apex, its light and power. Upon that faith it rests; in that faith it lives and labors; and by that faith it will conquer at last, when the noises and confusions of today have followed the tangled feet that made them into silence and oblivion.

2

Out of this simple faith grows, by inevitable logic, the philosophy which Masonry teaches in signs and symbols, in pictures and parables. Stated briefly, stated vividly, it is that behind the pageant of nature, in it and over it, there is a Supreme Mind which initiates, impels, and controls all. That behind the life of man and its pathetic story in history, in it and over it, there is a righteous Will, the intelligent Conscience of the Most High. In short, that the first and last thing in the universe is mind, that the highest and deepest thing is conscience, and that the final reality is the absoluteness of love. Higher than that faith cannot fly; deeper than that thought cannot dig. My little poem tries to tell it:

> No deep is deep enough to show
> The springs whence being starts to flow.
> No fastness of the soul reveals
> Life's subtlest impulse and appeals.
> We seem to come, we seem to go;

But whence or whither who can know?
Unemptiable, unfillable,
It's all in that one syllable—
God! Only God. God first, God last.
God, infinitesimally vast;
God who is love, love which is God,
The rootless, everflowing rod.

There is but one real alternative to this philosophy. It is not atheism—which is seldom more than a revulsion from superstition—because the adherents of absolute atheism are so few, if any, and its intellectual position is too precarious ever to be a menace. An atheist, if such there be, is an orphan, a waif wandering the midnight streets of time, homeless and alone. Nor is the alternative agnosticism, which in the nature of things can be only a passing mood of thought, when, indeed, it is not a confession of intellectual bankruptcy, or a labor-saving device to escape the toil and fatigue of high thinking. It trembles in perpetual hesitation, like a donkey equi-distant between two bundles of hay, starving to death but unable to make up its mind. No; the real alternative is materialism, which played so large a part in philosophy fifty years ago, and which, defeated there, has betaken itself to the field of practical affairs; where, too often, men who profess faith in God, live as if He did not exist. This is the dread alternative of a denial of the great faith of humanity, a blight which would apply a sponge to all the high aspirations and ideals of the race. According to this dogma, the first and last things in the universe are atoms, their number, dance, combinations, and growth. All mind, all will, all emotion, all character, all love is incidental, transitory, vain. The sovereign fact is mud, the final reality is dirt, and the decree of destiny is "dust unto dust!"

Against this ultimate horror, it need hardly be said that in every age Masonry has stood as a witness for the life of the spirit. In the war of the soul against dust, in the choice between dirt and Deity, it has allied itself on the side of the great idealisms, altruisms, and optimisms of humanity. It takes the spiritual view of life and the world as being most in accord with the facts of experience, the promptings of right reason, and the voice of conscience. In other words, it dares to read the meaning of the universe through what is highest in man, not through what is lower, asserting that the soul is akin to the Eternal Spirit, and that by a life of righteousness its eternal quality is revealed.[1] Upon this philosophy Masonry rests, and finds a rock beneath:

[1] Read the great argument of Plato in *The Republic* (book vi). The present writer does not wish to impose upon Masonry any dogma of technical Idealism, subjective, objective, or otherwise. No more than others does he hold to a static universe which unrolls in time a plan made out before, but to a world of wonders where life has the risk and zest of adventure. He rejoices in the New Idealism of Rudolf Eucken, with its gospel of "an independent spiritual life"—independent, that is, of vicissitude—and its insistence upon the fact that the meaning of life depends upon our "building up within ourselves a life that is not of time" (*Life's Basis and Life's Ideal*). But the intent of these pages is, rather, to emphasize the spiritual view of life and the world as the philosophy underlying Masonry, and upon which it builds—the reality of the ideal, its sovereignty over our fragile human life, and the immutable necessity of loyalty to it, if we are to build for eternity. After all, as Plotinus said, philosophy "serves to point the way and guide the

On Him, this corner-stone we build,
    On Him, this edifice erect;
And still, until this work's fulfilled,
    May He the workman's ways direct.

Now, consider! All our human thinking, whether it be in science, philosophy, or religion, rests for its validity upon faith in the kinship of man with God. If that faith be false, the temple of human thought falls to wreck, and behold! we know not anything and have no way of learning. But the fact that the universe is intelligible, that we can follow its forces, trace its laws, and make a map of it, finding the infinite even in the infinitesimal, shows that the mind of man is akin to the Mind that made it. Also, there are two aspects of the nature of man which lift him above the brute and bespeak his divine heredity. They are reason and conscience, both of which are of more than sense and time, having their source, satisfaction, and authority in an unseen, eternal world. That is to say, man is a being who, if not actually immortal, is called by the very law and necessity of his being to live as if he were immortal. Unless life be utterly abortive, having neither rhyme nor reason, the soul of man is itself the one sure proof and prophet of its own high faith.[1]

traveller; the vision is for him who will see it." But the direction means much to those who are seeking the truth to know it. (See the chapter, "The Last Landmark," in my interpretation, *The Religion of Masonry*.)

[1] *The Testimony of the Soul*, by Rufus Jones; the thesis of which is that if the human soul is to be put on trial for its life, surely its own testimony ought to be heard, else the trial is unfair and the verdict false.

Consider, too, what it means to say that this little, infinite soul of man is akin to the Eternal Soul of all things. It means that we are not shapes of mud placed here by chance—freaks and flukes of blind fate—but sons of the Most High, citizens of eternity, deathless as God our Father is deathless; and that there is laid upon us an abiding obligation to live in a manner befitting the dignity of the soul.[1] It means that what a man thinks, the purity of his feeling, the character of his activity and career are of vital and ceaseless concern to the Eternal. Here is a philosophy which lights up the universe like a sunrise, confirming the dim, dumb certainties of the soul, evolving meaning out of mystery, and hope out of what would else be despair. It brings out the colors of human life, investing our fleeting mortal years— brief at their longest, broken at their best—with enduring significance and beauty; inscribing an autograph of eternal value on our fleeting day. It gives to each of us, however humble and obscure, a place and a part in the stupendous historical enterprise; makes us fellow-workers with the Eternal in His redemptive making of humanity, and binds us to do His will upon earth as it is done in heaven. It subdues the intellect; it softens the heart; it begets in the will that sense of self-respect without which high and heroic living cannot be. Such is the philosophy upon

[1] Elsewhere I have discussed "Fate, Faith and God," in a book of essays, *The One Great Church*. Also, the Emerson essay on "Fate" in *The Conduct of Life*. It is the fate of man to be free, if he has the will to win his freedom, and the wit and wisdom to keep it.

which Masonry builds; and from it flow, as from the rock smitten in the wilderness, those bright streams that wander through and water this human world of ours.

3

Because this is so; because the human soul is akin to God, and is endowed with powers to which no one may set a limit, it is and of right ought to be free. Thus, by the logic of its philosophy, not less than the inspiration of its faith, Masonry has been impelled to make its historic demand for liberty of conscience, for the freedom of the intellect, and for the right of all men to stand erect, unfettered, and unafraid, equal before God and the law, each respecting the rights of his fellows. What we have to remember is, that before this truth was advocated by any order, or embodied in any political constitution, it was embedded in the will of God and the constitution of the human soul. Nor will Masonry ever swerve one jot or tittle from its ancient and eloquent demand till all men, everywhere, are free in body, mind, and soul. As it is, Lowell was right when he wrote:

> We are not free: Freedom doth not consist
> In musing with our faces toward the Past
> While petty cares and crawling interests twist
> Their spider threads about us, which at last
> Grow strong as iron chains and cramp and bind
> In formal narrowness heart, soul, and mind.
> Freedom is recreated year by year,
> In hearts wide open on the Godward side,

In souls calm-cadenced as the whirling sphere,
In minds that sway the future like a tide.
No broadest creeds can hold her, and no codes;
She chooses men for her august abodes,
Building them fair and fronting to the dawn.

Some day, when the cloud of prejudice has been dispelled by the searchlight of truth, the world will honor Masonry for its service to freedom of thought and the liberty of faith. No part of its history has been more noble, no principle of its teaching has been more precious than its age-long demand for the right and duty of every soul to seek that light by which no man was ever injured, and that truth which makes man free. Down through the centuries —often in times when the highest crime was not murder, but thinking, and the human conscience was a captive dragged at the wheel of the ecclesiastical chariot—always and everywhere Masonry has stood for the right of the soul to know the truth, and to look up unhindered from the lap of earth into the face of God. Not freedom from faith, but freedom of faith, has been its watchword, on the ground that as despotism is the mother of anarchy, so bigoted dogmatism is the prolific source of scepticism—knowing, also, that our race has made its most rapid advance in those fields where it has been free the longest.

Against those who would fetter thought in order to perpetuate an effete authority, who would give the skinny hand of the past a scepter to rule the aspiring and prophetic present, and seal the lips of living scholars with the dicta of dead scholastics, Masonry will never ground arms! Her plea is for government without tyranny and religion without superstition, and as surely as suns rise and set her fight will be crowned with victory. Defeat is impossible, the more so because she fights not with force, still less with intrigue, but with the power of truth, the persuasions of reason, and the might of gentleness, seeking not to destroy her enemies, but to win them to the liberty of the truth and the fellowship of love.

Not only does Masonry plead for that liberty of faith which permits a man to hold what seems to him true, but also, and with equal emphasis, for the liberty which faith gives to the soul, emancipating it from the despotism of doubt and the fetters of fear. Therefore, by every art of spiritual culture, it seeks to keep alive in the hearts of men a great and simple trust in the goodness of God, in the worth of life, and the divinity of the soul—a trust so apt to be crushed by the tramp of heavy years. Help a man to a firm faith in what Stevenson called "the ultimate decency of things," in an Infinite Pity at the heart of this dark world, and from how many fears is he free! Once a temple of terror, haunted by shadows, his heart becomes "a cathedral of serenity and gladness," and his life is enlarged and unfolded into richness of character and service. Nor is there any tyranny like the tyranny of time. Give a man a day to live, and he is like a bird in a cage beating against its bars. Give him a year in which to move to and fro with his thoughts and plans, his purposes and hopes, and you have liberated him from the despotism of a day. Enlarge the scope of his life to fifty years, and he has a moral dignity of attitude and a sweep of power impossible hitherto. But give him a sense of Eternity; let him know that he plans and works in an ageless time; that above his blunders and sins there hovers and waits the infinite—then he is free!

Nevertheless, if life on earth be worthless, so is immortality. The real question, after all, is not as to the quantity of life, but its quality—its depth, its purity, its fortitude, its fineness of spirit and gesture of soul. Hence the insistent emphasis of Masonry upon the building of character and the practice of righteousness; upon that moral culture without which man is rudimentary, and that spiritual vision without which intellect is the slave of greed or passion. What makes a man great and free of soul, here or anywhither, is loyalty to the laws of right, of truth, of purity, of love, and the lofty will of God. How to live is one matter; and the oldest man in his ripe age has yet to seek a wiser way than to build, year by year, upon a foundation of faith in God, using the Square of justice, the Plumb-line of rectitude, the Compasses to restrain the passions, and the Rule by which to divide our time into labor, rest, and service to our fellows. Let us begin now and seek wisdom in the beauty of virtue and live in the light of it, rejoicing; so in this world shall we have a foregleam of the world to come—bringing down to the Gate in the Mist something that ought not to die, assured that, though hearts are dust, as God lives what is excellent is enduring!

4

Bede the Venerable, in giving an account of the deliberations of the King of Northumberland and his counsellors, as to whether they should allow the Christian missionaries to teach a new faith to the people, recites this incident. After much debate, a gray-haired chief recalled the feeling which came over him on seeing a little bird pass through, on fluttering wing, the warm bright hall of feasting, while winter winds raged without. The moment of its flight was full of sweetness and light for the bird, but it was brief. Out of the darkness it flew, looked upon the bright scene, and vanished into the darkness again, none knowing whence it came nor whither it went.

"Like this," said the veteran chief, "is human life. We come, our wise men cannot tell whence. We go, and they cannot tell whither. Our flight is brief. Therefore, if there be anyone that can teach us more about it—in God's name let us hear him!"

Even so, let us hear what Masonry has to say in the great argument for the immortality of the soul. But, instead of making an argument linked and strong, it presents a picture—the oldest, if not the greatest drama in the world—the better to make men feel those truths which no mortal words can utter. It shows us the black tragedy of life in its darkest hour; the forces of evil, so cunning yet so stupid, which come up against the soul, tempting it to treachery, and even to the degradation of saving life by giving up all that makes life worth living; a tragedy which, in its simplicity and power, makes the heart ache and stand still. Then, out of the thick darkness there rises, like a beautiful white star, that in man which is most akin to God, his love of truth, his loyalty to the highest, and his willingness to go down into the night of death, if only virtue may live and shine like a pulse of fire in the evening sky. Here is the ultimate and final witness of our divinity and immortality—the sublime, death-defying moral heroism of the human soul! Surely the eternal paradox holds true at the gates of the grave: he who loses his life for the sake of truth, shall find it anew! And here Masonry rests the matter, assured that since there is that in man which makes him hold to the moral ideal, and the integrity of his own soul, against all the brute forces of the world, the God who made man in His own image will not let him die in the dust! Higher vision it is not given us to see in the dim country of this world; deeper truth we do not need to know.

Working with hands soon to be folded, we build up the structure of our lives from what our fingers can feel, our eyes can see, and our ears can hear. Till, in a moment—marvelous whether it come in storm and tears, or softly as twilight breath beneath unshadowed skies—we are called upon to yield our grasp of these solid things, and trust ourselves to the invisible Soul within us, which betakes itself along an invisible path into the Unknown,—a mystery as impossible to understand as it is to interpret the voices of the winds. It is strange: a door opens into a new world; and man, child of the dust that he is, follows his adventurous Soul, as the Soul follows an inscrutable Power which is more elusive than the wind that bloweth where it listeth. Suddenly, with fixed eyes and blanched lips, we lie down and wait; and life, well-fought or wasted, bright or somber, lies behind us—a dream that is dreamt, a thing that is no more. O Death,

> Thou hast destroyed it,
> The beautiful world,
> With powerful fist:
> In ruin 'tis hurled,
> By the blow of a demigod shattered!
> The scattered
> Fragments into the void we carry,
> Deploring
> The beauty perished beyond restoring.
> Mightier
> For the children of men,
> Brightlier
> Build it again,
> In thine own bosom build it anew!

O Youth, for whom these lines are written, fear not; fear not to believe that the soul is as eternal as the moral order that obtains in it, wherefore you shall forever pursue that divine beauty which has here so touched and transfigured you; for that is the faith of humanity, your race, and those who are fairest in its records. Let us lay it to heart, love it, and act upon it, that we may learn its deep meaning as regards others—our dear dead whom we think of, perhaps, every day—and find it easier to be brave and hopeful, even when we are sad. It is not a faith to be taken lightly, but deeply and in the quiet of the soul, if so that we may grow into its high meanings for ourselves, as life grows or declines.

> Build thee more stately mansions, O my soul,
>   As the swift seasons roll!
> Leave thy low-vaulted past!
> Let each new temple, nobler than the last,
> Shut thee from heaven with a dome more vast,
>   Till thou at length art free,
> Leaving thine outgrown shell by life's unresting sea!

NOTE—Here lies the meaning of the three grips whereby Masons know one another in the dark as well as in the light. (1) Science, assuming that the seat of the soul is in the brain, lays bare the skull, dissects its hemispheres, traces its convolutions and nerves. Then it subjects the brain of a dog to the same tests, and finds that it and the brain of man are alike; obtains from both the same elements, found everywhere. Science, so far from proving the immortality of the soul, lays aside its instruments unable to prove that there is a soul. Not by that grip can man be raised from a dead level to a living perpendicular. (2) Logic then tries to demonstrate that the soul, in its nature, is indivisible, indestructible, and so immortal. Plato, Cicero, and the rest formulated this argument; but if they convinced others they did not convince themselves. Doubts returned; for at the most critical point upon which the conclusion depended, there was a juggling of words. Not by that grip can man be raised to walk in newness of life. (3) There remains the strong grip of Faith—the profound, ineffaceable intuition of the soul itself; the voice of God speaking within; the Divine Word abiding in the heart. How else has God ever revealed truth to man? How else could He? Once we know that the soul is akin to God—man a little brother of Him whom he seeks—we have a reach and grasp and power of faith whereby we are lifted out of shadow into the light. (Ms. *Lessons in Masonry*, by Albert Pike. House of the Temple, Washington, D.C.)

How many Masons fail to grasp the master truth of the Master Degree! And yet the candidate is not altogether to blame, since the historical lecture does not even mention it, much less expound it. That lecture only reminds the candidate that Masonry cherishes the hope of a glorious immortality—that is all. Whereas in the Degree itself immortality is not a vague hope to be cherished here and realized hereafter. It is a present reality into which the candidate is symbolically initiated; a fact to be realized here and now. If our ritual does not convey this truth, it behooves us to see that it does, first by laying hold of the truth ourselves, and second by so shaping our ceremony, or at least by so explaining it, as to make the truth unmistakable. Manifestly, if we are immortal at all, we are immortal now, and to know that fact is the one great human experience.

THE SPIRIT OF MASONRY

The crest and crowning of all good,
Life's final star, is Brotherhood;
For it will bring again to Earth
Her long-lost Poesy and Mirth;
Will send new light on every face,
A kingly power upon the race.
And till it comes we men are slaves,
And travel downward to the dust of graves.

Come, clear the way, then, clear the way:
Blind creeds and kings have had their day.
Break the dead branches from the path:
Our hope is in the aftermath—
Our hope is in heroic men,
Star-led to build the world again.
To this event the ages ran:
Make way for Brotherhood—make way for Man.
                    —EDWIN MARKHAM, *Poems*

Chapter Three

THE SPIRIT OF MASONRY

1

OUTSIDE OF the home and the house of God there is nothing in this world more beautiful than the Spirit of Masonry. Gentle, gracious, and wise, its mission is to form mankind into a great redemptive brotherhood, a league of noble and free men enlisted in the radiant enterprise of working out in time the love and will of the Eternal. Who is sufficient to describe a spirit so benign? With what words may one ever hope to capture and detain that which belongs of right to the genius of poetry and song, by whose magic those elusive and impalpable realities find embodiment and voice?

With picture, parable, and stately drama, Masonry appeals to lovers of beauty, bringing poetry and symbol to the aid of philosophy, and art to the service of character. Broad and tolerant in its teaching, it appeals to men of intellect, equally by the depth of its faith and its plea for liberty of thought —helping them to think things through to a more satisfying and hopeful vision of the meaning of life and the mystery of the world. But its profoundest appeal, more eloquent than all others, is to the deep heart of man, out of which are the issues of life and destiny. When all is said, it is as a man thinketh in his heart whether life be worth while or not, and whether he be a help or a curse to his race.

> Here lies the tragedy of our race:
> Not that men are poor;
> All men know something of poverty.
> Not that men are wicked;
> Who can claim to be good?
> Not that men are ignorant;
> Who can boast that he is wise?
> But that men are strangers!

Masonry is Friendship—friendship, first, with the great Companion, of whom our own hearts tell us, who is always nearer to us than we are to ourselves, and whose inspiration and help is the greatest fact of human experience. To be in harmony with His purposes, to be open to His suggestions, to be conscious of fellowship with Him—this is Masonry on its Godward side. Then, turning manward, friendship sums it all up. To be friends with all men, however they may differ from us in creed, color, or condition; to fill every human relation with the spirit of friendship; is there anything more or better than this that the wisest and best of men can hope to do?[1] Such is the spirit of Masonry; such is its ideal, and if to realize it all at once is denied us, surely it means much to see it, love it, and labor to make it come true.

Nor is this Spirit of Friendship a mere sentiment held by a sympathetic, and therefore unstable, fraternity, which would dissolve the concrete features of humanity into a vague blur of misty emotion. No; it has its roots in a profound philosophy which sees that *the universe is friendly,* not a "malevolent wonderland," and that men must learn to be friends if they would live as befits the world in which they live, as well as their own origin and destiny. For, since God is the life of all that was, is, and is to be; and since we are all born into the world by one high wisdom and one vast love, we are brothers to the last man of us, forever! For better for worse, for richer for poorer, in sickness and in health, and even after

[1] Suggested by a noble passage in the *Recollections* of Washington Gladden; and the great preacher goes on to say: "If the church could accept this truth—that Religion is Friendship—and build its own life upon it, and make it central and organic in all its teachings, should we not have a great revival of religion?" Indeed, yes; and of the right kind of religion, too! Walt Whitman found the basis of all philosophy, all religion, in "the dear love of man for his comrade, the attraction of friend to friend" (*The Base of all Metaphysics*). As for Masonic literature, it is one perpetual pæan in praise of the practice of friendship, from earliest time to our own day. Take, for example, the *Illustrations of Masonry,* by Preston (first book, sect. i-x); and Arnold, as we have seen, defined Masonry as Friendship, as did Hutchinson (*The Spirit of Masonry,* lectures xi, xii). These are but two notes of a mighty anthem whose chorus is never hushed in the temple of Masonry! Of course, there are those who say that the finer forces of life are frail and foolish, but the influence of the cynic in the advance of the race is—nothing! As for Masonry, it does not believe that "the things we value most are at the mercy of the things we value least."

death us do part, all men are held together by ties of spiritual kinship, sons of one eternal Friend. Upon this fact human fraternity rests, and it is the basis of the plea of Masonry, not only for freedom, but for friendship among men.

Thus friendship, so far from being a mush of concessions, is in fact the constructive genius of the universe. Love is ever the Builder, and those who have done most to establish the City of God on earth have been the men who loved their fellow-men. Once let this spirit prevail, and the wrangling sects will be lost in a great league of those who love in the service of those who suffer. No man will then revile the faith in which his neighbor finds help for today and hope for the morrow; pity will smite him mute, and love will teach him that God is found in many ways, by those who seek Him with honest hearts. Once let this spirit rule in the realm of trade, and the law of the jungle will cease, and men will strive to build a social order in which all men may have opportunity "to live, and to live well," as Aristotle defined the purpose of society. Here is the basis of that magical stability aimed at by the earliest artists when they sought to build for eternity, by imitating on earth the House of God.

2

Our human history, saturated with blood and blistered with tears, is the story of man making friends with man. Society has evolved from a feud into a friendship by the slow growth of love and the weld-

ing of man, first to his kin, and then to his kind.[1]
The first men who walked in the red dawn of time
lived every man for himself, his heart a sanctuary of
suspicions, every man feeling that every other man
was his foe, and therefore his prey. So there were
war, strife, and bloodshed. Slowly there came to the
savage a gleam of the truth that it is better to help
than to hurt, and he organized clans and tribes. But
tribes were divided by rivers and mountains, and the
men on one side of the river felt that the men on the
other side were their enemies. Again there were
war, pillage, and sorrow. Great empires arose and
met in the shock of conflict, leaving trails of skele-
tons across the earth. Then came the great roads,
reaching out with their stony clutch and bringing
the ends of the earth together. Men met, mingled,
passed and repassed, and learned that human nature
is much the same everywhere, with hopes and fears
in common. Still there were many things to divide
and estrange men from each other, and the earth was
full of bitterness. Not satisfied with natural barriers,
men erected high walls of sect and caste, to exclude
their fellows, and the men of one sect were sure that
the men of all other sects were wrong—and doomed
to be lost; the most awful dogma ever taught in times

[1] *The Neighbor*, by N. S. Shaler. Also, *Self and Neighbor*, by E. W.
Hirst, which deals with the psychology, as well as the philosophy, of
fraternity. So far, we have no History of Brotherhood—a strange omis-
sion—except, perhaps, a little book entitled *The Growth of Brotherhood*, by A. T. Dakin, tracing the slowly developing sense of solidarity
from A.D. 50 to 1920. What a theme for a masterpiece, if only the
materials were more abundant and available!

not actually barbaric. Thus, when real mountains no longer separated man from man, mountains were made out of molehills—mountains of immemorial misunderstanding not yet moved into the sea!

Barriers of race, of creed, of caste, of habit, of training and interest separate men today, as if some malign genius were bent on keeping man from his fellows, begetting suspicion, uncharitableness, and hate. Still there are war, waste, and woe! Yet all the while men have been unfriendly, and, therefore, unjust and cruel, only because they are unacquainted, or else the victims of blind drives and neurotic torments in the depths of their unconscious life. Amidst feud, faction, and folly, Masonry, the oldest and most widely spread order, toils in behalf of friendship, uniting men upon the only basis upon which they can ever meet with dignity. Each lodge is an oasis of equality and goodwill in a desert of strife, working to weld mankind into a great league of sympathy and service, which, by the terms of our definition, it seeks to exhibit even now on a small scale. At its altar men meet as man to man, without vanity and without pretense, without fear and without reproach, as tourists crossing the Alps tie themselves together, so that if one slip all may hold him up. No tongue can tell the meaning of such a ministry, no pen can trace its influence in melting the hardness of the world into pity and gladness.

The Spirit of Masonry! He who would describe that spirit must be a poet, a musician, and a seer— a master of melodies, echoes, and long, far-sounding cadences. Now, as always, it toils to make man better, to refine his thought and purify his sympathy, to broaden his outlook, to lift his altitude, to establish in amplitude and resoluteness his life in all its relations. All its great history, its vast accumulations of tradition, its simple faith and its solemn rites, its freedom and its friendship are dedicated to a high moral ideal, seeking to tame the tiger in man, and bring his wild passions into obedience to the will of God. It has no other mission than to exalt and ennoble humanity, to bring light out of darkness, beauty out of angularity; to make every hard-won inheritance more secure, every sanctuary more sacred, every hope more radiant! [1]

The Spirit of Masonry! Ay, when that spirit has its way upon earth, as at last it surely will, society will be a vast communion of kindness and justice, business a system of human service, law a rule of beneficence; the home will be more holy, the laughter of childhood more joyous, and the temple of prayer mortised and tenoned in simple faith. Evil,

[1] If Masons often fall far below their high ideal, it is because they share in their degree the infirmity of mankind. He is a poor craftsman who glibly recites the teachings of the Order and quickly forgets the lessons they convey; who wears its honorable dress to conceal a self-seeking spirit; or to whom its great and simple symbols bring only an outward thrill, and no inward urge toward the highest of all good. Apart from what they symbolize, all symbols are empty; they speak only to such as have ears to hear, and eyes to see. At the same time, we have always to remember—what has been so often and so sadly forgotten—that the most sacred shrine on earth is the soul of man; and that the temple and its offices are not ends in themselves, but only beautiful means to the end that every human heart may be a temple of peace, of purity, of power, of pity, and of hope!

injustice, bigotry, greed, and every vile and slimy thing that defiles and defames humanity will skulk into the dark, unable to bear the light of a juster, wiser, more merciful order. Industry will be upright, education prophetic, and religion not a shadow, but a Real Presence, when man has become acquainted with man and has learned to worship God by serving his fellows. When Masonry is victorious every tyranny will fall, every bastile crumble, and man will be not only unfettered in mind and hand, but free of heart to walk erect in the light and liberty of the truth.

Toward a great friendship, long foreseen by Masonic faith, the world is slowly moving, amid difficulties and delays, reactions and reconstructions; if it does not become a City of Friends, it will be a City of Destruction—a human volcano. Of that day which will surely arrive, though long deferred, when nations will be reverent in the use of freedom, just in the exercise of power, humane in the practice of wisdom; when no man will ride over the rights of his fellows; when no woman will be made forlorn, no little child wretched by bigotry or greed, Masonry has ever been a prophet. Nor will she ever be content until all the threads of human fellowship are woven into one mystic cord of friendship, encircling the earth and holding the race in unity of spirit and the bonds of peace, as in the will of God it is one in the origin and end: one race, the Human Race. Having outlived empires and philosophies,

having seen generations appear and vanish, it will
yet live to see the travail of its soul, and be satisfied—

> When the war-drum throbs no longer,
> And the battle flags are furled;
> In the parliament of man,
> The federation of the world.

3

Manifestly, since love is the law of life, if men are
to be won from hate to love, if those who doubt and
deny are to be wooed to faith, if the race is ever to
be led and lifted into a life of service, it must be by
the fine art of Friendship. Inasmuch as this is the
purpose of Masonry, its mission determines the
method not less than the spirit of its labor. Earnestly
it endeavors to bring men—first the individual man,
and then, so far as possible, those who are united
with him—to love one another, while holding aloft,
in picture and dream, that temple of character which
is the noblest labor of life to build in the midst of
the years, and which will outlast time and death.
Thus it seeks to reach the lonely inner life of man
where the real battles are fought, and where the
issues of destiny are decided, now with shouts of
victory, now with sobs of defeat. What a ministry
to a young man who enters its temple in the morning of life, when the dew of heaven is upon his days
and the birds are singing in his heart! [1]

[1] Read the noble words of Arnold on the value of Masonry to the
young as a restraint, a refinement, and a conservator of virtue, throw-
ing about youth the mantle of a great friendship and the consecration
of a great ideal (*History and Philosophy of Masonry*, chap. xix).

From the wise lore of the East, Max Müller translated a Parable of Man—as the story of the Prodigal Son is the Parable of God—which tells how the gods, having stolen from man his divinity, met in council to discuss where they should hide it. One suggested that it be carried to the other side of the earth and buried; but it was pointed out that man is a great wanderer, and that he might find the lost treasure on the other side of the earth. Another proposed that it be dropped into the depths of the sea; but the same fear was expressed—that man, in his insatiable curiosity, might dive deep enough to find "the pearl of great price" even there. Finally, after a space of silence, the oldest and wisest of the gods said: "Hide it in man himself, as that is the last place he will ever think to look for it!" And it was so agreed, all seeing at once the subtle and wise strategy. Man did wander over the earth, for ages, seeking in all places high and low, far and near, before he thought to look within himself for the divinity he sought. At last, slowly, dimly, he began to realize that what he thought was far off, hidden in "the pathos of distance," is nearer than the breath he breathes, even in his own heart.

Here lies the great secret of Masonry—that it makes a man aware of that divinity within him, wherefrom his whole life takes its beauty and meaning, and inspires him to follow and obey it: making his existence a process of self-discovery, self-mastery, and self-spending. Once a man learns this deep secret, his life is new, and the old world is a valley all dewy to the dawn with a lark-song over it. There never was a truer saying than that the religion of a man is the chief fact concerning him.[1] By religion is meant not the creed to which a man will subscribe, or otherwise give his assent; not that necessarily; often not that at all—since we see men of all degrees of worth and worthlessness signing all kinds of creeds. No; the religion of a man is that which he practically believes, lays to heart, acts upon, and thereby knows concerning this mysterious universe and his duty and destiny in it. That is in all cases the primary thing in him, and creatively determines all the rest; that is his religion—"the doing of all good, and for its sake the suffering of all evil." It is, then, of vital importance what faith, what vision, what conception of life a man lays to heart, and acts upon.

At bottom, a man is what his thinking is,—"what he thinks about when he is alone," as Emerson said—thoughts being the artists who give color to our days. Optimists and pessimists live in the same world, walk under the same sky, and observe the same facts. Sceptics and believers look up at the same great stars—the stars that shone in Eden and will flash again in Paradise. Clearly the difference between them is a difference not of fact, but of faith—of insight, outlook, and point of view—a difference of inner attitude and habit of thought with regard to the worth and use of life; "a queer little turn of

[1] *Heroes and Hero-worship*, by Thomas Carlyle, lecture i.

the heart," as someone put it. By the same token, any influence which reaches and alters that inner habit and bias of mind, and changes it from doubt to faith, from fear to courage, from despair to sun-burst hope, has wrought the most benign ministry which a mortal may enjoy. Every man has a train of thought on which he rides when he is alone; and the worth of his life to himself and others, as well as its happiness, depends upon the direction in which that train is going, the baggage it carries, and the country through which it travels. It is as we think in our hearts, the secrets of our souls, whether we are victims of life or victors over it; whether we stumble through our days, or strike our stride and walk erect, free and unafraid. If, then, Masonry can put that inner train of thought on the right track, freight it with precious treasure, and start it on the way to the City of God, what other or higher minis-try can it render to a man? And that is what it does for any man who will listen to it, love it, and lay its truth to heart.

High, fine, ineffably rich and beautiful are the faith and vision which Masonry gives to those who foregather at its altar, bringing to them in picture, parable, and symbol the lofty and pure truth wrought out through the ages of experience, tested by time, and found to be valid for the conduct of life. By such teaching, if they have the heart to heed it, men become wise, learning how to be both brave and gentle, faithful and free; how to renounce super-stition and yet retain faith; how to keep a fine poise of reason between the falsehood of extremes; how to accept the joys of life with glee, and endure its ills with patient valor; how to look upon the folly of man and not forget his nobility; how to be "a little kinder than necessary,"—in short, how to live cleanly, kindly, calmly, open-eyed and unafraid in a sane world, sweet of heart and full of hope; and even in an insane world how to keep his poise, and not give up, let down, and sink into a sour cynicism. Whoso lays this lucid and profound wisdom to heart, and lives by it, will have little to regret, and nothing to fear, when the evening shadows fall. Happy the young man who in the morning of his years makes it his guide, philosopher, and friend.[1]

Such is the ideal of Masonry, and fidelity to all that is holy demands that we give ourselves to it, trusting the power of truth, the reality of love, and the sovereign worth of character. For only as we

---

[1] If the influence of Masonry upon youth is here emphasized, it is not to forget that the most dangerous period of life is not youth, with its turmoil of storm and stress, but between forty and sixty. When the enthusiasms of youth have cooled, and its rosy glamour has faded into the light of common day, there is apt to be a letting down of ideals, a hardening of heart, when cynicism takes the place of idealism. If the judgments of the young are austere and need to be softened by charity, the middle years of life need still more the reënforcement of spiritual influence and the inspiration of a holy atmosphere. Also, Albert Pike used to urge upon old men the study of Masonry, the better to help them gather up the scattered thoughts about life and build them into a firm faith; and because Masonry offers to every man a great hope and consolation. Indeed, its ministry to every period of life is benign. Studying Masonry is like looking at a sunset; each man who looks is filled with the beauty and wonder of it, but the glory is not diminished. (See two addresses by the author, entitled "The Patriarchs" and "Albert Pike, a Master Genius of Masonry," in *The Men's House*.)

incarnate that ideal in actual life and activity does it become real, tangible, and effective. God works for man through man and seldom, if at all, in any other way. He asks for our voices to speak His truth, for our hands to do His work here below—sweet voices and clean hands to make liberty and love prevail over injustice and hate. Not all of us can be learned or famous, but each of us can be loyal and true at heart, undefiled by evil, undaunted by error, faithful and helpful to our fellow souls. Life is a capacity for the highest things. Let us make it a pursuit of the highest—an eager, incessant quest of truth; a noble utility, a lofty honor, a wise freedom, a genuine service—that through us the Spirit of Masonry may grow and be glorified.

When is a man a Mason? When he can look out over the rivers, the hills, and the far horizon with a profound sense of his own littleness in the vast scheme of things, and yet have faith, hope, and courage—which is the root of every virtue. When he knows that down in his heart every man is as noble, as vile, as divine, as diabolic, and as lonely as himself, and seeks to know, and to love his fellow-man. When he knows how to sympathize with men, even in their sins—knowing that each man fights a hard fight against many odds,—and still believe in them when they do not believe in themselves. When he has learned how to make friends and to keep them, and above all how to keep friends with himself. When he loves flowers, can hunt the birds without a gun, and feels the thrill of an old forgotten joy when he hears the laugh of a little child. When he can be happy and high-minded amid the meaner drudgeries of life. When star-crowned trees, and the glint of sunlight on flowing waters, subdue him like the thought of one much loved and long dead. When no voice of distress reaches his ears in vain, and no hand seeks his aid without response. When he feels a social iniquity as a personal sin, and a human calamity as a private bereavement—sharing the guilt and sorrows of his fellows. When he finds good in every faith that helps any man to lay hold of divine things and to see majestic meanings in life, whatever the name of that faith may be. When he can look into a wayside puddle and see something beyond mud, and into the face of the most forlorn fellow-mortal and see something beyond sin. When he knows how to pray, how to love, how to hope, how to meet defeat and not be defeated. When he has learned how to give himself, to forgive others, and to live with thanksgiving. When he has kept faith with himself, with his fellow-man, with his God; in his hand a sword for evil, in his heart a bit of a song —glad to live, but not afraid to die! Such a man has found the only real secret of Masonry, and the one which it is trying to give to all the world.

THE UNKNOWN BUILDERS

Find out first, if you can what is true in Masonry, and you will not be overburdened with Masonic reading. When you have gained some real knowledge, the rest cannot harm you, and may even be of benefit.

—THEODORE SUTTON PARVIN

THEODORE SUTTON PARVIN

A pioneer in the field of Masonic education, who founded the internationally known Iowa Masonic Library in 1844, and served as its librarian until his death in 1901. He was succeeded by his son, Newton Ray Parvin, connected with the library from 1872 until his demise in 1925. Father and son together gave 110 years to the service of the Grand Lodge of Iowa.

Chapter Four

THE UNKNOWN BUILDERS

WILL THERE ever be a great epic in honor of the anonymous goodness and hidden fidelity of our race? Never upon this earth; absorbed in the present, striving for the future, the past and those who with it depart fades too quickly out of mind, out of memory. But somewhere, in the archives of God, a Book is kept in which all high human worth is recorded and appraised, and in that Book is the secret of our human advance. For, that things are as well with us as they are is due, not to our own efforts, but to the faithfulness of innumerable lives gone before us, whose fleeting days melted into the stream of influence, law and faith by which the race is hallowed and guided.

In the Church, by the poetry of its faith, a day is set apart in honor of All Saints, in memory of every brave and beautiful spirit who has ascended in victory from the moral battlefields of time. It is a festival in thanksgiving for every noble soul, every love-anointed act, inspired by the Grace of God since ever time began—however lowly and obscure the soul, however unknown and unsung the act—awaiting that anthem which in the future it will be ordained shall be sung in gratitude and praise. Also, a day is dedicated to All Souls, of every race and land, who have walked lightly or sadly, striding in joy and hope or stumbling in sorrow and sin, along the old-worn human road—that as little as possible may be lost of the precious treasure of mankind.

In the Lodge, too, we need a Day of Celebration and Dedication, in tribute to the multitudes of Unknown Builders, forgotten of fame, unrecorded by history, unsung by poetry, who by their love and loyalty built their lives into the Temple, and left only their "marks" upon it. Their names are lost—like autumn leaves blown by winter winds—save in the memory of God, who does not forget; they sleep in the indistinguishable dust, with no hope of record by man, content to live in the work they wrought and the good they did, vanishing as if they had never been. They are the real Builders of the Temple, as it stands stately in the sunlight, or touched by the mysticism of the moonlight—it is at once their monument and their memorial. Into their labors the Craft enters, and because of their faithfulness we have a finer, firmer faith with which to face the morrow.

How swiftly Time passes, sweeping all its sons away in a flood of years; how few are remembered

for a decade, and fewer still adown the ages. Even
the most famous name is soon emptied by oblivion,
and becomes a vacancy that is vacated by the passing
of the age in which it shone. Man, pursued by Time,
overtaken by Death, seems as frail as a mist; yet
something in his dreaming soul defies Death and
refuses to let it have the last word. If a Roman poet
could call our mortal life "the dream of a shadow,"
in it and through it, as we learn in the Lodge, if we
work and watch, if we pray and trust in God, the
Eternal, we shall find in our own hearts an Eternity
that will never pass away, in which no true thought
fades, no faithful deed is forgotten, and "love can
never lose its own." So mote it be!

BIBLIOGRAPHY

THE LITERATURE of Freemasonry is bewilderingly vast and varied, much of it the product preceding the advent of the modern spirit and method of critical historical research, and therefore more interesting than valuable. More than sixty thousand titles of Masonic books, brochures, articles and the like have been recorded in the original volumes and the Beyer-Quint continuation of the Wolfstieg *Bibliographie der freimaurerischen Literatur* (1911-1930). The text and notes of the foregoing pages indicate, often with brief characterizations, such books as the writer found particularly helpful in the course of his study, whereof he makes acknowledgment. Much has been written since this book appeared in the first edition, and many books are out of print and no longer available.*

Anderson, *Book of Constitutions.*
Anderson, *Masonic Token.*
Armitage, *Short Masonic History,* 2 vols.
Arnold, *Philosophical History of Freemasonry.*
Arnold, *Rationale and Ethics of Freemasonry.*
Ashmole, *Diary.*
Aubrey, *The Natural History of Wiltshire.*
Aynsley, *Symbolism of the East and West.*
Bacon, *New Atlantis.*
Barker, *The Mahatma Letters* to A. P. Sinnett.
Bayley, *Lost Language of Symbolism; A New Light on the Renaissance.*

* *Macoy's Guide to Masonic Literature* lists various available titles and will be sent free to any address upon application to the Macoy Publishing & Masonic Supply Co., 35 West 32nd Street, New York, N. Y.

Blake, *Realities of Freemasonry.*

Blavatsky, *The Secret Doctrine; Isis Unveiled.*

Borlase, *Antiquities of Cornwall.*

Boutelle, *The Man of Mount Moriah.*

Breasted, *The Dawn of Conscience; Religion and Thought in Egypt.*

Bromwell, *Restorations of Masonic Geometry and Symbolry.*

Buck, *Symbolism, or Mystic Masonry.*

Budge, *Book of the Dead; The Gods of the Egyptians.*

Callahan, *Washington, the Man and the Mason.*

Calvert, *The Grand Lodge of England; Grand Stewards and Red Apron Lodges.*

Campbell, *Life of Ashmole.*

Capart, *Primitive Art in Egypt.*

Carlyle, *Heroes and Hero-worship; Sartor Resartus.*

Carr, *The Swastika.*

Castells, *Our Ancient Brethren; Genuine Secrets of Freemasonry; Apocalypse of Freemasonry.*

Catholic Encyclopaedia, art. "Masonry."

Cheethan, *Mysteries Pagan and Christian.*

Churchward, *The Arcana of Freemasonry; Signs and Symbols of Primordial Man.*

Conder, *Records of the Hole Crafte and Fellowship of Masons.*

Crowe, *Things a Freemason Should Know.*

Cumont, *Mysteries of Mithra; Oriental Religions.*

Da Costa, *Dionysian Artificers.*

Dakin, *The Growth of Brotherhood.*

Dallaway, *Architecture in England.*

Darrah, *The Master's Assistant.*

Davidson & Aldersmith, *The Great Pyramid: Its Divine Message.*

Daynes, *The Birth and Growth of the Grand Lodge of England.*

De Clifford, *Egypt, the Cradle of Masonry.*

De Quincey, *Works,* vol. xvi.

De Villars, *Comte de Gabalis.*

Dill, *Roman Life.*

Drummond, *History of Symbolic Masonry in the United States.*

Edinburgh Encyclopedia.

Emerson, *The Conduct of Life.*

Encyclopaedia Britannica, art. "Freemasonry."

Evans, *Tree and Pillar Cult.*

Fergusson, *History of Architecture.*

Findel, *The Principles of Freemasonry in the Life of Nations.*

Finlayson, *Symbols and Legends of Freemasonry.*

Forbes, *Rambles in Naples.*

Fort, *Early History and Antiquities of Freemasonry.*

Frazer, *The Golden Bough.*

Fryar, *La Place des Victores.*

George, *Seventeenth Century Men of Latitude.*

Gibson, *Builders of Men.*

Gilchrist, *Freemasonry in Ancient Egypt.*

Giles, *Freemasonry in China.*

Gorringe, *Egyptian Obelisks.*

Gotch, *Architecture of the Renaissance in England.*

Gould, *Atholl Lodges; Concise History of Freemasonry; Essays on Freemasonry; History of Freemasonry; Military Lodges.*

Haige, *Symbolism.*

Hallam, *History of the English Constitution; History of the Middle Ages.*

Hall, *The Lost Keys of Freemasonry, or The Secret of Hiram Abiff.*

Harrison, *Ancient Art and Ritual.*

Hartland, *Ritual and Belief.*

Hastings, *Encyclopaedia of Religion,* art. "Freemasonry."

Hawkins, *Concise Cyclopaedia of Freemasonry.*

Hayden, *Washington and His Masonic Compeers.*

Heckethorn, *Secret Societies of All Ages and Countries.*

Heindel, *Freemasonry and Catholicism; Rosicrucian Cosmo-Conception.*

Higgins, *Anacalypsis,* 2 vols.

Hirst, *Self and Neighbor.*

Holland, *Freemasonry from the Great Pyramid.*

Hope, *Historical Essay on Architecture.*

Hughan, *Origin of the English Rite of Freemasonry; Masonic Sketches and Reprints.*

Hughan and Stillson, *History of Freemasonry and Concordant Orders.*

Hunt, *Masonic Symbolism.*

Hutchinson, *The Spirit of Masonry.*

Hyamson, *History of the Jews in England.*

James, *Some Problems of Philosophy.*

Jamieson, *Dictionary of Scottish Language.*

Jewish Antiquities.

Jewish Encyclopaedia, art. "Freemasonry."

Johnson, *Beginnings of Freemasonry in America.*

Kennedy, *St. Paul and the Mystery-Religions.*

Kingsford and Maitland, *The Perfect Way, or the Finding of Christ.*

Kipling, *Kim; Debits and Credits; Traffics and Discoveries; Puck of Pook's Hill; In the Interests of the Brethren; The Man Who Would be King.*

Kissick, *Irish Prince and the Hebrew Prophet.*

The Koran.

Laurie, *History and Illustration of Freemasonry.*

Lawrence, *Practical Masonic Lectures.*

Lawrence, *Sidelights on Freemasonry; The Keystone; Byways of Freemasonry.*

Legge, *Chinese Classics.*

Leicester Lodge of Research, *Transactions.*

Lennhoff, *The Freemasons.*

Lessing, *Ernst and Falk; Fragments; Nathan the Wise.*

Lethaby, *Architecture.*

Lockyear, *Dawn of Astronomy*.

Lundy, *Monumental Christianity*.

Lyon, *History of the Lodge of Edinburgh*, *(Mary's Chapel)* No. 1.

MacBride, *Speculative Masonry*.

MacGregor Mathers, *The Kabbalah Unveiled*.

Mackey, *Encyclopedia of Freemasonry; Symbolism of Freemasonry; Lexicon of Freemasonry*.

Manchester Lodge of Research, *Transactions*.

Marshall, *Nature, a Book of Symbols*.

Maspero, *Dawn of Civilization*.

Materlinck, *The Blue Bird*.

Mead, *Quests New and Old*.

Melville, *The Life and Writings of Philip, Duke of Wharton*.

Mills, *Our Own Religion in Persia*.

Moehler, *Symbolism*.

Mommsen, *De Collegia*.

Moret, *Kings and Gods of Egypt*.

Morris, *Lights and Shadows of the Mystic Tie; The Poetry of Freemasonry*.

Morse, *The Guilds of China*.

Müller, *Hibbert Lectures*.

Oakesmith, *The Religion of Plutarch*.

Old Charges.

Oliver, *Antiquities of Freemasonry; History of Initiation; Signs and Symbols of Freemasonry; Masonic Sermons; Revelations of a Square; Theocratic Philosophy of Freemasonry*.

Papworth, *Notes on the Superintendents of English Buildings in the Middle Ages*.

Paton, *Freemasonry: Its Symbolism*.

Pierson and Steinbrenner, *Traditions, Origin and Early History of Freemasonry*.

Pike, *Morals and Dogma; Lectures on Masonic Symbolism*.

Plato, *The Republic*, book vi; *Phaedo*.

Plott, *Natural History of Staffordshire.*
Plutarch, *De Iside et Osiride;* "On the Cessation of Oracles."
Poole, *The Old Charges.*
Pound, *Lectures on the Philosophy of Masonry.*
Powell, *The Magic of Freemasonry.*
Preston, *Illustrations of Masonry.*
Quatuor Coronati Lodge No. 2076, *Transactions.*
Ravenscroft, *The Comacines.*
Rawlinson, *History of Phoenicia.*
Reade, *The Veil of Isis.*
Regius MS.
Reisner, *Egyptian Conceptions of Immortality.*
Richardson, *The Great Work.*
Rogers, *History of Agriculture and Prices in England.*
Ruskin, *Seven Lamps of Architecture.*
Sachse, *Benjamin Franklin as a Freemason.*
Sadler, *Masonic Facts and Fiction.*
St. Andrew's Lodge, *Centennial Memorial.*
Schure, *Hermes and Plato; Jesus, the Last Great Initiate;
    Pythagoras and the Delphic Mysteries.*
Scott, *The Cathedral Builders.*
Shaler, *The Neighbor.*
Sibley, *The Story of Freemasonry.*
Smith, *Dictionary of the Bible.*
Smith, *English Guilds.*
Smith, *Unwritten Sayings of Our Lord.*
Speth, *Royal Masons; Builders' Rites and Ceremonies.*
Steiner, *The Way of Initiation.*
Stevens, *Cyclopedia of Fraternities.*
Stewart, *Symbolic Teaching, or Masonry and Its Message.*
Sue, *The Wandering Jew.*
Tatsch, *Freemasonry in the Thirteen Colonies; Facts About
    George Washington as a Freemason.*
Toland, *Socratic Society.*
Tolstoi, *War and Peace.*
Tuttle, *Environmental Factors in Christian History.*

Tyler, *Oaths, Their Origin, Nature, and History.*

Underhill, *Mysticism.*

The Upanishads.

Van Dyke, *The Lost Word.*

Vibert, *Freemasonry Before the Existence of Grand Lodges.*

Waite, *Real History of the Rosicrucians; Secret Tradition in Freemasonry; Studies in Mysticism; A Book of Mystery and Vision; Strange House of Sleep; Steps to the Crown; Life of Saint-Martin; The Way of Divine Union; Deeper Aspects of Masonic Symbolism; Mysteries of Magic; The Hidden Church of the Holy Grail; The Secret Doctrine in Israel; Emblematic Freemasonry.*

Ward, *Interpretations of Our Masonic Symbols; Outline History of Freemasonry; Who Was Hiram Abiff?*

Watts, *The Word in the Pattern.*

Webster, *Primitive Secret Societies.*

Whiston, *The Works of Josephus.*

Wilmshurst, *Masonic Initiation; Meaning of Masonry.*

Wright, *Indian Masonry.*

Yarker, *Arcane Schools; Recapitulation of All Masonry; Ancient Constitutional Charges of the Guild Freemasons.*

The Publishers express grateful acknowledgment to J. Ray Shute II for permission to reproduce the *Nocalore* initial letters used throughout this text.

INDEX

Index